AMC's COMPLETE GUIDE TO
TRAIL BUILDING
& MAINTENANCE

Fourth Edition

By the Staff of AMC's Trails Department

Appalachian Mountain Club Books
Boston, Massachusetts

The AMC is a nonprofit organization and sales of AMC books fund our mission of protecting the Northeast outdoors. If you appreciate our efforts and would like make a donation, contact us at Appalachian Mountain Club Books, 5 Joy Street, Boston, MA 02108.

http://www.outdoors.org/publications/books/

Book design by Eric Edstam

Library of Congress Cataloging-in-Publication Data

AMC's complete guide to trail building and maintenance / the staff of AMC's Trails Department.—4th ed.
    p. cm.
    Prev. ed. published under title: Complete guide to trail building and maintenance.
    Includes index.
    ISBN 978-1-934028-16-2 (alk. paper)
    1. Trails—Design and construction. 2. Trails—Maintenance and repair. I. Demrow, Carl. Complete guide to trail building and maintenance. II. Appalachian Mountain Club. III. Title: Complete guide to trail building and maintenance.

    TE304.D46 2008
    625.7'4—dc22

                 2008010603

Distributed by The Globe Pequot Press, Guilford, Connecticut.

Printed in Canada.

9 8 7 6 5 4 3 2 1   08 09 10 11 12 13 14 15 16

CONTENTS

FOREWORD

While the Appalachian Mountain Club's experience in trail building and
maintenance dates back to 1876 when the club was founded, much has changed
from the days when AMC's first "Councillor of Improvements" and others built
their trails in the White Mountains.

Trails are still built to inspire the imagination and take people to remark-
able places. Trails are still cleared of brush and blazed to help people find their
way. Yet much of trail work today is about preserving trails for the future with
techniques to conserve soil and protect fragile plant life. Trails that are newly
built are created with an eye toward both aesthetic appeal and minimizing
potential environmental impact caused by users and natural forces. Trails are
marked to guide the way, but trails may also be hardened with bog bridges or
step stones to keep feet on the trail and preserve soils, vegetation, and water
quality around the trail. Many trails are still primarily used for hiking, and
many are now also enjoyed for mountain biking or trail running. New trails
are being constructed on local land trust and conservation land as people seek
outdoor recreation opportunities close to home. Increasingly, trails are also
incorporating considerations to make them universally accessible when the
natural terrain allows.

The techniques described in this book comprise a conservationist approach
to trail building and maintenance. It is about making enjoyable trails and protecting the environment in the spirit of the AMC's mission to promote the
protection, enjoyment, and wise use of the mountains, rivers, and trails of the
Appalachian region. This book builds on the foundation laid by the knowledge
and experience imparted in the first, second, and third editions.

Chapters 1 through 5 provide guidance in visioning, planning, and laying
out a new trail. Chapter 4 has been expanded to include more detail on the
steps of planning and laying out a new trail, and Chapter 5 provides new information to help trail planners determine the costs and resources needed for
a project. Chapter 6 includes updated safety information, including appropriate
personal protective equipment to make sure your crews are productive, safe,
and enjoying themselves. Chapters 7 and 8 on trail construction, reconstruction, and erosion control build on many years of field experience and have
been expanded to include newer techniques that have been proven effective as

well as techniques that will be useful on multiuse trails. Chapter 9 has been expanded to include additional information on bridge construction, and Chapter 10 includes instructions on how to maintain trails. Chapter 11 has been greatly expanded with more detailed information about ski trail layout and construction, in part based on AMC's recent program in new ski trail construction in central Maine. Since trail protection also relies heavily on responsible use, and in response to inquiries AMC receives about trailhead structures, Chapter 12 offers new content on kiosk design and trailhead user education.

The contributions of the original and previous authors of this book cannot be over-appreciated. The first and second editions by Bob Proudman and Reuben Rajala were groundbreaking. Carl Demrow and David Salisbury followed with a third edition that updated trail construction and reconstruction techniques, and added guidance on safety and preparation. All have been based on hands-on field work for the dual goals of trail building and conservation.

This edition draws on the collective experience of AMC's current and past Trails and Recreation Management Department staff. The Appalachian Mountain Club Trails Program is dedicated to the protection and care of trails and backcountry shelters and the experiences they provide. We promote stewardship, public service, and ethical recreation. Today, AMC's dedicated volunteers and staff maintain over 1,700 miles of trail from Maine to Washington, D.C, including 350 miles of the Appalachian Trail. A number of these trails are among the steepest, most exposed, and most used in the nation; we feel confident in saying our experience will apply to most trail situations in other parts of the country. Many of the suggestions for this edition came from AMC's volunteer trail work community, members who continue to give extraordinary time every year to the care of beloved trails and to sharing their expertise and enthusiasm with all willing newcomers.

ACKNOWLEDGMENTS

Many members of the AMC Trails and Recreation Management Department contributed to this edition. Andrew Norkin, the Director of Trails and Recreation Management, brought his long-time experience in trail project planning, trail construction, and bridge construction in particular. Mariah Keagy, White Mountain Trails Supervisor, incorporated many new techniques for trail construction and erosion control that she and the AMC Trail Crew have found to be reliable in their never-ending efforts to protect trails and their surrounding environment. Alex DeLucia, North Country Trails Volunteer Supervisor, brought his many years of experience in training volunteers, teaching trail maintenance and reconstruction techniques, and leading crews in safe, productive, and fun trail projects. Alex also lent his artistic skills to create many new illustrations in Chapter 6. Sara Sheehy, Southern New England Regional Trails Coordinator, contributed her considerable experience in leading trail crew projects across the nation. Mike Cooper, Maine Trails Supervisor, imparted his experience in designing and building truly enjoyable hiking and skiing trails. Jennifer Heisey, Mid-Atlantic Recreation Planner, brought her experience in visioning new trails and getting them off the ground so they can get on the ground. Nancy Ritger, Interpretative Naturalist, contributed to the new chapter on kiosks and user education with Alex DeLucia and Alexandra Kosiba, Camp Dodge Programs Coordinator, who also offered her skills and experience to over half the chapters in this book. Hawk Metheny, Backcountry Recreation Management Specialist, also offered his years of insight to creating a useful trail building and maintenance guide. Heather Clish, Deputy Director of Conservation, coordinated the contributors for meaningful updates to the text and brought her experience in trail protection.

Thanks is also due to Lester Kenway, who developed much of the material on the use of rigging and winches for earlier editions, and continues to impart his knowledge to the trails community both in organized training sessions and by training scores of individuals through the Maine Conservation Corps.

The AMC Books and Communications staff also deserves a hearty thanks: Kevin Breunig for his support and encouragement in getting this edition off the ground; Dan Eisner for his patience and help in bringing all the pieces together; and Heather Stephenson for taking this book through to completion.

CHAPTER 1
PLANNING A TRAIL
PROJECT

AT-A-GLANCE

Before you are ready to build a trail, you will first need to do some planning and become familiar with trail jargon.

- **Work with others:** Consult with stakeholders to ensure the public will be satisfied with the trail.

- **Get to know the land:** Familiarize yourself with the proposed trail site to confirm that trail construction will not harm the environment.

- **Terminology:** Learn the most common terms used by trail builders and maintainers.

Planning a new trail construction project can be one of the most rewarding and challenging experiences that outdoor enthusiasts will undertake in their lifetimes. There are many reasons to build a trail. These include the promotion of physical fitness, the encouragement of enjoying nature (e.g., bird watching), providing users a vista or other scenic feature, the creation of a "tool" for future conservation efforts, and the establishment of a place of solitude. There are a host of other reasons to construct a new trail, but regardless of the reasoning or rationale, the vision or concept must be valid and shared by others for the vision to become reality.

When envisioning a new trail project, most individuals are eager to tramp through the woods and hang flagging tape. Perhaps a major reason individuals are so eager to take on a trail building project is that because it happens on a large tract of land, a project such as this provides a unique opportunity to create something on such a grand scale. After all, how often do folks have a hand in something that can last an "eternity," will be open for all to use, and will exist on a scale far greater than anything most people do in their daily job?

More than 75 years ago, many trails in the Northeast were laid out and constructed for use by a select group of individuals, especially affluent travelers who had time to recreate. Most trails were constructed as a way to get from point A to point B. Generally, the trails were built so people could reach the summit of a mountain via the quickest and most straightforward route. While the trails may have withstood the use when initially constructed, many years of use and erosion greatly changed the character of those trails. Today, trail maintainers face the sometimes overwhelming task of combating the cumulative effects that years of use and erosion have caused. Some trails have been nearly washed away (especially steep trails with poor soil), leaving an unsightly scar on the landscape.

By maintaining old networks of trails through the years, maintainers have learned to approach any new trail design with a more complete understanding of both future resource impacts and trail users' experience. Today, trail professionals know that a thorough and comprehensive trail plan is essential to the development of a trail that will withstand the rigors of erosion and user traffic for many years. Each year, professionals meet at conferences throughout the world to share new ideas, discuss positive findings, and share information about what does not work so that financial and human resources are put to use well. Today, trail professionals use an arsenal of tools to help them make informed choices when deciding where to locate a trail. The AMC strongly recommends that professionals be employed to act as trail designers or project consultants to ensure that the trail be designed correctly.

When proposing the construction of a new trail, it is necessary to get many other people involved. Unlike many years ago, proposed trails that would cross public lands go through an approval process that incorporates many different interests and individuals. Today, a wide range of specialists should review proposed trails to ensure they will not adversely affect natural, historical, and economic interests. Agency personnel will also prepare an information packet and hand it out to those who are interested or involved with the planning process.

Trails proposed across private lands may also face the same level of public involvement and environmental assessment. Planning boards, conservation commissions, land regulatory commissions, and wetland bureaus may help determine the suitability of a trail, as well as the positive and negative effects of a proposed trail over the long and short term. It would be advantageous to speak with local officials before immersing yourself in a potential project to be certain that the trail concept is allowable.

Often, a trail designer/advocate prematurely determines which groups will use a trail. It is usually wise *not to* limit your intended users until others have commented on the proposal. However, you may establish broad generalizations about a trail's proposed users and determine that a trail will be non-motorized, motorized, or multiuse ahead of time because this can be conceptualized beforehand. The trail's designer should know who will be using the trail, the estimated frequency of usage, safety considerations, and major obstacles or needs (such as bridges). The designer should also first research landowner information and have preliminary discussions with the owners before submitting the proposal to the public. This is especially important when a landowner's permission is necessary for the project to be successful (see Chapter 2).

WORKING WITH STAKEHOLDERS

To ensure a trail system's sustainability, it must have an agreed-upon need and be supported by the local community and the intended user groups. After a concept is created by the individual or group proposing the trail, the proposal should be submitted to all affected and interested parties so that it can be scrutinized and evaluated for feasibility. Stakeholders can be nonprofit organizations, federal, state and local governments, schools, hospitals, civic groups, local businesses, and private landowners. Support from these stakeholders is essential to the long-term success of your endeavor. You may learn that groups you thought would support your proposal are opposed and vice-versa. Identifying supportive stakeholders also can help to narrow down a trail's intended use. For example, without support of an equestrian group, you will not need to design the trail to accommodate horses.

As part of the planning process, it is also equally important to identify those who may be potentially adversely affected by it. They could include area home owners, other sporting clubs who use the land (e.g., hunting clubs/organizations), emergency responders, police, and departments of transportation. If your trail will be in a remote area, its presence may have limited potential conflicts with other user groups or interests. These potential conflicts are often identified during public hearings, planning board meetings, notices of intent and other public forums. Therefore, it is important to have thought of who could be affected and discuss your plans ahead of time with those individuals.

Once you finalize the trail's course, you must prepare an initial project cost estimate for fund raising or budgeting efforts. An experienced individual should complete the cost estimate to give the proposal credibility. The project budget must account for factors such as design standards, local government needs (e.g., search and rescue and police requirements), contractor estimates, engineering services, use of volunteer labor, and permitting fees.

Research possible options for who will be used to construct the trail. Many urban trails are designed by civil engineering firms, landscape architectural firms, and landscaping companies, for example. Local contractors are also often hired to provide the necessary equipment and labor, following the design standards set forth by the professional design team. On the other hand and quite the opposite, is the use of volunteers that are used to construct and maintain an entirely new trail.

It is equally important to draft a realistic project schedule to share with the potential stakeholders and others involved or interested in the project. At this time cost and time estimates should identify the differences between projects using professional contractors and engineers and those relying solely on volunteer labor.

Too often, a trail has the necessary support for construction but not the commitment from an organization or group to maintain the trail long after it has been built. It is becoming increasingly common for project funders to ask for a long-term maintenance commitment before approving any funding request.

RESEARCHING THE ENVISIONED LOCATION

Someone who has an intimate knowledge of the surrounding land will usually conceive a trail project. This individual may have spent many days tramping around the woods, locating appealing features, or finding unique forest types.

As part of the trail visioning process, one must find a site that will be both environmentally sound and attractive to the user. While instructions on how to lay out a trail will be detailed in Chapter 4, remember that the planner/trail designer should know the general characteristics of the topography and terrain to get a comprehensive feel of what will be involved to make the project a reality. Will the trail be passing through wetlands? If so, for how long (costs, wildlife disturbance, environmental impacts, for example, need to be considered)? Are there sensitive areas such as deer wintering yards that need to be avoided? Are there rare communities of plants or species and if so, where and how will they be protected? What are the unique features that will make this an attractive project for others to support?

Use soil characteristics to determine whether constructing a new trail system is feasible and if it will be sustainable. Certain soil types hold up well, while other soils are poor choices for constructing a natural tread trail. Consider topography, too. Flat terrain or steep slopes may prove to be equally challenging when determining a sustainable location for the trail and will factor in the project's costs. Both steep slopes and flat terrain, especially if combined with poor soil conditions, potentially pose a challenge for water drainage. Flat terrain can be susceptible to water pooling and steep terrain susceptible to rapid soil erosion. Streams and other water courses also deserve special attention during the planning stage as suitable bridge or ford areas should be identified ahead of time so that the final trail location doesn't greatly deviate from the conceptual plan.

During the planning stage, bring a camera to document the special features throughout the property. You should also bring (and know how to use) a topographic map and consider taking a global positioning system unit (GPS) to pinpoint features and reference photos on a map location. The photos and points on a map will be beneficial when presenting and selling the conceptual plan to those unfamiliar with the land. Before heading out, obtain landowner permission where necessary.

UNDERSTANDING TRAIL ANATOMY

Before getting started on your new trail project, it is important to understand the different components of a sustainable trail system. All the components of a trail comprise the trail landscape, or the environment seen by the hiker. These components complement each other as a hiker experiences a trail.

All trails have *terminuses*, which are the *trailhead*, or start of the trail (usually at roadside), and the destination, which could be a mountain summit,

Fig. 1.1. The treadway is the surface where the hiker makes direct contact with the ground.

waterfall, mill site, or other notable feature. Destinations in a system of trails will, for any single trail, include other trails and possibly campsites or other overnight facilities.

The trail *treadway*, or trail tread, is the surface upon which the hiker makes direct contact with the ground (see figure 1.1). All improvements to a natural surface trail treadway are made to conserve soil resources. These improvements (which often also make hiking easier) usually involve the hardening and stabilizing of soils to prevent them from shifting, eroding, or becoming muddy. Popular trails in sensitive areas, such as slopes and wet terrain, will inevitably get damaged; therefore, good maintenance of the treadway occasionally requires reconstruction and rehabilitation of the original soil profile. The treadway is the most important component of any foot trail.

The *trail right of way* is the area around the treadway that is cleared for passage of the hiker. It is usually 4- to-6-feet wide, depending on vegetation density. If a trail has other uses besides hiking, such as cross-country skiing or mountain biking, the right of way should be wider. The term "right of way" also refers to legal right of passage, as would be the case with a protected trail on private land.

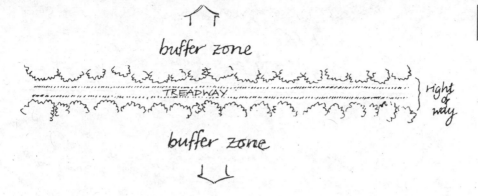

Fig. 1.2. Buffer zones insulate hikers . . .

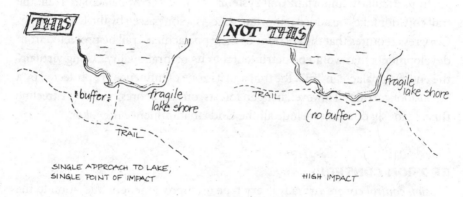

Fig. 1.3. . . . or insulate fragile areas from hiker impact.

The *buffer zone*, or *protective zone*, is the land area on each side of the trail treadway (see figure 1.2). Buffer zones diminish the impact on the hiker from activities detrimental to the hiking experience, such as second-home development, mining, or logging. While the hiker may still hear, see, or even smell such activities, the buffer does provide some degree of mitigation for hikers and their experience. Buffers can also be used to protect particularly fragile areas from hikers. Trail layout around sensitive plant life, lake shores, and springs should include buffers to protect these fragile areas from becoming trampled (see figure 1.3).

The *trail corridor* includes the treadway, right of way, buffer zones, and all the lands that make up the environment of the trail that a hiker experiences (see figure 1.4). The Forest Service has called it the "zone of travel influence." This area affects the hiker's perception of the trail environment.

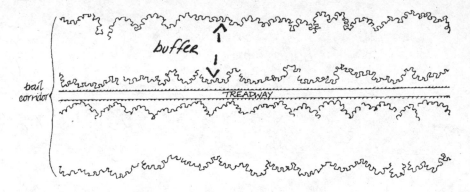

Fig. 1.4. The trail corridor includes the treadway, right-of-way, buffer zones, and all the lands that make up the environment of the trail as experienced by the hiker.

In particularly important trail systems, such as the Appalachian Trail, the trail corridor takes on added importance. Legislation passed by the United States Congress requires that the corridor of the Appalachian Trail be protected from developments that would be detrimental to its natural quality. Along virtually the entire Appalachian Trail, the trail and its zone of influence are protected by a 1,000-foot corridor. However, in open forests, on lake shores, and above treeline this obviously does not include all the lands that influence the hiker.

EROSION CONTROL

Erosion control covers virtually every type of improvement or alteration to the trail tread. Erosion control measures fall into four different categories that will be covered in Chapter 7.

Drainage consists of devices or structures—such as water bars, drainage dips, and ditches—that remove water from the trail tread or prevent water from getting on the tread. The purpose of drainage is to limit or eliminate the effects of erosion on the trail tread.

Stabilizers are used to hold soil in place and prevent erosion caused by water, feet, gravity, or other forces. Stabilizers include rock steps (used to stabilize steep gullied or eroding slopes) and cribbing (used to anchor soil above or below a trail on a slope).

Hardeners are used to eliminate the impact of foot travel through wet areas, and include bog bridges, step stones, and turnpiking.

Definers are used to channel or focus foot traffic onto a hardened or harder tread, thus protecting soils that may be wet, thin, or home to fragile plant life.

Scree, often used in alpine zones or to define a rock staircase, is a good example. Rock steps are also considered definers.

These are broad categories, and elements of more than one category can be found in a water bar, bog bridge, or stone step. More importantly, all types of erosion control should be used in concert to provide a trail with its own, custom-made erosion control system.

TRAIL FORMATS

There are three major trail formats that can be combined to comprise a trail system.

The loop (see figure 1.5) is a popular format for day-use trails because it enables easy access and parking. Hikers do not have to return on the same trail, thus maximizing hiker interest and satisfaction.

The horseshoe (see figure 1.6) can be a valuable trail format, especially in areas where public transportation is available. It can be used also as an appropriate alternative to auto travel on roads where distances between terminuses are

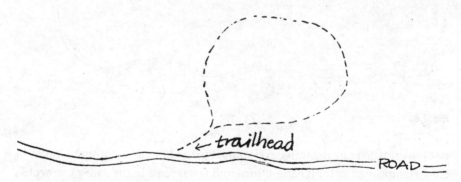

Fig. 1.5. Loop.

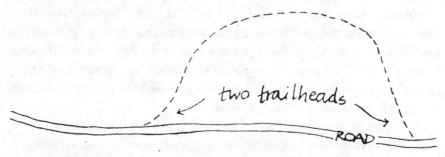

Fig. 1.6. Horseshoe.

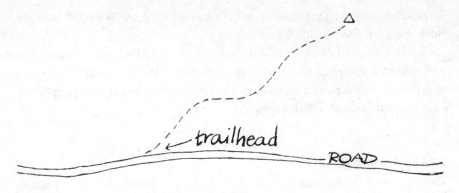

Fig. 1.7. Line.

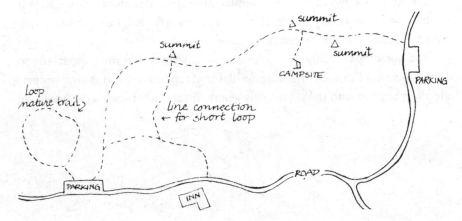

Fig. 1.8. Trail system.

not too great. Ski touring trail development in the Mount Washington Valley of New Hampshire has trailheads at inns and restaurants in the valley connected by trails in the horseshoe format. Many hiking trails are horseshoes.

The line (see figure 1.7) is the simplest and most common format for trails. It connects two points—the roadside trailhead and the destination. Good examples of trails in the line format are fire warden's trails to lookout towers on mountain summits. Long-distance trails such as the Appalachian Trail and Pacific Crest Trail are prime examples of trails in the line format. These trails on public lands with high scenic value are augmented with side trails, alternate routes, and connectors to form trail systems.

A trail system (see figure 1.8) can combine these different formats to satisfy a diversity of recreation needs. Careful design will provide trails for different users with different expectations. Multiday backpackers, day hikers, and others can be served by a well-designed trail system.

CHAPTER 2
TRAILS ON PRIVATE LAND

AT-A-GLANCE

Learning about landowners is an important step in the trail building process.

- **Research landowners:** Consult local records and speak with residents and government officials to learn who owns the land on a potential trail site.

- **Communication:** Talk to landowners to determine their concerns.

- **Permission and protection:** Make legal arrangements with landowners to establish a trail right of way.

Trail building in the East, where much of the land is privately owned, often involves constructing a trail on someone's property. In addition to the standard challenge of considering soils, topography, and vegetation, trail builders face the requirements of multiple landowners and conditions for the use of their properties.

The benefits of creating trails that incorporate private land are numerous. Greenway and suburban hiking and recreation paths, which increasingly cross private land, provide recreational opportunities close to population centers. Trails crossing private land can enhance access to town and county parks and offer recreational opportunities normally reserved for vacations and landscapes farther afield. Local trails also enhance environmental education opportunities, and school curricula can often use trail maintenance and development as part of nature study. Finally, local trails can imbue the public with conservation values.

Despite these community benefits, landowners have legitimate concerns about allowing trails to be built on their land. Although many landowners are primarily concerned about liability and future use, trail builders and maintainers may encounter a wide range of landowner concerns. Use the information in this section to make your best effort at securing permission and the best possible level of future protection for your trail.

DETERMINING OWNERSHIP

Once you've documented trail needs and decided to proceed with the construction of your trail, you'll need to investigate ownership of the land along your proposed trail corridor. In order to maintain flexibility for negotiations with owners, your initial stages of planning should include a broad trail corridor including alternate trail locations. Inflexible trail plans that rely on one key parcel of privately held land can be foiled if that owner refuses to cooperate.

1. *Review town tax maps (if they exist).* Such maps are usually kept by the assessor's office or the town clerk. The maps are public information and are available for anyone to examine. The information on the maps is extensive, although the boundary lines are not always accurate. The maps are usually cross-referenced with owners' names and addresses; they also indicate acreage and may indicate the existing easements and right of ways across properties. Many towns now also have digitized tax maps that can be reviewed and analyzed using Geographic Information Systems (GIS) software.
2. *Research deeds in the county registry of deeds.* In addition to checking names and addresses, looking for any easements or restrictions which might al-

ready apply to the property is also important. If the town has no tax maps, the process is far more complex—a bit like solving a jigsaw puzzle. Here are some suggestions:

- Get to know the locals. Local residents are probably the most useful sources of information because they are familiar with the use of land over time, attitudes toward conservation, financial status of individual owners, and future plans for the region. Ask local residents who are sympathetic to the trail project about general landownership, patterns, specific owners (if known), and ideas on who they think would be most favorably inclined toward the idea of a trail and land preservation. Discuss which other people know landowners and, if necessary, ask to be introduced.

- Talk to members of the town Select Board. If they support a proposed trail, they can be a good source of information because they often know who owns that land. The selectmen's office should have complete lists of property owners that includes acreage, addresses, and taxes paid. (However, they may have not have boundary maps.) The selectmen's office can give an idea of how much land is being sold in the town, what the various land uses are, and what future plans might affect the trail. Maintain a good working relationship with the town Select Board members, because they may be useful when you talk to landowners; in very small towns, their opinions may be quite influential.

- Talk with surveyors who have surveyed land in the area. Often, a few surveyors have been working a region for a number of years and know the land and landowners well, particularly the larger landholdings. Surveyors are a good source of information about existing woods roads, current use of the land, and outstanding natural features. Use sympathetic surveyors who have good relations with landowners and the town as references when you call landowners.

- Contact conservation officers of state fish and game departments, county foresters, and consultants from the USDA Natural Resource Conservation Service. Often they know a particular area well and can recommend landowners who would be more favorably inclined to the project than others. Their greatest contribution, however, is their knowledge of the land and its features.

- The chairpersons of town conservation commissions are extremely helpful in most cases, especially since they are aware of the prevalent conservation attitudes in the town. Again, they can be most useful when actually contacting landowners.

The types and patterns of landownership play an important role in the design and layout of a trail. Studying overall types and patterns of landownership will help to determine which landowners are most approachable and, by extension, where it will be easiest and most economical to lay a trail.

TYPES AND PATTERNS OF OWNERSHIP

Corporate Owners: Pulp and Paper Companies, Agricultural Ownerships

Land owned by corporations for timber harvesting and agriculture can be ideal for trail use. Well-planned trail use can be easily adapted to the land management programs of these owners and provide them an opportunity to communicate their management values to the public. Additionally, negotiations with one corporate owner often can yield access to large tracts of land. These agricultural lands are not disrupted to the same extent as residential land. Hikers are less bothersome to absentee owners than they are to residential owners who are closely affected by the use of their land.

However, corporate owners tend to have some very specific concerns. Before you approach these owners with a trail proposal, develop your vision in a manner that acknowledges their concerns, which generally are related to ways the trail will affect future use of the land. Allowing a public trail is often beneficial for corporate public relations. However, corporate decisions tend to be based on financial concerns, and not hiker satisfaction. Enthusiastic use by the public would make subsequent trail closure a bad public relations issue. Accidents could pose an unacceptable liability burden to the corporate owner. Genuine concerns about fire hazards, parking congestion, vandalism, and sanitation problems can also make obtaining endorsement of trail proposals by these owners difficult.

Corporate Owners: Developers and Subdividers

Owners whose purpose is to develop their land holdings sometimes have negative attitudes about proposals for trail use. From their perspective, trails may limit future development options. However, an increasing number of developers now see recreational trails as a potential selling point for residential development.

Designating land for development virtually precludes the possibility of high-quality trail design because such land tends to be subdivided into small units. Existing trails sometimes must be closed because access had been cut off by development. Many informal, unmaintained paths in and around cities and towns have been effectively closed by sprawl, such as limited-access highways, airports, and strip malls. Land held for development may present only limited trail options and narrow the possibility of successful public trail use.

However, if town boards and developers recognize the value and desirability of recreational trails as integral to a vibrant community and a selling point to potential buyers, trail systems or connections can be designed as part of a subdivision plan. For this approach to be successful, it is important to have town planning boards and open space committees support the overall trail vision as well.

Residential Owners

In urban and suburban centers, most ownerships are residential, with owners on or near their property. These owners require close and thorough follow-up for trail construction. Owner attitudes are varied and, in order to satisfy these different perspectives, trail design necessarily becomes more complex.

Negotiating with conservation-minded owners is easier because they can understand the social and environmental goals of the proposed trail. Document owner attitudes during initial research and note which owners are most sympathetic. Approaching them first will facilitate further negotiations. Endorsements from these owners may encourage their less sympathetic neighbors to accept the idea of public trail use. Depending on the situation, protection of trails on residential land can be so complex as to be unrealistic for trail projects.

TALKING TO LANDOWNERS

The utilization of land protection devices for trail corridors is a vast subject that at some stage usually requires legal counsel, a considerable financial investment, and time-consuming negotiations. This chapter offers a cursory review of some of the available mechanisms, as well as their benefits and drawbacks when applied to trail development and protection.

Crystal-clear communication is essential. All parties involved must clearly understand the goals of the trail project, how they will be accomplished, the role each party will play, and how the project will affect them. If policies and modes of implementation are not clearly understood and collectively acknowledged, negotiations for agreements will likely be unsuccessful.

Tact and enthusiasm are critical for the person negotiating with owners, and a good public relations profile in the proposed trail region helps pave the way to the owner's door. To establish strong public relations, the policies underlying implementation of the project must be clearly understood. Conflicting information sows seeds of landowner distrust and reticence. Develop a solid vision with a flexible plan before you talk to landowners.

Many landowners feel defensive about their rights, so use a low-key, soft-sell approach to reduce the likelihood that an owner will feel threatened. This is especially important today, when the demands on the private sector are growing. Despite the need for a soft-sell approach, you must be firm. Legal agreements that do not bind the owner to promise a high-quality environment for the trail may help get a trail initially constructed. However, these agreements won't assure the protection that trails desperately need. A legal agreement must guarantee that a trail will be sustained and preserved for a long period of time and throughout changes in landownership for the trail to be successful.

Your negotiator must be thoroughly familiar with the characteristics of the land on which the trail is proposed. Before approaching an owner, the negotiator should know about the owner's perspectives and views on trail use to help the development of a successful pitch and proposal that best suits the landowner's needs. Although individual trail arrangements can be adapted for each owner, they should all receive equal treatment. Mistrust can develop among neighboring owners if special accommodations are made for one particular owner.

LEGAL FORMS OF TRAIL PROTECTION

There are five legal arrangements that can establish a trail right of way: oral agreements, licenses, leases, easements, and land acquisitions. Between the two extremes of oral agreement and a complete fee purchase, there are three limited legal interests that can be placed on trail corridor land. These nonpossessory interests in land offer much flexibility and are excellent techniques for realizing private wishes with respect to the land. To protect a trail and its corridor, the goal is to use the arrangement the landowner finds agreeable that also provides the longest protection to the trail and is the most binding. Any legal arrangement requires careful consideration of its respective characteristics.

Oral Agreements

Generally a contract involving the sale of real estate is not binding unless it is in writing. An *oral agreement* that transfers ownership of land is not legally binding. Although some types of agreements for the use of land do not need to be in writing, enforcing an oral agreement will always be difficult because the parties may disagree over the original terms of their contract. An oral agreement is, therefore, inappropriate for use in a trail project except during the preliminary planning stages.

License

The most limited nonpossesory interest in land is the *license*, which is revocable at the will of either party to the agreement. Unlike an easement, a license does not run with the land; the death of the licensor generally will terminate the license, and the licensor often retains the ability to terminate the license at any time. A license simply permits the licensed party to enter the land of the licensor and maintain a trail without being deemed a trespasser. The license is the simplest legal device and the least formidable to the owner, who will be assured that there will be no threat of litigation should he or she decide that the arrangement is no longer in his or her best interest. The nonbinding nature of the license makes it fairly easy to consummate with owners; however, it has obvious limitations as a device to secure land for trails.

When negotiating a right of way for a trail, it is important to include an agreement about whether and how the landowner can use the right of way. This way, the trail will not include unnecessary obstacles and encroachments. Establish a minimum distance around the trail that will be free of incompatible developments and aesthetic concerns such as highways, structures, and timber-harvesting activity.

Lease

The *lease* involves the granting of an interest in land upon the payment of an agreed-upon fee. The fee does not have to be monetary, but to assure that the lease will be legally binding some consideration must be given for the right to use the land. The benefit of a lease agreement to the landowner is its ability to be terminated after a certain period of time. Remember, though, that the power of termination is limited to the terms of the written arrangement.

Easement

The *easement* is the strongest of the nonpossessory interests in land. An easement grants a non-owner the right to use a specific portion of the land for a specific purpose. The extent of the interest conveyed needs to be explicitly outlined in the deed of conveyance, which is recorded in public records of title. An easement may be limited to a specific period of time or may be granted in perpetuity. The termination of the easement may also be predicated upon the occurrence of a specific event (for example, the easement could include the following language: "so long as the bridge is maintained" or "unless and until the property is zoned for commercial development"). A trail corridor easement can range from eight feet to a quarter of a mile wide, depending on the owner, the financial resources of the trail sponsor, and the vision for the proposed trail. An easement agreement "runs with the land," meaning it survives transfer of land ownership and is generally binding upon future owners until it expires on its own terms.

Ownership-in-Fee

Ownership-in-fee is a complete transfer of ownership from landowner to trail steward. Ownership-in-fee may not be financially feasible or necessary, except perhaps where permanent facilities such as parking lots and campsites will be provided. However, a landowner may find the donation of land to a nonprofit appealing because of tax or estate planning concerns. If comfortable, your negotiator may want to explore this with the landowner.

CONCERNS OF PRIVATE LANDOWNERS

A legally binding agreement may require a commitment too great for an owner to accept. Remember that the freedom to make decisions about property is a highly-valued constitutional right.

Owner concerns regarding public trail development and any accompanying proposed legally binding arrangement are entirely legitimate. To see a trail proposal from the owner's perspective, consider the following points:

Future Use of the Proposed Trail Property

The major concern for protecting trail rights of way or easements is the landowner's future right to use property proposed for the trail. Trails need not be protected with highly restrictive agreements, but without some protection a trail's future cannot be securely guaranteed.

Try to anticipate the owner's reaction so that the trail proposal does not sound unreasonable. The trail sponsor must enter negotiations with a firm sense of the owner's attitude. In initial transactions, it may be best simply to secure a written pledge from the owner to continue to work with the trail sponsor toward construction and eventual protection.

Trails can easily bisect property into compartments, which can seriously constrain the property's future use. The trail agreement should permit motorized crossing of the corridor and possibly allow limited use of vehicles along the trail treadway. For working forest land, this concession and the latitude to cut timber according to a simple prescription will protect the trail while giving the owner essential freedom to manage his or her lands.

On a trail route with no alternative routes, you'll need to adapt the agreement to the owner's conditions. Sometimes the owner's plans may preclude trail development completely. In this case, nothing can be done to change the situation and alternative trail routes must be found. Remember, when relatively little commitment is required from landowners an agreement will be easier to reach.

In some cases, the best course of action may be to begin simply by getting verbal or basic written permission from the owner to build the trail. This approach may work well with reticent owners. If construction of the trail proceeds with minimal trouble to the landowner, maintenance work is top-notch, and the owner's use of the land is not restricted, the landowner may be won over and could be willing to agree to progressively more trail-protective agreements. Unfortunately, obtaining simple verbal or written permission for trail use is unlikely to actually protect the trail well into the future because of its very limited nature. The tenuous status of most trails on private land must eventually be fortified with viable agreements to protect and perpetuate these hiking opportunities.

Liability for Hiker Injury and Costs of Legal Self-Defense

Landowners are frequently concerned that by approving a proposed trail, they are tacitly accepting liability for accidents that hikers may have on their property. Landowners fear that failure to warn hikers about dangerous conditions on the land, or failure to inspect trails regularly and draw attention to possible hazards on the trail, will cause an injured hiker to sue the landowner. These lawsuits are usually based on an argument that the landowner has been legally negligent by failing to protect the hiker from hazards even though the landowner knew that the hiker was going to use his or her land. In order to establish that a landowner has been legally negligent, the plaintiff must prove four elements, which are covered below.

Duty

The plaintiff must prove that the landowner had some obligation or duty recognized by law to protect the plaintiff from unreasonable risk. In law, the actions of the landowner are judged by a standard of conduct. For example, if landowners generally prune dead branches off trees that overhang a public walkway to make the walkway safe, a landowner who does not do so would not have lived up to the legal standard of conduct for landowners. In this case, the landowner might be liable for the injuries of a hiker who gets hit by a dead branch while using the walkway.

Breach

The failure on the owner's part to conform to the standard of conduct that the law requires is considered a breach. In the previous scenario, the landowner has not pruned the branches on the tree, and therefore he has breached his duty to do so.

Proximate Cause

The plaintiff must also establish a reasonably close causal connection between the conduct and injury. Using the example above, the landowner's neglect was the actual reason the dead branch remained on the tree until it fell and hit the passerby. There is a direct relationship between the landowner's actions (or inactions) and the harm to the hiker.

Damage

The action or inaction of the negligent party must result in actual quantifiable loss or damage to the injured party. Following the same example, the hiker only has a cause of action if he is injured by the falling tree limb. If the hiker sustains a head wound and must be rushed to the hospital he has been damaged. If the branch startles him and he is annoyed or momentarily frightened when it falls, no actual injury has occurred and he cannot recover for the landowner's actions.

Burden of Proof

In a lawsuit for negligence, the burden of proof is on the injured party. This means that the injured party must prove each element of his or her case by a preponderance of the evidence. The defendant landowner, however, must still pay for a legal defense. Even though landowner liability is often limited by state recreational-use statutes, these statutes do not eliminate the right to sue, and defending yourself against even a frivolous lawsuit can be expensive. Landowners are legitimately concerned about legal costs, even though few, if any, cases have caused serious financial peril.

Extent of Duty

Identifying the extent of the duty that the landowner has to the hiker is important because, as indicated in the outline of requirements for negligence, landowner liability is predicated upon the breach of the duty owed to another person. The extent of the duty owed by a landowner to users of his land depends on the legal status of the person using the land.

Case Law

In some states, the law provides for categories of persons entitled to use land, and establishes a hierarchy of land users (most generally called trespassers), licensees, and invitees. However, most states have abolished this hierarchy. Instead, the law considers whether the landowner's conduct toward a person on his land is reasonable. Some discussion of the different categories is useful to demonstrate "reasonable" treatment by the landlord.

A trespasser is a person who enters the landowner's property intentionally and without privilege or consent of the landowner. The landowner owes no duty to the trespasser to use reasonable care to keep his lands safe for the trespasser; however, the landowner may not set traps for the trespasser. If the landowner knows of the trespasser's existence, the landowner has a duty to warn the trespasser of serious or life-threatening conditions.

A landowner may have an additional duty to protect trespassing children, because children cannot judge the degree of risk the way an adult can. This is particularly true when the landowner knows that children are trespassing; in this situation, his responsibility to protect them from dangers on his land is high. For example, the law finds it unreasonable for a landowner to leave unsecured dangerous equipment where children might play. It would also be illegal to fail to warn of thin ice on a pond if he knows children often skate on the pond and he knows that the ice is thin.

To licensees—people who have been given permission to use land but who do so for their own reasons without benefit to the landowner—the landowner owes a greater duty. The landowner does not need to inspect his property for safety, nor must he warn of hazards that should be obvious to the licensee. The landowner owes the greatest amount of duty to invitees, people whom the owner invites to enter the property at some benefit to the owner—social, financial, or otherwise. The landowner must protect invitees from known hazards, but the landowner also has an affirmative duty to protect invitees against hazards that he or she, with reasonable care, might discover when exploring the land.

The reasonableness test does not make a clear distinction between the licensee and the invitee but instead examines the landowner's conduct. The court looks at what a particular person was doing on the land and what that person could reasonably have expected from the landowner. For example, if the landowner lets people fish in his pond, he may only have a duty to warn them of known dangers. However, if he suspects that the bank of the pond is eroding and unsafe, the court may determine that the landowner had a duty to check the bank of the pond and ensure that the fishers were safe.

Opening land to the public implies that it has been prepared for their reception. While there may seem to be some inherent risks involved with hiking, the legal duty owed to a hiker has not been established clearly, and no determination would cover every circumstance. It seems likely that the courts will enforce greater responsibility on owners in the future because of a generally increasing concern for safety.

Statutory Law

Many states have recreational-use statutes that limit the liability of owners who allow the public to use their lands for recreational purposes such as hiking, skiing, or mountain biking. Generally, these laws protect only landowners who permit use of their lands without charge. The statutes may also provide a specific level of care below which the landowner is liable. To encourage landowners to allow the recreational use of their land these laws help to minimize the duty of landowners toward recreational land users. These statutes also serve to keep the cost of liability insurance premiums fairly low, which makes it feasible for landowners to purchase insurance to protect themselves when they open their lands to recreational use. While these laws limit liability, they do not eliminate the threat of lawsuits or the legal burden of self-defense. So, landowners do have a legitimate concern about the cost of defending themselves against a frivolous or malicious lawsuit.

Indemnifications

Indemnification of landowners by the responsible trail club is one way to alleviate the very real concern over liability. Indemnification should only be done on a case-by-case basis and then only after the trail club has obtained a qualified legal opinion.

Insurance spreads risk over a population large enough so that no insured party would suffer unacceptable losses if a mishap occurs. Insurance is available to private landowners concerned with the liability they may incur by opening land to hiking. Most landowners have homeowner's insurance policies that adequately cover their risks. However, if the landowner lacks insurance, or if additional coverage is deemed necessary, the trail sponsor could purchase it, with the landowner as the beneficiary.

When seeking proper insurance, a local agent usually knows a landowner's needs. It is important for the agent to understand the nature of the recreational program, as well as the volume of recreational use and potential hazards. The agent should be informed of state laws limiting landowner liability.

SPONSORS

Two basic types of liability insurance policies are available to managers (sponsors) of recreation facilities on private land: the Owner, Landlord, and Tenant policy (OL&T) and the Comprehensive General Liability policy. If possible, someone familiar with insurance terms and definitions should review policies to determine the extent of the coverage.

The OL&T policy is the basic method for covering legal liability to the public. Campgrounds and parking areas may be covered by this type of policy. The Comprehensive General Liability Policy offers extensive coverage unless specific risks are excluded. Its major advantage is its coverage of almost all trail hazards.

OVERUSE, VANDALISM, PARKING, AND OTHER MANAGEMENT PROBLEMS

If the owner's reservations regarding future use and liability are quelled, concerns over the actual management of the proposed trail may become the greatest cause for reticence in an owner's support. All of the problems that can develop on public trails can develop on trails on private land. These problems range from physical concerns such as soil erosion to the social problems of overcrowding, vandalism, parking congestion, and littering. These trail management problems and their attendant solutions are described later in this book. A responsible trail organization will convince owners that problems have solutions, that these problems can be controlled by effective management, and that the organization has the knowledge to effectively manage the trail.

The basic point, then, is to inspire trust in the maintenance organization that will be responsible for the trail. It is presumed that the sponsoring organization will have determined that it has the capability to meet this responsibility. This is essential before winning landowner support; if management tasks exceed capabilities when problems develop, the owner's trust in the organization will be diminished.

A prudent procedure for new trails is to limit information on the trail's availability and to clearly explain landowner's property rights in trail information. This approach allows traffic to increase gradually and increases the likelihood that users will respect landowners. Management problems are almost directly proportional to the level of trail use and also a factor of perceived hiker and landowner rights. A maintaining organization will obviously not be as heavily taxed on a trail with low or moderate public use. Gradually increasing the dissemination of information about a trail serves to gradually increase the number of hikers on the trail. The gradual start will help the trail manager develop and adapt a management style to support the higher profile that comes with increasing use. This way, problems can be solved earlier and not after they become full-blown irritants to the landowner.

Once the trail is constructed and in use, the trail managing organization should remain in regular contact with the landowners to ensure continued support of the trail. This work includes tracking changes in ownership and establishing communication with new landowners, ensuring landowners know whom to contact with management issues or questions, and sharing general updates about the trail.

CHAPTER 3
DEVELOPING & USING
TRAIL MAINTENANCE
INVENTORIES

AT-A-GLANCE

Prior to doing new construction or performing maintenance, go into the field to assess problem areas and determine which work needs to be done.

- **Objectivity vs. subjectivity:** Consider the experience of the assessor and the type of reporting to determine whether information gathered is objective or subjective.

- **Trail condition reports and logs:** Write down or make an audio recording of work to be done on the trail.

Before beginning work on a trail project, it can be helpful to create inven- tories or assessments of trail conditions and maintenance needs. They are useful in a variety of ways to trail maintainers, land managers, and others and can be used for project planning, scheduling maintenance, budget preparation, specific project guidance, and many other aspects of trail management. Their uses can range from the prioritizing of small, specific project areas to the creation of baseline data on trails conditions in a land management area.

OBJECTIVE AND SUBJECTIVE ASSESSMENTS

Most of the types of trail condition assessments tend to be completed by either a trails staff person or volunteer who hikes and takes note of general conditions. In the case of a trail log (which will be discussed in detail later in this chapter), a measuring and recording device is used to note problem areas on the trail. These assessments are subjective for the following reasons: information gathered by this type of assessment is not quantifiable. Assessments often include a rating system; for example, the assessor will decide whether a section of trail is "good" or "bad," which can be difficult to determine since a finding of "good" or "bad" will vary depending on overall conditions and user/land manager expectations of the area.

It's also important to note that because smaller organizations and nonprofits are often in charge of these assessments, people with varying levels of trail management experience work on them. Sometimes the workers have very little experience, which can make assessments unpredictable. Aside from experience with trail management, experience in the region and with a certain character of trail can also vary.

Despite the limitations of subjective trail condition assessments, they can also be beneficial. A plus is that they can be done by a variety of people who do not need any special training, aside from general trail maintenance experience. They also can be done quickly.

Other types of trail condition assessments are considered objective. One example is the measuring and calculating of the amount of soil that is displaced in one eroded section of the trail. Objective, scientific assessments do provide valuable and accurate information on trail conditions, but because a high level of training and a significant time commitment are necessary to collect the data properly, it is not very practical for most trail managers. However, for those who have the time and resources, scientific assessments can provide accurate, quantifiable trail condition information for many levels of trails management. An example of a training program is one taught through Beneficial Designs and American Trail, called UTAP (Universal Trail Assessment Process). This process includes in-depth assessment and the measuring and recording of trail features along a certain segment of trail. Parts of this process involve multiple people and can be quite labor-intensive, measuring the grade of each section and measuring all features and trail improvement needs. Trainings in UTAP are offered at different locations around the United States.

Despite their tendency to be subjective, there are certainly ways to make trail condition assessments more accurate and consistent. One way is to create clear standards and communicate them to all reporters. This can include written descriptions of what constitutes "bad" or photographic examples of "bad" versus "moderate." Another way to ensure consistency is to be sure that reporters have a certain amount of training and experience and are familiar with the local standards. Also, before planning a project, have a qualified person take a field assessment if the quality of the initial trail assessment is in question.

TRAIL CONDITION REPORTS

Most maintainers use reports completed by assessors in the spring to prepare for the summer maintenance effort. Like other organizations and trail systems, the AMC trail crew hikes all AMC trails in the White Mountains in the spring to remove winter blowdowns and identify trail problems; the crew leaders then fill out a Trail Condition Report (see figure 3.1) for each trail. Volunteer trail adopters also file reports on minor and major maintenance needs.

Most trail groups have their own assessment forms to collect information on specific problems (e.g., a missing sign) or general maintenance needs (e.g., a boggy or eroded section of trail). Specific problems may require a follow-up field check to thoroughly assess the situation and prepare for eventual correction. Some forms provide spaces for comments about guidebook descriptions, facilities along the trail, parking accommodations, off-trail or bootleg camping, and other trail-related matters. Some also double as work reports.

Bear in mind that the degree of detail provided will vary depending on the questions asked and the trail maintenance experience of the person recording the inventory. Not only does the reporter's experience and knowledge of standards count, but he or she will rarely provide more information than asked for on the form. So, firstly, be sure your report covers the right amount of information, and then be sure that the standards and experience of those collecting the information is up to par, as well. Lastly, get additional input from both maintainers and hikers to compensate for the biases you may get if only one or two evaluations are considered. Those not trained in trail problems and their

TRAIL CONDITION REPORT
AMC TRAILS PROGRAM

Date: _____/_____/_____
Name: _____

Trail:_____

Section:_____
Wilderness   AT   Alpine_____**Miles**

Crew (List names)
Leader: **Hours**   **Hours**

_____   _____
_____   _____
_____   _____
_____

                                        ***Total Patrol Hours:** _____

Please Comment on All the Following Observations

Weather Conditions (During inspection): _____

General Trail Condition (Due to recent weather)
❑ Very Wet   ❑ Wet   ❑ Normal   ❑ Dry   ❑ Frozen   ❑ Other:_____

Blazes

Condition	Quality	Quantity	Color	Note Problems and Solutions (What and Where):
❑ Good	❑ Neat	❑ Right	❑ White	_____
❑ Fair	❑ Messy	❑ Too Few	❑ Yellow	_____
❑ Bad	❑ Big/Small	❑ Too Many	❑ Blue	_____

Brushing (4′ x 8′ Standardizing) Condition   Note Problem Locations and Lengths:
❑ Good   ❑ Needs Some (Soon)   _____
❑ Too Wide   ❑ Needs Lots (Now)   _____

General Drainage Maintenance Condition   Note Problems and Locations:
❑ Clean (Good or done)   ❑ Needs Normal Cleaning   _____
❑ Needs Extensive Cleaning   ❑ Needs Rebuilding   _____

Use (By Hikers): ❑ Low   ❑ Moderate   ❑ High   ❑ Can't Tell

Overall Trail Section Condition and Priority

Condition	Priority for Work	
❑ Great	Low	Needs little or no work (annual maintenance; clean drainages, brush, blaze, etc.) - Adt.
❑ Good	Low/Med	Needs some minor work later, stable for now (replace & add a few WB, RS, SS, etc.) - VC, Adt.
❑ Fair	Med	Needs some work soon to control moderate damage (some RS, SS, BB, drainages, etc.) - VC, TC
❑ Bad	Med/High	Needs abundant work now to repair and stop damage (lots of rock work, WB, SS, BB) - TC, VC
❑ Very Bad	High	Needs major work now to repair and stop much serious damage (major reconstruction/relo) - TC

Fig. 3.1a.

Problems, Work Needed, and Locations (Please be specific)

Drainage Needs. What type of drainage is needed, how many of each are needed, and where? Please Estimate Amount of Each Needed:

Old work to be improved/replaced   **New** work needed   ←Hey! Don't double count!

RWB _____ #   RWB _____ #
WWB _____ #   WWB _____ #
DIP _____ #   DIP _____ #
SideDitch _____ feet   SideDitch _____ feet
RXR _____ #   RXR _____ #

Is there running water, erosion from lack of drainage, wet areas that won't drain, etc. that can be repaired of controlled by replacing, improving, and/or installing additional drainages? What are the general problems and their specific locations?

Trail Tread Stability and Hardening Needs. Please estimate amount of each needed:

Old work to be improved/replaced   **New** work needed ←Hey! Don't double count!

RS _____ #   LDR ____ feet   RS _____ #   LDR ____ feet
CRB ____ feet   BB _____ feet   CRB ____ feet   BB _____ feet
SCR ____ feet   SS _____ #   SCR ____ feet   SS _____ #
SH _____ feet   SH _____feet   RELO ___ feet

Are there trail tread problems or erosion that require replacing, improving, and/or installing structures? What are the general problems and their specific locations?

Trail Defining and Marking Needs

Cairns   Condition   Quantity   Note Problems and Solutions (What and Where):
         ❑ Good   ❑ Right   _____
         ❑ Fair   ❑ Too Few   _____
         ❑ Bad   ❑ Too Many   _____

Old work to be improved/replaced   **New** work needed   ←Hey! Don't double count!

CRN _____ #   CRN _____ #
SW _____ feet   SW _____ feet
RUBBLING _____feet   RUBBLING _____feet
                                Bootlegs/BI _____ feet

Are there sections that are difficult to follow (why?), are too wide, have bootleg trails, require better signs, cairn work (be specific), special blazes, scree walls, brushing in, etc.? What and where are the problems?

Special Needs: Are there any such as major stream bridges, difficult stream crossings, ladders, difficult ledges, bootleg campsites, trailhead problems, etc.? Please elaborate on problem(s) and solution(s).

Fig. 3.1b. Crew leaders fill out a Trail Condition Report to identify problems on the trail.

solutions can find help in various trails manuals such as this book, the *Appalachian Trail Field Book: A Self-Help Guide for Trail Maintainers* (developed by the Appalachian Trail Conservancy), or the Student Conservation Association's *Lightly on the Land*. However, none of these substitute for the experience of building and maintaining a trail first-hand.

TRAIL LOGS

One method of collecting very specific, detailed information on a particular section of trail is by creating a trail log, also called a work log. A trail log consists of an inventory of each problem on a trail, or trail deficiency, and possible solutions for each specific site. Logs are done using a measuring wheel which measures distance as it is rolled across the ground. It can be used to create distance reference points along the trail, so as to be as specific and detailed as possible. Work logs are especially helpful for prioritizing and scheduling projects, as well as estimating time and expenses. They provide a way for project managers/planners to learn about potential projects, while also helping them create detailed project plans for field crews. Because they also serves as a way to quantify the amount of work to be done, logs are also used to calculate the amount of time the crew and project managers need and the money that must be budgeted.

Work logs should be prepared by experienced trail people. Two people are ideal because their expertise and knowledge can be combined to evaluate and develop a prescription for a difficult trail problem. Generate work logs while traveling uphill; the view of treadway is better when going uphill. Also travel tends to be slower going uphill. Many say that spring is the best time to do work logs and see water-related problems that might not be evident in summer or fall. This timing coordinates well with pre-season project planning. However, it is always very important to note the weather while creating the log, because recent precipitation will cause an entire trail to be wet, making some sections appear to be in worse shape than they actually are. Though many of these drainage problems may exist in drier weather, they may not be as dramatic without a serious water event.

Good, detailed work logs require time. On a trail requiring extensive work, it may take an experienced person a full day to log three or four miles.

Creating a Trail Log

Before you begin your work, you will need the following tools:

- Sturdy Measuring Wheel (preferably 1-foot or 5-foot increments)
- Tape/digital recorder, batteries, cassette (if using a tape recorder)
- Spare batteries and extra cassette (if using a tape recorder)
- Paper and Pen
- Your gear for the day
- Optional: GPS or measuring wheel with GPS, camera

Note: Test the recorder to be sure it is working properly, and check frequently.

1. Begin by pressing play on your recorder, and record the name of the trail, the date, names of those generating the log, weather conditions and trail conditions (e.g., wet, snowy patches, etc.), the wheel conversion rate (if any), and a description of the exact location of where the log begins. As you encounter signs, note their placement and information.
2. Head up the trail. Look for notable features, existing structures, and problem areas.
3. When you reach a feature or proposed work site, note your location by speaking clearly and crisply as you read the number on the wheel. Also, briefly describe the feature or problem and be sure to take a moment to think of the best possible solution if a problem exists. Then suggest the solution in a clear, concise, quantifiable way. For example, a person might say, "Problem: trail eroded and gullying. Solution: install four to five rock stairs." List all trail junctions, streams, and outlooks.
4. Continue noting features, trail problems, and suggested solutions for the entire section of trail. Check your recorder often to be sure it is working. You may also choose to record notes about priority of work, possible camp options, or water sources. Also, if the recorder fails, use your pen and paper as needed.
5. Transcribe the work log directly off the tape onto a computer. This process is tedious and time consuming, but if you do this immediately after completing the log, you will remember more details about problems you did not clearly describe on your recorder.
6. Don't forget that someone else is most likely going to be using this log in the field, so make it as detailed—yet concise and comprehensible—as possible, with adequate reference points for those who are pacing, not using a measuring wheel (see figure 3.2).

ETHAN POND TRAIL LOG
From Ethan Pond Shelter to Shoal Pond Trail

LOGGED BY JUSTIN PREISENDORFER AND ALEX DELUCIA

DATE: November 28, 2001
Ground Wet

WHEEL READING (5' INCREMENTS)	ITEM	WORK NEEDED
0002	2 EXISTING BB	REMOVE AND INSTALL 2 NEW BB
0011	2 EXISTING BB	REMOVE AND INSTALL 2 NEW BB
0020	3 EXISTING BB	REMOVE AND INSTALL 4 NEW BB
0026	EXISTING DIP RIGHT	
0030	1 EXISTING BB FOLLOWED BY SS AND DIP RIGHT	REPLACE WITH 1 BB
0058	EXISTING DIP RIGHT	IMPROVE
0075	1 EXISTING BB, DRAINAGE DIP RIGHT	REPLACE BB AND IMPROVE DIP
0094	6 EXISTING SS	
0107	1 EXISTING BB	REPLACE WITH NEW BB
0111	1 EXISTING BB, DIP RIGHT	REPLACE WITH 1 NEW BB IMPROVE DIP RIGHT
0116	2 EXISTING BB WITH DIP RIGHT	REPLACE WITH 2 NEW BB IMPROVE DIP RIGHT
0122	2 EXISTING BB WITH SS IN BETWEEN	REPLACE WITH 4 NEW BB
0130	SS WITH DIP RIGHT	IMPROVE DIP
0133	5 EXISTING BB	REPLACE WITH 8 BB
0153	DIP RIGHT WITH 2 EXISTING BB	REPLACE WITH 3 BB AND IMPROVE DIP RIGHT
0164	1 EXISTING BB	REPLACE WITH NEW BB
0169	2 EXISTING BB	REPLACE WITH 3 BB
0185	1 EXISTING BB	REPLACE WITH NEW BB

Fig. 3.2. Trail log example.

DIGITAL/GPS WORK LOGS

There are many different types of GPS devices on the market, many of which have varying capabilities of storing specific data. Because technology is constantly changing and new capabilities are always being invented, conduct enough research before investing in a GPS system, the GIS program, and any other software needed for collecting, organizing, and managing the data.

Once you have purchased a GPS device and appropriate technological support to work with the data to be collected, you're ready to think about heading out into the field. Check and double check your settings before beginning the log, make sure your device is charged, pack spare batteries, and be prepared to spend the day in the field. Once you are ready to start, walk along the trail collecting points. Know what your parameters are for the desired data before you begin to collect and be sure to maintain consistency.

Digital work logs can be useful in many different trail management applications, though due to the price and complexity of the device and software needed, it can be less accessible to certain trails managers.

In addition to trail management, GPS devices can also have field project benefits. Though most trail crews very rarely bring GPS devices into the field, if they do, it would be possible to locate very specific work sites and location of materials according to GPS coordinates.

USING A WORK LOG IN THE FIELD

Because a trail log is literally a list of work needed on a trail, it serves as a "to do" list of projects on a specific section of trail. It should be detailed enough that, with a little discussion on prioritizing certain sections, an experienced crew leader will be able to take this trail log into the field. Using the detailed reference points, the crew leader should be able to identify all the trail deficiencies and proposed solutions.

As mentioned earlier, work logs provide a relatively accurate inventory of the needs of a specific section of trail. However, no work log can ever be considered completely accurate or contain the best solution for every trail problem—two logs done by the same person for the same trail at different times will vary. Flexible procedures should be planned to accommodate variations from the work log.

To save time for the work crew and to support the log descriptions, flag the work on the trail shortly before the project begins. Use flagging tape to mark each location where work is needed, and write on each piece of tape either the instruction (e.g., three rock steps) or a reference point from the log using a permanent marking pen. Remove all flagging when the work is completed. The crew leader can also use the log to note which projects are completed each week to supplement weekly work reports.

TRAIL PROJECT PLANNING AND PRIORITIZING

Detailed work logs are also an invaluable tool when prioritizing projects and estimating time and expenses. Setting priorities not only requires using the information on the trail log, but also taking into account many other factors, such as: Who are the users? How popular is the trail? What is the destination of the trail? What is the character? What is the general trail condition? From here, the planner can then start to prioritize which sections of trail to work on, as well as which projects to prioritize in these sections. For example, one might decide that a poorly laid-out, badly-eroded trail (whether popular or not) in need of major reconstruction is a lower priority than a trail in adequate shape that has no drainage. Because installing drainage over a section of trail is faster and cheaper than major reconstruction and will stabilize an entire section of trail, it may be for the greater good. However, the opposite decision could also be made, prioritizing the popular, severely-eroded trail since it is in such disrepair and goes to a very popular local destination. Decisions such as this one, once you have all the information, are made based on management style, management plans, and funding availability.

CREATING TIME AND COST ESTIMATES

Logs are obviously helpful to estimate the time and money required to do a project. However, in order to use them, you must be knowledgeable about the productivity of the crew assigned to work on the project. This can also fluctuate according to availability of material, commute time to the project site, and difficulty of the project. Often, volunteer crews can take more time to do a project than a professional crew, but a larger volunteer crew size can often compensate for that. So, keeping a general record of work reports and knowing your crews can be useful to get an average feel for productivity, which can then be applied to make an estimate for project planning, which will be discussed in Chapter 5.

WORK LOGS FOR THE FUTURE

Since trails are as dynamic and prone to change as the water that often flows down them, detailed work logs might become outdated quickly. AMC crews have found little change overall in tread condition on most trails over a few years, but conditions always get worse, never better. Trail conditions can change considerably if use levels change dramatically or a natural catastrophe occurs (e.g., a landslide, or a stream jumps its course and floods the trail). The work prescription should be similar over time, with slightly more work needed. For planning purposes, work logs should prove to be good for up to four years, though obviously the most recent, the most accurate.

CHAPTER 4
CREATING NEW TRAILS:
PLANNING & LAYOUT

AT-A-GLANCE

Careful attention must be given to planning and layout for a trail to be successful.

- **Planning:** Consider elements such as topography, elevation gain, vegetation, and soil when determining the course a trail will take.

- **Layout:** Familiarize yourself with the area, organize your data on a map, and place flagging tape to mark the route the trail will take.

Creating a trail has four major phases: visioning, planning, layout, and construction, with each successive phase requiring greater focus on the details. *Visioning*, which you already learned about in Chapter 1, starts with the big picture and often includes broad-brush ideas for possible trail locations. Planning is a conceptual stage where various factors are analyzed and carefully considered. Planners develop ideas about how the proposed trail area should look by considering how users' needs mesh with the landscape. During layout, trail builders go into the field and apply results from the planning stage to the proposed area of the trail. Once information is gathered during this phase, thought of as a field survey, conceptual plans are revisited and altered. Layout prepares the area for trail construction and is the final step before actual construction. With new trails, the planning and layout phases blend together with field scouting and various feasibility studies. Construction is the process of physically building the trail and implementing the project plans. Overall, good planning is the single most important factor in a trail's success and can help ensure that a trail is pleasant and that it lies on the land as lightly as possible, insuring that it won't have an adverse impact on the environment.

This chapter covers issues relevant to trail building, but it is advised that you anticipate and think beyond just the trail surface and become familiar with the wide range of potential trail issues. During the planning phase consider the following before going into the field.

- Social issues: Think about trail use conflicts and work toward providing high-quality user experiences.
- Environmental issues: Make sure natural resources will be protected.
- Management: Consider regulations and enforcement and well as assuring user safety.
- Historical and cultural resources: Insure that they will be protected.

PLANNING

Anyone can thoughtlessly scratch out a trail route on a map but a well-developed plan is necessary to ensure a successful trail. The purposes of the planning phase are to develop a trail that will be interesting and satisfying, as well as anticipate possible problems and provide corrective or preventive action. First determine the type of trail that is appropriate for the setting, which will aid in planning the attributes of the trail.

Then start where your trail starts—the proposed parking area or trailhead—and mentally walk through the trail to anticipate potential problems.

Settings and Trail Characteristics

Setting	Evidence of Human Activity	Surroundings of Natural Environment	Trail Surface	Use
Urban	High	Low	Paved	Multiuse
Rural/Roaded Natural	Medium	Medium	Gravel	Multiuse
Semi-Primitive	Medium-Low	Medium-High	Natural	Single- or Multiuse
Primitive	Low	High	Natural	Single-Use

Trailhead and Parking Facilities

The proposed location of a trailhead needs careful study during the planning phase. If it will be near major recreational areas, visitor use may be high. The location and size of trailhead parking can, to some degree, limit the number of users. If the designer wants a small number of visitors, parking should be nonexistent or limited. If parking is plentiful and accessible, visitor use may become high, and increase trail maintenance needs. However, some trails become popular even where parking is limited, so careful analysis of the area's recreation needs and the expected number of users is critical.

Parking facilities provide the first impression of a trail and can be the most problematic part of a trail. Be certain to involve abutting landowners, local businesses, and the appropriate governmental agencies in the planning process. For safety, the location of parking facilities on highways must be carefully planned and must be coordinated with the state's highway department or local municipality. Their specifications for a parking facility will likely determine the location of the trailhead.

Try to coordinate parking facilities with other recreational uses. Use an existing picnic area for your trailhead to eliminate the need for a new parking lot. If a snowmobile trail has a parking area, then a summer hiking trail placed in the same vicinity will eliminate the cost of building a parking lot. However, weigh your options carefully because this may invite unwanted users on your trail.

Place a signboard or kiosk at your trailhead to post rules and regulations, allowed trail uses, map(s), management and emergency material, and other important information about the trail (see Chapter 12). Reduce the possibility of vandalism by locating the signboard out of sight of the road, or fifty feet in on the trail. Proactive trailhead management can prevent problems associated with litter and human waste; remember that some preventive educational efforts (e.g., Leave No Trace Ethics) are considerably less expensive than building new facilities to combat these problems. If you do need a more developed trailhead that could include toilet facilities and fee boxes, plan your facilities carefully to avoid problems after installation.

Noise Impacts on Trail Experiences

Buffer the hiker from the sight and sounds of unnatural features such as roads, railroad tracks, industrial facilities, logging operations, and residential developments. In cases where the trail must cross a road or industrialized area, place the trail to reduce exposure to them. Cross these areas in the shortest practical manner, preferably at right angles. Right-angle crossings are also safer for road and railroad crossings (see figure 4.1).

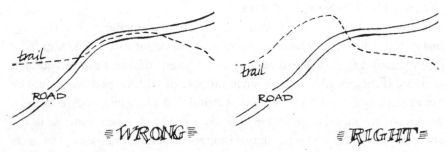

Fig. 4.1. Design trails to cross roads at a perpendicular angle with good lines of sight.

Private Lands

When a trail crosses private land, insist that trail users respect the private land they are using and consider acknowledging the generosity of the landowner with a sign or mention in a brochure. If your trail crosses the property of a large paper or timber company owner, you may want to educate users about timber management and the partnership you have with the corporate owner (see Chapter 2 for details on trails on private land).

Topography

During the planning phase, study and use topographical maps for ideas about possible trail routes. Check these maps to determine the lay of the land and decide the best location for the trail. Topographic features such as ledges, knolls, and views are elements that make trails interesting. Let the trail drift across the land; this limits difficult construction and allows hikers a greater sense of anticipation when traveling. To provide visitors with an interesting and satisfying experience, include subtle turns and undulations in grade steepness, dramatic climbs to a view, or the sudden appearance of a waterfall.

Rocks, cliffs, ledges, caves, and other potentially dangerous areas offer points of interest along a trail. Do not avoid these rigors of the landscape when designing the trail, but use caution when placing trails over shale slides, talus slopes, or cliff edges. Scarred tree and talus with recently fractured surfaces indicate falling rock. It is unreasonably dangerous to locate trails under these ledges and cliffs. Clearly define trails skirting the tops of cliffs. Wet, mossy areas that form ice in the spring and fall are as dangerous as any cliff side location and must be avoided. If these limiting conditions are not serious, the trail should take every advantage of dramatic topography.

Prudent topography management is essential to minimizing potential environmental impacts. Gullies caused by erosion could develop on trails that ascend long, steep gradients. You must find a balance between the trail's need to gain elevation and the tendency of foot traffic and water to erode trails. Often trail designers choose to build climbing contours on the sides of hills; this allows designers the flexibility to choose appropriate grades and to take advantage of short-levels, small dips, or low spots that allow for natural drainage. Because *sidehill trails* also allow running water to cross over the trail, they can reduce water volumes that aggravate erosion.

Significant Elevation Gain

To climb a long, steep grade on a mountain, a sidehill trail alone cannot provide the needed rise in elevation. Often the lateral area available for the trail is limited, so the trail must turn and start a lateral motion in the opposite direction. This turn, aptly named a *switchback*, has been used for centuries in road and trail design. When planning a series of switchbacks seek enough area to maneuver around unforeseen problems, such as a spring or ledge bands. Ideally, the area available is quite wide and allows room for switchbacks, climbing turns, and contouring trail sections.

Draining water from the trail is difficult around switchback turns, and usually involves shedding the same water several times. Plan long stretches between switchbacks and minimize the number of turns to avoid monotonous repetition.

On a well-designed trail, one switchback leg is not visible from another. Switchbacks often fail when their upper and lower legs are built within sight of each other. Descending visitors who can clearly see the turn ahead will shortcut the turn by dropping off the trail before the turn. Watercourses will develop on these shortcuts once they are trampled, causing erosion and forcing maintainers to manage multiple steep trail sections.

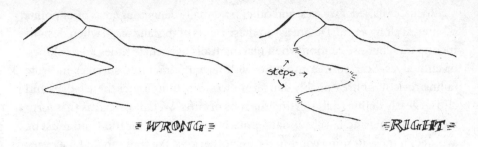

Fig. 4.2. Narrow switchbacks lead to shortcutting; wide turns fortified with steps help prevent shortcutting.

Control shortcutting on switchbacks by using a wide turn (see figure 4.2). You may have to run a small section of the turn straight up the fall line, but where the danger of shortcutting is great, such as in open hardwoods or above tree line where hikers can see for long distances, a wide turn running straight up the grade may be the best choice. Harden the trail on the steepest part of the turn with steps to keep the turn stable and durable.

When possible, use natural features such as rock outcrops, boulders, and dense stands of vegetation to form barriers against shortcuts. Plan the outer edge of a turn near a good view to attract a user's attention and draw them to the corner and away from shortcuts. Placing large rocks, logs, and brush on the inside of a switchback often reduces shortcutting near the turn. Clearly mark switchbacks and any abrupt change in a route's direction to prevent hikers from walking off the trail at a turn.

Avoid areas with landslides, rockslides, and places with evidence of avalanches if the trail is used in winter. All such areas may be prone to severe soil and vegetation movement that can be hazardous to hikers.

Do not build switchbacks on short, frequently used trails, such as those between a water supply and a campsite or a parking lot and a view. Switchbacks need a large area and adequate vegetative screening between legs. Short trails do not cover enough area for proper switchback design.

Vegetation

The type and density of vegetation in areas proposed for trail development have two primary design functions: aesthetic, enhancing the hiking experience; and management, as a tool to assist the designer in protecting the environment.

Include a variety of vegetation along a trail route to make the trail more interesting and satisfying, especially for nature trails. Alternatively, continuity in species composition has its own special attraction: a prolonged stretch of dense woods can promote a hauntingly exciting feeling of anticipation and adventure. Generally, hikers are interested in natural environments. In some cases, though, modified vegetation—resulting from sound timber practices, farming, or other activities—can be interesting and educational, and valuable in providing views and wildlife.

There is no single criterion for settling on one type of vegetative cover over another when making an aesthetic decision. In fact, the aesthetic quality of vegetative cover will usually be a secondary consideration. Your primary design emphasis should be the characteristics of the soil and topography—their influence on trail stability in mountainous and unstable terrain is critical.

When designing a trail, vegetation can be used in many ways as a tool to protect the environment. It can be used to keep trail users on the trail and prevent them from creating widened treads and unofficial trails. Treadway boundaries are profoundly affected by the density of trailside trees and shrubs; therefore, dense undergrowth enables greater flexibility in trail layout. For example, bypassing switchbacks is much less likely if dense shrubbery lines the edge of the trail. In crowded areas, vegetation breaks up lines of sight and absorbs sound. A good example of the ability of vegetation to buffer sound is in snowmobile trail design. Proper buffering using vegetation, hillsides, and other features can reduce vehicle sound levels by one-third to one-half. Vegetation is also a valuable buffer between a trail with high public use and a sensitive environment such as a pond shore.

Trail designers often use vegetation to fight trail erosion. Roots of vegetation along trails anchor soil and retard erosion of the trail treadway. However, with particularly unstable soils, steep slopes, and high visitor use, root stability is not sufficient to prevent resource damage.

Trailside trees are a major source of building material for treadway construction, particularly when rock is not available. The availability of trees of suitable size for treadway hardening may be a factor in whether to route a trail through a fragile bog or marsh (see Chapter 7). Use of native trees for bog bridges, also known as puncheons, keeps costs low and adds a more rustic appearance than dimensional lumber.

Vegetation can indicate broad soil characteristics. Tree size and age indicate soil fertility—large, young trees indicate deep, well-drained soils while small, stunted trees and wetlands species indicate marginal soil conditions. The preponderance of a species can give clues to soil texture, depth, and wetness. Pines and red oaks grow in sandy soils, while balsam fir, spruce, and hemlock indicate shallow soil depths. Red maple, cedar, and tamarack grow in soils that are moist.

Compaction

Traffic on a trail causes compaction of the surface soil into cement-like hardness. Compacted surfaces lose their porosity and ability to absorb water. If this water is not absorbed it will either puddle on the trail and create an ever-widening mud hole for hikers to walk around or flow downhill and cause surface erosion. These tendencies make draining water off the trail critical for soil retention, even on flat trails.

Surface Erosion

Trail layout, existing soils, and number of users are the most important factors affecting erosion on trails. Erosion is a natural process in which soils are worn away by wind, water, and other natural elements. On trails, this natural process is aggravated by soil compaction and the churning agitation of foot traffic. Water flowing over the compacted soil surface detaches the smaller, lighter particles and carries them downhill. The greater the velocity of flowing water, the greater the mass of soil carried.

Trail gradient, water flow, and elevation increase surface erosion, especially when combined. Water velocity increases as slope steepness increases; increased water volume increases the force acting on the soil. Higher elevations tend to receive more precipitation and the ecosystem often possesses thinner soils. These large volumes of water, exacerbated by steep slopes and foot traffic, create significant erosion hazards for trails. This erosion can quickly destroy a trail treadway.

Erosion is easy to spot on a trail. Loose stones and gravel remain after the smaller stabilizing sand and silt particles have washed away (see figure 4.3). The loose material offers poor footing and often hikers walk the un-eroded edge of the trail to avoid the difficult surface. This starts the vicious cycle of trampling more plants, compacting soil, and initiating more erosion that can change a trail into a wide boulder-strewn gully.

Erosion can often cause resource damage beyond the trail. After sediment-loaded water settles on the forest floor, it suffocates smaller plant life. If these sediments find their way into streams and ponds, they can kill fish, degrade water quality, and add nutrients that eliminate the dissolved oxygen plants, a process called eutrophication. Soil loss around the base of trees can expose roots to disease and weaken their anchoring function, making them more susceptible to being blown down during wind events.

Due to the threat of resource degradation, those laying out and constructing a trail must carefully evaluate soil characteristics. Where possible, locate trails

Fig. 4.3. Erosion can turn a treadway into an obstacle course, complete with exposed rocks and roots.

on soils that are capable of withstanding the anticipated use without eroding or becoming wet and muddy.

Soil

Trail planners must pay close attention to soil characteristics and should know how different types of soils respond to foot traffic. If the plan calls for a trail to reach the top of a high mountain, you will likely have to deal with a delicate alpine environment. Or, if you want people to experience a bog, you will be dealing with a devolved mull. If a trail is on the seashore, expect peripatetic sand. The soil is also an important, yet subtle part of the outdoor experience—just as critical as the flora, or vistas.

Soil is a complex mix of minerals, organic matter, organisms, pore space, and water. The soil found in a given area from the ground to bedrock is called the soil profile (see figure 4.4). Each soil profile is composed of layers (sometimes very small or thin). Your local USDA Natural Resource Conservation Service office or Agricultural Extension office will have detailed soil maps that show prevalent soil profiles, including the approximate depth of each layer. These maps can be very helpful to the trail planner. Your local conservation district or conservation commission may also be helpful.

The ability of soil to withstand traffic depends on the combination of soil wetness, texture, structure, and depth. You must consider these qualities when determining the best location for a trail.

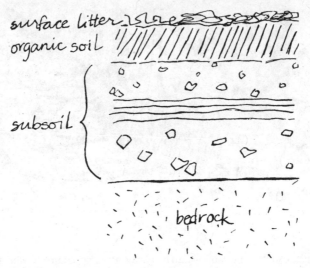

Fig. 4.4. The soil profile.

Soil Wetness

Ground water moves through the landscape and saturates the surface of soils, especially during periods of heavy rainfall and the spring thaw. The ground water fluctuates with the seasons. Seasonally high ground water in shallow or poorly drained soils will create problems on a compacted treadway. In very poorly drained soils, such as in bogs or depressions near lakes and streams, water moves so slowly that the soil surface may be wet for much of the year. Avoid building trails in these areas. If you must pass through them, use bog bridges from the outset to protect trailside vegetation and soils. (See Chapter 7.)

Evaluate soil wetness after long periods of rainfall or during the spring snowmelt. Assure minimal surface water is present. If water is flowing across the ground in many rivulets, the site may not be appropriate for a trail. You can also dig a shallow hole where the proposed trail would be; if it fills with water or if water placed in it does not percolate out of the hole, then the water table is high or dense soils inhibit drainage. Trails sited across soils like this will degrade quickly or demand significant amounts of work to stabilize. Often it is better to site the trail elsewhere.

Soil Texture

Soil texture refers to the relative proportions of various-sized groups of grains in soil. Texture is an important factor in how well soil can sustain foot traffic. In general, loam soils with a mixture of sand, clay, and silt will resist compaction and erosion most successfully. The smaller sizes of silt and clay particles add cohesion; sand and gravel lend porosity and water absorption. Coarse fragments in the treadway can increase the durability of the soil. Gravel-sized fragments embedded in the soil matrix help to hold the more easily eroded sand and silt in place. Rocks, stones, and loose gravel on the surface act as natural erosion retardants. Although they can cause uncertain footing, this is not a serious concern.

Moderately sandy soils will resist compaction and will absorb a large amount of rainfall, making them good for trail use. Use caution, however, when building trails across pure sand because it supports few plants for soil retention and blows when dry. Avoid building trails on soils made mostly of silt and clay. They become muddy when wet, cracked and dusty when dry, and erode easily.

Also avoid soils with high organic matter and minimal mineral material. Organics are five times lighter than the more common mineral soils, they compact quickly, wash away easily, and become mucky when wet. Organic soil can hold two to twenty times its dry weight in moisture, while a mineral soil will hold only about a fifth of its weight in water.

Soil Depth

Soil depth is the distance from surface level to bedrock. Avoid shallow soils when possible, especially on steeper terrain. Shallow soils over bedrock or hardpan (an impervious layer of subsoil) can lead to problems on hiking trails. Water cannot drain through the impervious substrate and will saturate the soils above. This saturated soil sloughs easily when walked on and erodes quickly. In steep terrain, steep rock slabs are dangerous for hikers when wet. To pass safely, hikers often grab hold of the plant life on the edge of the trail. This causes the plants to eventually be uprooted, forcing hikers to reach further from the trail for a plant to hold on to. This makes the trail wider, which is not enjoyable for the hiker, is disruptive to the natural environment, and creates major management challenges.

The limitations of soil depth are especially critical in the alpine environments, where soil is at most only a few inches thick and should be carefully preserved. Plant life is small, often shallow-rooted and easily damaged by foot traffic. In the alpine environments, maintainers must take special pains to mark the trail and avoid abrupt turns. Discourage shortcuts and help contain hiking traffic to rock surfaces by lining the path with low rock walls or by building bog bridges over vegetated areas.

In summary, remember that erosion from a simple footpath can add tons of soil to watersheds. Soil depth and trail gradient are the most important factors in determining appropriate trail locations. Both are easily measured in the

Summary of Indicators for Evaluation of a Proposed Trail Installation

Conditions	Conditions Posing Slight Limitations for Trail Installations	Conditions Posing Moderate Limitations for Trail Installations	Conditions Posing Severe Limitations for Trail Installations
Soil Wetness	Depth to seasonal high water table 4 feet or more; well drained to moderately well drained	Depth to seasonal high water table 1 to 4 feet; excessively drained	Depth to seasonal high water table less than 1 foot; poorly drained
Soil Texture	Particle mixture of sand, clay, silt; 20–50 percent of content gravel	High sand content; less than 50 but greater than 20 percent of content gravel	High clay content; no gravel
Soil Structure			Hardpans less than one foot from soil surface; peaty, mucky soils
Soil Depth to Bedrock	Greater than 3 feet	1.5–3 feet	Less than 1.5 feet
Slope*	0–5 percent	5–20 percent	Greater than 20 percent

* *Slope* is the number of feet of vertical rise per 100 feet of horizontal distance, expressed as a percentage—that is, a 10% slope rises 10 feet vertically for every 100 feet traversed horizontally.

field with a soil auger and clinometers. Evaluate these facets during the initial phases of a proposed trail and do your best to locate your trail on the most suitable soils.

TRAIL LAYOUT

This is the stage where the process of venturing into the woods and the physical task of building a trail begins. Trail layout relies on construction and maintenance as much as planning. Good designers apply the content of this book as they navigate, hang flagging tape, and apply aesthetic virtues to a trail line. Patience and experience are needed to keep the primary objective in mind: to provide for recreational interests with the least amount of impact on the land. Good layout can and should satisfy both objectives.

Before you start to nail down your route, talk to local people, especially older residents who are familiar with the land. Loggers, hunters, avid off-trail hikers, and foresters are usually very helpful. They may be able to point out all the significant features in a particular area and give a personal account of its history.

Aerial photographs can reveal features such as ledges, wetlands, watercourses, forest cover, and sometimes old roads that would be potentially usable for the trail. Stereoscopic aerial photographs are usually available and these can help you visualize what you could miss from reading a map. Aerial photos are available from your USDA Natural Resource Conservation Service office or from a managing agency in the case of state or federal land.

Often, an hour in a plane or helicopter can give you a much better sense of the landscape than hours of studying maps or days walking the area. You will want to fly over the proposed trail area several times at different elevations and from multiple directions. It is best to charter an aircraft or find a pilot willing to volunteer to fly you. Bring a topographic map, take photographs, and keep your eyes glued to what is on the ground. GIS data and satellite imagery available on the Internet can also be a good planning tool

Defining the Line

Once you reach the proposed area for your trail, get to know the neighborhood. Check the proposed route. Then check it again. Walk around to find the best soils and appropriate grades. The more time you spend in the field in this layout phase, the better the trail location will be. You will probably find that some part of the proposed route simply will not work, or you may find a solution to an unresolved problem. You may get lost or at least confused, and after hours or days of working the perfect line, you will meet dead ends. All of this is par for the course and will help you understand the environment you are working in. Use what you learn to build a better trail and be willing to drop what simply is not working. Remember that an hour of time while doing trail layout will often equal weeks of a trail crews' time and can save years of maintenance headaches.

This is not the time to learn orienteering skills. Skilled knowledge of maps and compasses are requirements for the job. Laying out a trail demands that you follow the best line for the trail; often this will not be a compass bearing line. Trail designers simply need to know where they are even if they drift into multiple dead ends. Bring someone else with you. Trail layout is safer, faster, and often provides better results when done in pairs. One person can scout ahead while the trailing person hangs the flag line, or two people can scout in different directions when unforeseen obstacles impede practical advancement.

A GPS receiver can be very helpful, but they are often fickle. They can allow you to mark features quickly, store data so you can easily track your movements, and they can be used to pinpoint location. They rely on clear signals from satellites traversing all corners of the sky on various trajectories. If you are in a deep valley, under a dense canopy, or other factors are limiting your GPS unit from calculating reasonable triangulations, the GPS will give you no data, or worse, undependable data. Bring a GPS unit as a supporting tool and use it if it is receiving a strong signal, but rely primarily on your maps and good sense.

Fall is the best time of the year to layout trails; leaves have fallen off the trees and sight lines are excellent. Once the ground is covered with ice and snow, it is unrealistic to continue with anything other than scouts to establish points of interest, mark difficult terrain, or check grades. Try to check your trail route at different times of the year. Check it in the spring for indications of drainage and wetness problems, check it in the summer to confirm your scenic objectives are visible, and check it in winter if the trail is intended for ski touring.

Organizing Trail Data

Use U.S. Geological Survey (USGS) topographical maps or their GIS map data sets to record information gathered for the route. If your project is particularly complex, make a GIS layer and data files that are referenced on your map. In these files, record all pertinent features for eventual use in the final on-the-ground layout. Describe the nature of each feature and whether it will improve or hurt the trail. Include other pertinent information, such as boundary lines and addresses of landowners or managing agency.

As this information file develops, each feature will become a control point that will either be avoided (a bog or a steep slope) or included if is a beneficial feature (a good view). The final choice of route will then involve connecting nice features and circumnavigating negative ones. As an alternative to computer files, buy a piece of mylar, then overlay natural, cultural, historic, and development features on the mylar. This can also complement a paper description taken at points.

The layout process is one of trial and error. As it proceeds, you will continually backtrack and reflag the route until finally the location meets the needs of the hiker and lies as lightly as possible on the land. Remember, hikers, like water, seek the path of least resistance. Refine the layout so the trail follows a route hikers will most likely take.

As you lay out the trail, pay careful attention to where you will install drainage devices in advance to prevent erosion problems in the future. See Chapters 7 and 8 for more information on drainage.

Flagging the Route

Use different colors of flagging tape. Choose one color for initial cruises (see figure 4.5). Flag control points (scenic features, boundary corners, unsightly areas, and difficult ground) in a separate color. Pick a bright color made of reasonably permanent tape to define drift lines (a generalized route that could support a trail). Use still another color tape of heavy-duty grade, to mark the centerline of the final trail route. Be sure to share the color scheme and particulars of your flagging system in detail with the workers who will be building the trail. Make relevant notes directly on the flagging tape with permanent marker, such as "Install switchback turn here." Use consistent abbreviations for regularly referenced information.

Place the flagging tape no more than 50 feet apart on the finish line or close enough so that the trail builders can see more than one flag at any one point. Sometimes in very dense growth, you may need to tie ribbons a foot to two feet apart. Tie ribbons securely on living trees and branches. Choose tree trunks whenever possible, as ribbons on branches break in the cold, blow off, or are yanked off more often. Avoid leaving long tails on your flags—they shred and become litter. Biodegradable tape, though reasonable for initial cruise lines, will break down too quickly to use for trail layout. Sometimes placing a few small flags with wire stems or wooden grade stakes in areas where trees are sparse,

Fig. 4.5. Use highly visible flags to mark your route in the woods.

can help builders decipher where to construct the treadway. Always keep the builders' ease in mind and remember the flag line is for their use.

As you are hanging your flag line in the field, keep these ideas in mind:

- During layout, pay careful attention to the environmental concepts covered in this chapter.
- Where possible, always use a sidehill trail location, and check soil characteristics at regular intervals. Keep the gradient below 20 percent if possible, unless you plan to harden the steep grades during construction.
- Blend your trail into the natural surroundings by maintaining continuity with the land. Be sensitive to various plant communities, avoiding rare plants and fragile areas. Avoid too much meandering or sudden changes in direction. Likewise, use long, straight sections rarely; they do not interest hikers.
- Record all important information for later discussion.
- Remind the trail builders to remove all flagging tape when the project is completed.

CHAPTER 5
DETERMINING THE COSTS OF TRAIL PROJECTS

AT-A-GLANCE

Before beginning a new trail project, you will need to estimate how much it will cost.

- **Break down costs:** Use the cost of each structure, number of weeks of labor, and cost of a trail per foot or mile to estimate a total cost.

- **Labor costs:** Consider the experience level of the trail builders when determining labor costs.

- **Funding resources:** Seek funding from the government or private donors.

Determining the cost to construct or perform maintenance on a trail is an important part of the planning and implementation process and requires a thorough understanding of many components and variables. Factors that influence project cost include site conditions, use of professional trail crews, volunteer labor and contracted services, terrain, use of native vs. non-native materials, engineering standards, and choice and use of equipment. Also consider land acquisition, permits, project management, and administrative expenses when determining cost. Your trail implementation plan should include a budget that identifies each item or major task. On larger, complex projects the cost estimates may need to be broken out into phases over a period of years due to availability of funding. A successful project requires that trail project costs be carefully thought out ahead of time to ensure that funds will be available to complete the project.

Because having an accurate cost estimate is essential, people with a solid background in trail construction should usually do the estimate before breaking ground on a new trail. Funding organizations will probably want to know up front what a project will cost and how the cost was determined before offering any financial support.

HOW TO ESTIMATE COSTS

Trail managers and designers often use one or more of the following methods to estimate trail project costs: unit costs, crew weeks of labor, and per foot or mile costs.

With unit costs, a cost has already been determined for each structure to be built along the trail. For example, to install a native rock water bar it may be determined that it would cost fifty dollars (considering materials, equipment, and labor) to construct. Sidehill construction may be determined to cost an average of ten dollars per linear foot. A tally of structures multiplied by their costs would equal a total project cost. It is important when using the unit cost method to have a completed trail work log (see Chapter 3) from which to work.

Often projects are estimated by using crew weeks of labor to determine the amount of time it will take to complete a project. For example, it might be determined that a professional trail crew of four people will contribute 160 hours per week of labor (or crew week) to a project. Experienced trail leaders can estimate how much work a crew is capable of completing in a week and divide the project into a number of crew weeks. Usually, project material costs are estimated separately and added to labor costs to provide an overall cost. The crew week method of determining trail project costs is widely used for both volunteer and professional trail crew labor. As with the other methods, the person estimating the project costs should have a solid background in trail work and first-hand knowledge of the work a crew can perform in a given time period.

Some trail projects are estimated using the per foot or mile method. This method is used when an accurate figure has already been successfully determined from previous experience or from another organization's previous experience. For example, a per foot cost may have been determined in the past for a 5-foot-wide wooden boardwalk of similar design or an 8-foot-wide Americans with Disabilities Act (ADA) trail that uses bituminous asphalt as surfacing. The per foot or per mile method isn't recommended when the trail has a range of variables incorporated into the design, such as a trail that requires a variety of involved structures.

Often, trail designers and managers use a combination of ways to determine project costs. They will use the methods discussed above and factor in other variables such as:

- the commute to the project site. How long will it take for the crew to drive to the trailhead and then pack-in to the project site?
- availability of native/project materials. Is rock needed for a retaining wall nearby and available or will it need to be transported a long distance?
- safety concerns. Is the project located in an area that could be dangerous to the crew members and/or the public? This may drive up project costs due to the need for additional materials or different trail construction methods to make the area safely passable.
- the tools and equipment that are available or prohibited from being used on the trail. Can motorized equipment be used or is the project limited to hand tools only?
- whether the project is located in an area that is susceptible to weather extremes, such as alpine regions or in areas that receive large amounts of precipitation. Extreme weather conditions can slow production or cause the crew to cease work for periods of time.
- the experience of the work crew and the quality of the soil and terrain.

These are general guidelines to use when considering the variables that may play a large role in reaching an accurate construction or maintenance cost figure. It is often best to consult those who are familiar with local conditions if in doubt.

Trail design, layout, and project management costs are sometimes underestimated or overlooked entirely when determining the expense of a project.

Too often the costs are not included in an overall trail project budget. Planning and oversight costs can be a significant expense and can quickly add up if not included. Trail design is often performed by those without an adequate background, which can lead to unforeseen problems and expenses. Design and management costs can often comprise 20 percent of total project costs, although that figure can vary widely from project to project.

SOURCES OF LABOR

Determine who will build or maintain your trail when preparing your cost estimate. Trails get built and maintained a range of ways. Nonprofit trail clubs who have professional and volunteer trail workers, such as the Appalachian Mountain Club, construct trails throughout the Northeast. Other trails are constructed by trail contractors, landscape companies, or construction firms. Youth conservation corps often construct trails on both public and private lands. On state and federal lands, agency personnel often perform the trail construction. For some projects, volunteers are solely responsible for getting a trail built.

Some projects use a combination of professional and volunteer labor. Regardless of who will build your trail, you must have an idea of who will be used ahead of time so that you can include the appropriate labor costs into the project estimate. Before finalizing your project budget, be sure to obtain estimates from contractors, youth conservation corps, or nonprofit trail clubs, because final numbers may vary widely depending on the source used. Be sure to include labor costs even if you are using only volunteers for your project since hidden costs such as food, safety equipment, and travel expenses are often missed.

RESOURCES FOR FUNDING

Once a cost estimate for your trail project has been established the question often asked is, "Where will the money come from to support a trail project?" Often, trail projects are funded through a combination of funding sources. Funds from federal, state, and local governments and private sources are often combined to pay for project costs. Sometimes user fees, taxes, or bonds are used. Other times, funds come from donations from area businesses, individual sponsors, foundation support, or creative ways such as "buy a mile" programs or fundraising events.

The trail administrator should seek funding sources and apply for grant opportunities. When considering whether to apply for federal or state grants, do research well ahead of time. Speak with past recipients, and discuss your project with the grant administrator to be certain your project and application will meet their requirements. Grants are often very competitive so set aside a sufficient amount of time to prepare a quality application. When applying for grants, be aware of application deadlines, award dates, and the reporting process to avoid surprises. Also, make allowances for moving the project forward if the grant is not awarded. It is always important to have a backup plan.

Raising funds for new trail projects is often easier than raising funds for trail maintenance projects. It is also easier to raise funds if strong partnerships with other organizations, businesses, and agencies are developed. Don't overlook the importance of having strong community support in place prior to seeking funding. Consider breaking down your project into components so that you can tailor your funding requests through a number of different sources. Be certain to follow up with donors by submitting progress reports and writing thank you notes where appropriate.

CHAPTER 6
SAFETY & PREPARATION:
WORK SAFE, WORK SMART

Protect yourself while working by taking precautions and using care with tools.

- **Personal protective equipment:** Prevent injury by wearing the appropriate attire.

- **Food, water, and first aid:** Eat and drink to prevent exhaustion and dehydration and administer first aid when necessary.

- **Tools:** Use the correct tools properly and ensure they are maintained well.

Trail work for most is satisfying, challenging, exhausting, frustrating, and usually fun, but the element of danger is always present. Cutting wood, digging ditches, and moving stones—the basics of trail work—are fraught with many perils and inconveniences, ranging from cuts, scrapes, and bruises to blisters, achy muscles, and dehydration. Any of these can temporarily affect your enjoyment of trail work and how much and how well you can contribute. Ignore these problems for too long, and they can keep you from performing your work on the trail.

There are other hazards that are more serious and require immediate attention to be taken. Hypothermia; heat stroke; injuries from tools, rocks, or falling trees; and similar serious conditions are usually caused by minor mistakes or blunders that culminate in a major mishap. Following are the fundamentals of preparation that are essential for protecting yourself and fellow trail workers when you work on a trail.

PERSONAL PROTECTIVE EQUIPMENT (PPE)

Use of personal protective equipment (PPE) while doing trail work can make the difference between having a successful, injury free day and one that is plagued with injuries. Having the appropriate PPE for the activity, and being sure it is functioning properly should be at the forefront of any trail maintainers mind.

Boots and Socks

Sturdy leather boots are one of the most important pieces of gear a trail worker can have (see figure 6.1). A well-made pair of boots will keep you comfortable and protect your feet while you work. Many people use lightweight cloth boots for hiking, but these boots provide inadequate protection for most trail work activities, such as moving large rocks or logs. If you are planning to do a lot of trail work purchase a pair of quality all-leather boots that are suitable for hiking as well as rugged enough to stand up to the rigors of trail work. Leather boots will last much longer than cloth boots and will better protect your feet; be sure, though, to break them in gradually before any long trips to avoid blisters. Steel-toed boots offer an extra level of protection, but they are usually found to be very uncomfortable for long hikes.

Help protect your feet from blistering by wearing the right socks. Use heavyweight wool or wool blend. Don't wear cotton socks that will absorb moisture and increase the chances of blistering. As soon as you feel the onset of a blister or a hot spot, stop working. Remove your boots, allow your feet to dry thor-

Fig. 6.1. A pair of well-made boots can be a trail maintainer's best piece of equipment.

oughly, and apply moleskin, molefoam, or duct tape to prevent further injury. Some choose to wear a light inner polypropylene liner to wick moisture away from their feet and reduce friction.

Gloves

Gloves (see figure 6.2) should be worn for most trail work activities, although certain tasks require finger mobility and additional dexterity that are limited

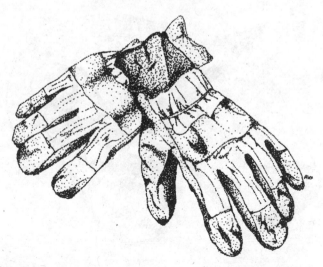

Fig. 6.2. Sturdy gloves can help protect hands from potential injury.

when using gloves. Some trail work activities, such as chain saw work, operating a griphoist, or similar activities, require the operator to wear gloves to protect their hands from a possible serious injury. Leather gloves are often the choice of trail workers as they offer more cut protection than cotton gloves and generally hold up better with heavy use.

Eye Protection

Safety glasses and safety goggles are inexpensive and lightweight. Use the impact-resistant kind that offers protection on the sides as well as the front (see figure 6.3). They can be clear or tinted and are designed to be shatter proof. Safety goggles (see figure 6.4) are designed to fit over prescription eye

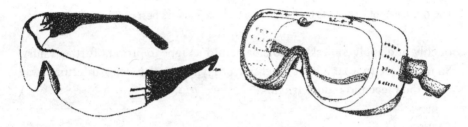

Fig. 6.3. Safety glasses.   **Fig. 6.4.** Safety goggles.

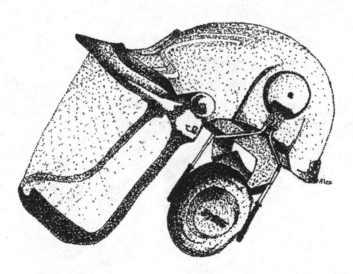

Fig. 6.5. Helmets can be outfitted with mesh face masks and ear protection.

glasses. While eye protection is suggested for all trail work, be sure to wear safety glasses/goggles during any ax work and all work involving hammers, chain saws, and the splitting or drilling of rocks. Be sure to use safety glasses/goggles that meet ANSI Z87.1-2003 standards or higher.

Helmet mounted, mesh facemasks (see figure 6.5) also serve as eye protection while operating a chain saw or brush cutter. However, it is recommended that the chain saw operator wear safety classes in addition to the mesh face guard.

Ear Protection

Some trail maintenance activities, such as using chain saws, rock drills and other forms of gas-powered equipment require users to wear ear protection to prevent hearing loss. Two types of ear protection are generally available: plastic ear muffs (see figure 6.6) worn on the outside of the ear and foam plugs (see figure 6.7), which are worn in the ear canal. Both are designed to reduce external noise to a level that prevents or limits hearing loss. It is important to know the decibel level of the equipment being used so you can choose the appropriate ear protection. Hearing protection should have a noise reduction rating (NRR) that specifies the number of decibels (dB) that is reduced when worn correctly. Use hearing protection that meets ANSI S3.19-1974 standards or higher. (Visit www.ansi.org for more information.)

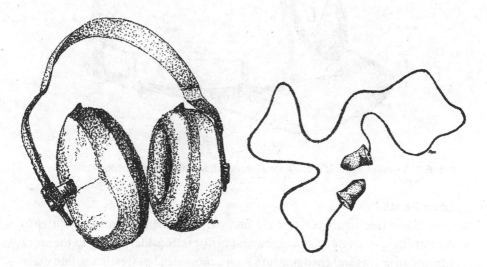

Fig. 6.6. Plastic ear muffs.   **Fig. 6.7.** Foam ear plugs.

Hard Hats

Hard hats (see figure 6.8) should be required when doing trail work activities and must be worn in any situation in which falling or flying objects could present a danger. For example, you should always wear a hard hat when you work in an area with unstable rocks overhead, when you fell trees, and when you work around standing trees with dead limbs (such limbs are known as widow makers for good reason). Hard hats should meet all OSHA–ANSI Z89.1-1997 safety standards in its design for the intended activity. Helmets that are not designed or approved for trail work/construction activities should not be worn because they might not provide adequate protection. Hard hats should be replaced if they have been damaged or if they have reached their expiration date (usually stamped on the inside of the brim) as UV exposure, sweat, and repeated use contribute to the breakdown of materials. Color, though seemingly insignificant, can make a difference, as lighter colored ones are much cooler on hot, sunny summer days.

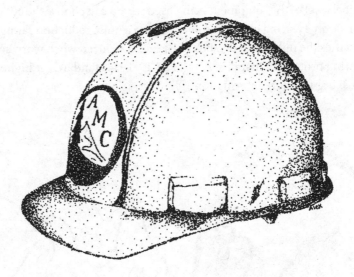

Fig. 6.8. A helmet will help protect a trail worker from falling or flying objects.

Long Pants

Long pants (see figure 6.9) should be used for most trail work activities to protect the user from cuts, scrapes, and bruises. Consider hiking to the work site in short pants and changing into long pants when hot weather would make wearing long pants uncomfortable for hiking.

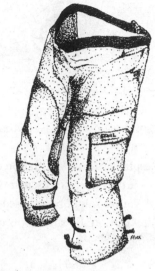

Fig. 6.9. A properly dressed trail worker. **Fig. 6.10.** Chain saw chaps.

Chain Saw Chaps

Chain saw chaps (see figure 6.10) are worn over pants and cover a person's legs and lower torso to provide cut-resistance and prevent a serious injury from occurring. Chaps purchased should be approved by Underwriter's Laboratories (UL) and the American Pulpwood Association and must fit the operator correctly to provide maximum protection. The fibers in chaps catch and clog the drive sprocket which in turn stops the chain rotation quickly and ideally before serious personal injury occurs.

Dust Masks and Respirators

Dust masks and respirators (see figure 6.11) filter out undesirable contaminants from the air. It is important for a trail worker to acquire training on hazardous material identification and safety practices to choose the proper mask or respirator. Dust/particle masks are intended to filter airborne particulates created when doing activities such as drilling and splitting rock, crushing stone, or sanding wood. Be sure to check the directions and instructions for proper application and wear.

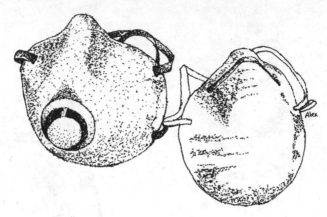

Fig. 6.11. Respirator (L) and dust mask (R).

Respirators have a filtration component that filters out things such as hazardous fumes from stains, paints, epoxies, chemicals, or gaseous materials that a trail worker might be exposed to. Respirators and dust masks vary in quality and application. Be sure to purchase the correct model and carefully read the directions.

Rain Gear and Insulation

Wearing and carrying quality outerwear that will protect you from the elements is important (see figure 6.12). Pack rain gear and insulating layers appropriate for your location and activity. For example, a rain jacket and light sweater might be appropriate to have in your pack in protected or low-lying areas in summer, but those working in alpine areas or above treeline should also pack rainwear, wind suit, and insulating layers appropriate for a worst-case weather scenario. This might require packing several layers of clothing, including a warm hat and gloves, even in the summer. Be sure to use wool or synthetic blends that are designed to keep the worker warm even when wet.

Maintenance, Inspection, and Retirement of Personal Protective Equipment

All PPE should be stored appropriately and inspected on a scheduled basis. Clean all PPE before putting it in storage when the season ends. It will be easier to detect damage after it has been cleaned. Look for hairline cracks in helmets, cracked safety glasses, tears in gloves, and any other damage to your PPE. Store helmets, safety glasses, ear protection, and similar plastic items out of direct sunlight to prevent prolonged exposure to UV rays, which break down some plastics prematurely. It is a good idea to label and date all PPE at time of pur-

Fig. 6.12. Proper rain gear can help keep you warm and dry while out on the trail.

chase, unless already marked. Keep timely records of the number of uses and of the stress that has been placed on that piece of equipment.

Replace your PPE when the item has reached its expiration date or sooner, depending on use and wear. Certain events, like severe helmet impact, dropping your helmet a long distance to the rocks below, or cutting into your chain saw chaps, exposing the protective layers, could force you to retire a piece of PPE much earlier than its expiration. Your PPE is far too important to be negligent in its care and use.

First-Aid Kit and Other Considerations

Every trail crew or worker should have a first-aid kit with them at all times. The contents should be based on the number of people in the crew, hazards posed by the work, and the remoteness of the work location. Inventory your first-aid kit regularly and replenish any used or damaged supplies. See page 66 for suggested first-aid kit contents for a one-person crew and an eight-person crew. Trail workers should, at the very least, receive training in wilderness first

PERSONAL FIRST-AID KIT FOR THE TRAIL WORKER

- 1 package of moleskin or molefoam
- aspirin or ibuprofen
- 1 triangular bandage and safety pins
- an assortment of Band-Aids
- 1 Ace bandage
- 3, 4-inch-by-4-inch gauze dressings
- 1 roll of tape or Kling bandage
- gloves
- pocket mask
- antihistamine capsules
- iodine antiseptic or iodine antiseptic wipes
- shears or scissors

FIRST-AID KIT FOR A TRAIL CREW OF UP TO EIGHT PEOPLE

- 1 roll of tape
- 4 triangular bandages and safety pins
- 3, 3-inch Kling bandages
- 6, 4-inch-by-4-inch gauze pads
- 15 band-aids
- 2 packages of moleskin or molefoam
- 1 pair of bandage scissors
- 1 pair of tweezers
- 2, 5-inch-by-9-inch combine dressings
- 1 Sam Splint
- 2 Ace bandages
- 1 pen
- 5 "SOAP" notes or incident report forms
- 1 pocket mask
- 1 eye wash
- 1 bottle of iodine antiseptic
- 12 ibuprofen
- 6 pairs of gloves
- 1 tube of glucose
- 1 cold pack

aid and CPR to be prepared for emergencies. It is recommended that trail crew leaders obtain more advanced training in first aid.

Know how to identify and protect yourself from the local poisonous plants and insects. Warn others if they will be working in an area infested with poison ivy, poison oak, or other poisonous plants. Bring Tecnu or Fels Naptha soap so workers can wash off the irritating oil if they are exposed. The same applies to poisonous snakes; warn the crew, identify the species to avoid, and have a first-aid and evacuation plan should someone get bitten and become ill.

Insects can test a trail worker's patience, and in extreme cases their bites may produce an allergic reaction. Carry plenty of bug repellent that has been proven to be effective. Individuals allergic to bees or other stinging insects should have their own EpiPen or anaphylaxis kit. It is also desirable to have the crew leader or person responsible for medical emergencies to be trained in administering (epinephrine) EpiPens for those undergoing anaphylactic shock. The crew member responsible for first aid should also consider obtaining an EpiPen for medical emergencies involving anaphylactic shock. (Note: EpiPens and anaphylaxis kits can be obtained only with a prescription.) All crew leaders should have undergone first-aid training when leading any work party.

FOOD AND WATER

Stay properly hydrated—you'll be a safer, happier, and more efficient trail worker. Being properly hydrated will help you avoid hypothermia, heat exhaustion, and heat stroke. A dehydrated person often is sluggish, susceptible to injuries, and can have impaired judgment. Bring at least two quarts of water in the field with you; take more if the weather is hot and humid. Drink small amounts often rather than a quart in one sitting. Headaches are often an indicator of dehydration. Follow the guideline that if you are thirsty that you are already dehydrated. Another indicator is the color of your urine. A properly hydrated person will have clear and copious urine.

Never drink water directly from untreated water sources, such as ponds, streams, and rivers as you risk getting ill. If you obtain your water from untreated water sources, several methods for water treatment are recommended. Boil the water for 5 minutes, use a commercial water purifier, or treat with iodine. For the trail maintainer working for a day, iodine tablets or a lightweight commercial water purifier might be best.

Bring plenty of food with you and eat it. Don't scrimp on food. If you are doing a lot of hard work, you'll need more food than you would for a day of sitting on the couch. Eat food you know is healthy and will provide energy.

SAFETY

Before you set out on the trail, get in the right mindset. The safety of yourself and the others in your work party should be your first priority. When making decisions, always lean on the side of safety. Remember that if you or another member of your party gets hurt you cannot expect an immediate response from emergency workers in the woods. While the leader is usually responsible for ensuring safe work habits and techniques are used, it is important to stress that all individuals are responsible for their safety.

Crew leaders should hold a safety meeting each morning before work begins to go over proper techniques. Run through the fundamentals of preparation with your group. Make certain that everyone has adequate layers, appropriate PPE, and enough food and water for the day. Go over the goals for the day and tools you'll need. Do not assign people to work for which they have not been trained. Crew leaders should always have an evacuation plan. Leaders should monitor crew safety levels continually and communicate with the crew if changes are needed. They should be especially aware of their own behaviors and practices, since their actions will set the tone.

Safe Working Techniques

Before going into the woods on their first trip, trail workers must know minimally how to lift heavy items safely, carry tools safely, and identify the circle of danger. These topics can be covered in a safety talk at the trailhead or other starting point. Other techniques can be taught on the project site.

Lifting
Many trail workers have back problems because they failed to heed this simple advice: Lift with your knees, not with your back! Improper lifting may lead to an injured back.

Fig. 6.13. Bend your knees and keep a straight back when lifting or rolling objects.

Trail work often requires lifting everything from branches to logs, rocks, and tools (see figure 6.13). Most trail work activities can cause a sore back, but lifting improperly can lead to more serious problems. Always consider your back and how you can limit the stress on it. When lifting, start with your knees bent, back straight, and feet shoulder-width apart. Keep your shoulders and neck straight. Lift the object gradually rather than jerk it up. If you are moving (pushing) a heavy object along the ground, keep your back straight and parallel with the direction you are pushing. Exert force on the object again with your knees.

Carrying Tools

There is a right way and a wrong way to carry tools. When carrying a tool with sharp teeth, a blade, point, or sharpened surface, carry the tool at your side with the sharp or pointed end pointed away from you (see figure 6.14). Should you trip, stumble, or fall (and you will), simply toss the tool to your side to avoid injury to yourself or the person in front of or behind you. Distance yourself from the person in front of you, especially when carrying hard-to-hold tools. Use blade guards and sheaths on sharp edges when you are hiking on to or out of a work site. Switch hands often to avoid fatigue and if you can do it comfortably, strap your tools onto your pack to leave your hands free. Don't carry tools on your shoulder, as you increase the likelinhood of personal injury if you should fall.

Fig. 6.14. Carry tools to your side and with sharp edges pointed down.

Circle of Danger

The *circle of danger* is the area that surrounds a worker who is using or carrying a tool (see figure 6.15). The primary, or inner, circle of danger extends as far as the tool can reach while the worker is using it. The secondary, or outer, circle of danger is the distance the tool could travel if the worker were to let go of the tool. Be especially aware of the outer circle when tools like axes and swizzle sticks are in use; the quick swinging motion of those tools spell danger when combined with a broken handle or a lost grip. Workers should never enter someone's primary circle of danger while he or she is working, and should never enter the outer circle in the direct path of a swing. The person using the tool must always be aware of people in the immediate area and ask others to move away if they are too close.

Fig. 6.15. Be aware of your circle of danger when using a tool.

ACQUIRE THE SKILLS

Obtain additional training from a local club or agency. Training with other trail workers is fun, increases your ability, and gives you an opportunity to ask questions about trail work. With many trail maintaining clubs, training is often required for those who wish to maintain a section of trail on their own.

Leading crews is challenging and requires skills beyond basic trail work. If you want to lead crews, acquire first-aid certification and leadership training. First-aid training will give you an extra measure of risk management and is required by most organizations in order to lead groups of individuals. Leadership training helps with the finer points of group management and can be obtained through many trail maintaining organizations

Use common sense and go through the fundamentals of preparation before you head out. Work safe and work smart.

Managing Your Crew

Set an attainable goal each day—one that is ambitious but not out of reach and do your best to accomplish it. Examples of good goals would be to clean all the drainages on a section of trail, brush one mile of a trail, or install six rock steps. Goals will keep you focused and give you a sense of accomplishment at the end of the day.

Be sure to check in regularly with your crew. Trail work can be more exhausting than some people anticipate. Offer breaks for people to drink water, eat a snack, care for their feet, and enjoy their surroundings. Finding appropriate tasks for your crew can be challenging as well. Plan a variety of tasks that offer something for everyone in your crew. Above all, be sure your crew is safe, busy, and having fun on the trails.

THE RIGHT WORK PLAN AND TOOLS

Plan and prepare your trail work project ahead of time, and determine the type of tools and the number you'll need. Know exactly what work you plan to do and the location of the work site. If necessary, have the work site marked in advance of your trip. If you are leading a volunteer crew, marking your work ahead of time is especially important. It will minimize the amount of time the leader will need to orient him- or herself to the work; during this time volunteers are likely to be stand around, waiting for someone to instruct them.

It is critically important that you bring the proper tools, as well as the correct amount, so that you and your crew can work effectively. There is no formula for this—use your experience and judgment. Of course, don't hedge excessively and bring unneeded tools that will slow you down or make your crew doubt your leadership ability. The more you know about your work ahead of time, the better able you will be to select the right tools and the right amount. Avoid doing extra work that requires additional tools. Focus on one task, such as cleaning drainage, and bring only the tools you will need for that job.

Tools: Use and Care

The types of tools used in trail maintenance will vary depending on the type of work. One should always have the proper tools for the job. The purpose of this section is to educate the trail maintainer about various types of tools and equipment and to outline their proper use, care, and applicable safety procedures.

In addition to describing hand tools, this section will discuss some basic power tools. However, the information provided is limited. Professional users and manufacturers can supply significantly more information about selecting and safely operating power equipment. Remember, proper training is very important for safe and efficient use of all power tools.

Strive to purchase top-quality tools. Bargain tools will usually cause headaches for trail workers and could possibly compromise their safety and efficiency, especially in a backcountry setting.

Cutting Tools

Cutting tools are one of the most important types used in trail work. They are used to clear trees and brush from trails during their initial development and annually thereafter. Also, cutting tools are used to build all sorts of wooden trail structures.

Cutting tools are the most difficult and elaborate in terms of the maintenance they require; in addition, high-quality tools may be difficult to find. Many stores carry simple tools such as axes, saws, and pruners; however, most won't stand up to the rigors of heavy use. Purchase quality tools that are designed to withstand the use. Sometimes, the best-quality hand tools are hand-forged antique tools found at flea markets and antique stores. The removal of a light patina of rust might reveal a tool superior to any commercially available today.

The Ax

The ax is one of the world's oldest tools. It has played a tremendously important role throughout history. In America, the ax reached its highest form; nowhere else in the world has it been used so much, undergone so many changes, and seen so many adaptations to different uses. Unfortunately, the ax is losing its importance and popularity. This makes it very difficult to find a good ax made of high-quality steel.

Although fewer people use the ax today, it continues to be an important tool in trail work. For example, it is the AMC trail crews' primary tool for cutting logs for trail reconstruction and removing winter blowdowns. If used correctly and maintained properly, the ax can be a very effective, efficient, and safe tool for removing blowdowns and harvesting project wood. It is lighter than the chain saw and does not require as many accessories. In addition to being a very practical tool for trail work, the ax is also an aesthetically pleasing tool which, because of its ancient roots, has great appeal for many trail workers. Aside from replacing the handle when necessary, maintaining an ax is a relatively expense-free proposition, unlike the continued cost of operating a chain saw.

The two basic kinds of axes are the single bit and the double bit (see figure 6.16). Both can be used for removing blowdowns, felling trees, limbing, cutting notches and water bars, and topping bridges. The double-bit ax was more popular in the past, but the single-bit ax is the most popular type of ax used today. The flat head of the single-bit ax can also be used occasionally for pounding stakes or driving wedges. It is best to use a sledgehammer for heavy pounding or when driving spikes or other metal. Both types of ax heads can have different shapes (see figure 6.17).

The size of the ax is a personal preference. Often, chopping work is done with a 3- to 3½-pound ax head, although some prefer to use a heavier head. The correct handle length is a function of height and body type. Accidents can more easily occur when folks use a handle of incorrect length.

A high-quality ax is often made of two different kinds of steel. Mild steel, which is softer and more resistant to impact, comprises the body of the ax, or the eye. The edge of the ax is made of harder carbon steel that is forged to the

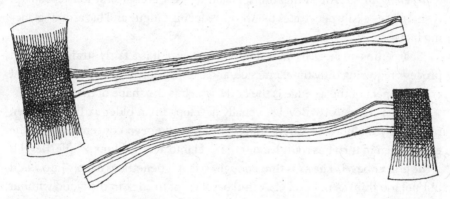

Fig. 6.16. Double-bit ax and single-bit ax.

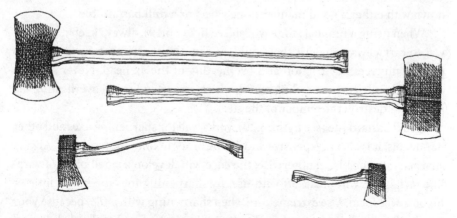

Fig. 6.17. Some different ax head patterns (top to bottom): Michigan; Maine or square head; Hudson Bay; hatchet.

body; it will take and hold a sharp edge. Most axes purchased today are drop-forged and made of soft steel which often doesn't hold a sharp edge for very long. When shopping for an ax look for a seam and hammer marks between the eye and the edge of the ax; this indicates that it is made of two different kinds of steel. An ax head that is painted or otherwise obscured, especially in the vicinity of the edge, is probably drop-forged. A good place to look for a high-quality two-piece ax is an antique store. The older axes found in such circumstances are often handmade and of generally higher quality than those purchased in the store.

In addition to axes for cutting clean timber, most crews also have a root ax, usually a lower-quality single bit. Root axes are used when cutting in or close to the ground where use of a good ax would be damaged.

Sharpening an Ax. All cutting tools, including axes, are safest when kept sharp. A sharp edge easily penetrates the wood, reducing fatigue and hazardous glancing blows.

Sharpening an ax well can be tedious; however, it is a fairly straightforward process, requiring only time, practice, and a few simple implements. The most critical aspect of the ax edge is the *bevel*, which is the shape of the edge itself.

Look at figure 6.18. Bevel A usually develops in an older ax that has been improperly maintained. Sharpening has obviously been concentrated on the edge, which in turn has rounded out the steel into a fairly blunt profile. Bevel B is the proper bevel. The ax is thin enough so that it penetrates deeply into wood but not too thin, as in bevel C. A thin bevel is apt to stick in the wood without knocking the chips loose and makes the edge fragile and prone to breaking. To work a bevel down and get it into shape, as in illustration B, work the steel down with either a good manual stone wheel or a mill bastard file.

When using a manual stone wheel (see figure 6.19), always keep its surface wet to carry away any grit that could clog up the sharpening surface and to prevent unnecessary friction and overheating of the ax head. Never sharpen an ax with an electric grinding wheel, which can often lead to overheating the metal and destroy the temper of the steel.

A mill bastard file (see figure 6.20) works well for sharpening axes and other hand tools; it is also inexpensive and can be brought onto the work site. Always sharpen into the blade; otherwise, the edge will develop a small piece of wire-like metal that will break off with use. By sharpening into the blade, little or no burr will form. Use extreme care when sharpening with a file, because your hand will be pushing toward the blade. A file can be fitted with a handle and hand guard. Cut a 4-inch square of leather or old fire hose, cut a hole through

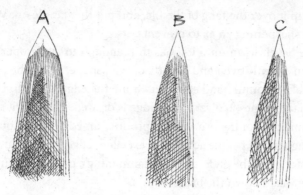

Fig. 6.18. Sharpen your ax to look like bevel B.

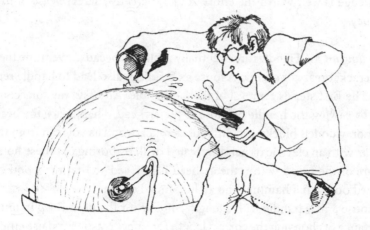

Fig. 6.19. Use a low-speed wheel and keep it wet. Also note angle of ax to wheel.

Fig. 6.20. File diagonally into edge. Watch you fingers.

the center, slip it over the tang of the file, and put the handle on. Wear leather gloves when sharpening an ax to prevent cuts.

Work the bevel down until it looks thin enough to cut properly (bevel B) and has a consistently even and slightly curved shape. Once the proper bevel is attained, take a round hand stone and hone the edge smooth. Use water or light oil on hand stones. If a very keen edge is desired, a finer grit stone can be used. This final part of the process can produce an edge fine enough to shave a hair, although many people achieve an excellent edge with just using a file. A sharpening stone may be preferable for maintaining a good edge, since frequent filing rapidly wears down the blade.

Again, an ax should be kept as sharp as possible at all times. Maintaining a keen edge is well worth the effort as it will greatly increase ease of use and efficiency.

Rehandling an Ax. Handles are eventually replaced, because over time they will warp, crack, break, or shrink. A loose ax head can also lead to handle replacement. The first step is removal of the old handle. An easy way to accomplish this is by sawing the handle off close to the ax head. Then, place the head in a vise or on wooden blocks and drill out as much wood as you can from the eye of the ax with an electric or hand-operated drill. By boring out these holes, the pressure of the wood within the ax head is relieved so that the wood can be pounded out with a hammer and a blunt metal object.

Choose a new handle with a length suitable for the user. Keep in mind the importance of choosing the correct length for safety reasons and use efficiency. When purchasing a new handle closely observe the grain of the wood. It should be fairly straight, close together, and parallel with the axis of the handle and the ax head (see figure 6.21). Always avoid knots and other defects in the wood. Hickory is often considered the best choice for handles because of its overall strength and spring-like qualities. Avoid purchasing handles that are painted, since painting often conceals faults in the wood and the paint can contribute to blisters forming.

The next step is fitting the handle into the eye. The handle needs to be shaped to closely match the eye of the ax in order to fit tightly. Use a draw knife, wood rasp, or spoke shave to whittle the top of the handle down to the size of the eye. Remove wood cautiously, a little at a time, so that you do not make the handle too thin. Once you can get the handle to slide into the top third of the eye, test the fit by pounding the handle into the head. Hold the handle, ax head down, and drive the handle down into the eye by pounding the base of the handle with a wooden or leather mallet or old mattock handle. You can also drive the ax head

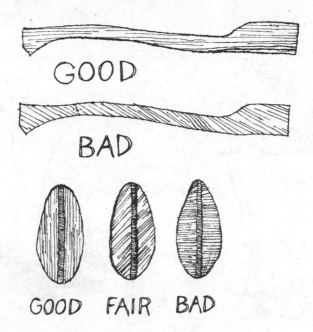

Fig. 6.21. The grain of the handle should be parallel to the ax head.

down onto the handle by setting the head onto the handle and pounding the base of the handle straight down onto a block of wood on the floor or a stump. Be careful to prevent the head from springing off the handle. See how it fits and where you need to take off more wood. Knock the head off the handle with a block of wood or mattock handle and shave off more wood where needed. Try the fit again. You'll probably need to test the fit and fine-tune the handle a few times until you achieve the desired fit.

Once you get a snug fit, pound the handle home so the ax head wedges tightly on the handle at its proper place (see figure 6.22). An inch or so of the top of the handle should be sticking out past the top of the ax head; saw off this excess wood, leaving a quarter to half an inch protracting above the eye; when this wood swells with moisture it tightens the handle's fit. Next, drive a hardwood wedge into the cut handle slot, now inside the eye of the ax head. Cut off any excess wedge when it will not go deeper. Wooden wedges, usually supplied with a new handle, compress as they are driven in and expand inside the head, wedging it on tightly. The wedge may split as you drive it in; that's fine, as some pieces will go deeper and fill wider gaps. Avoid small steel wedges and save them for the field if the ax head becomes loose. Once steel wedges are driven into the ax, the grain of the handle becomes cracked and weakened. Thus, it is hard to reuse the same handle to re-hang your ax.

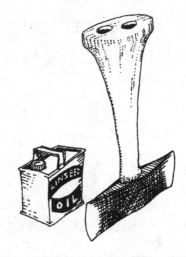

Fig. 6.22. Drive handle into head with a wooden or leather mallet.

Fig. 6.23. Feed your ax. Put linseed oil in the holes in the handle—adds life!

Care of the Handle. When purchased, new handles are often either painted or have a hard varnish finish that can cause blistered hands and cause the handle to dry out and crack. Sand off the finish and rub in a coat of boiled linseed oil with a rag; this keeps the handle flexible and protects it from rot and drying, which can lead to cracking and shrinking. A periodic coating of boiled linseed oil will help prevent these problems and give the handle a smooth finish.

To help extend the life of a handle, linseed oil should be periodically placed in one or two holes drilled in the end of the handle (see figure 6.23). The holes should be about ¼ inch in diameter and ½ inch deep. At the end of the work trip, place several drops of linseed oil in the holes and set the ax handle upright to soak overnight. The natural capillary action of the wood will draw the oil into the grain.

If a handle shrinks and loosens within the head of the ax, you can sometimes solve this problem temporarily by soaking the ax head in a bucket of water overnight. Soaking in water causes the wood to swell and tighten within the head. Remember, this is only a temporary solution. Replacing or adding a wedge may help, but the handle should eventually be replaced.

Do not store an ax for a long period of time by leaning it in a corner, as the handle could develop a bend. Hang it up instead.

Ax Sheaths. Axes should be sheathed when transported or stored to protect both the edge of the ax and people. Many kinds of sheaths can be purchased (see figure 6.24) or made. The most common ones are leather sheaths with snaps or straps.

Sheaths can be made using rubber from an old garden or fire hose. Cut the hose the width of the blade and slit it lengthwise. The hose is pinned against the edge of the ax with a piece of rubber inner tube. Another type of sheath can be made by hollowing a block of wood to fit over the edge of the ax (see figure 6.25). Wood is less prone to slip off the blade and is stronger than rubber hose. Staple or screw the inner tube to the wood sheath to hold it in place against the ax.

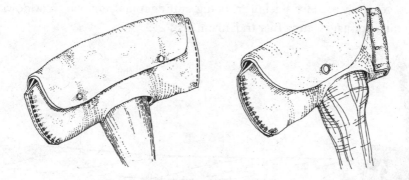

Fig. 6.24. Store-bought leather ax sheaths.

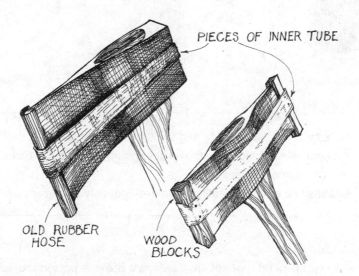

PIECES OF INNER TUBE

OLD RUBBER HOSE

WOOD BLOCKS

Fig. 6.25. Homemade ax sheaths.

Pulaski

This tool is a single-bit ax with a small adze/hoe blade (see figure 6.26). Though
originally created for use digging fire line in wild land fire fighting, because it
combines two traditional wood working tools—the ax and the adze—a well-
sharpened Pulaski is a versatile wood working tool. A Pulaski sharpened to be
a wood tool should be marked as such and never used in the dirt. Pulaskis are
most generally used for sidehill grubbing, cutting roots, removing blowdowns,
cleaning drainages, and other trail maintenance.

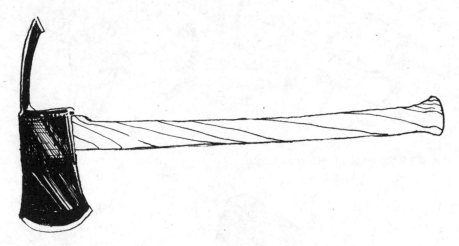

Fig. 6.26. Pulaski.

Crosscut Saws

There are two general types of crosscut saws: the one-person crosscut, generally 3 to 4½ feet in length, and the two-person crosscut, usually 5 to 8 feet in

Fig. 6.27. One-person crosscut saw, with handle for two-person option (top): two-person crosscut saw (bottom).

length (see figure 6.27). There are two basic two-person saw patterns. The *felling saw*, for cutting down trees, has a concave back and is relatively lightweight and flexible. The *bucking saw*, for cutting up felled trees, has a flat back and is heavier and stiffer.

Three common tooth patterns are available, each designed for a specific type of wood. The perforated-lance-tooth style is best for cutting softwoods (see figure 6.28). The champion-tooth style (see figure 6.29) is ideal for cutting hardwoods or frozen timber and is most often used with one-person saws. The plain-tooth style (see figure 6.30) is designed for cutting dead, dry wood.

The teeth of a plain-tooth saw both cut the wood and remove the shavings. On perforated-lance- and champion-tooth saws, the cutting teeth sever the wood fibers on each side of the cut. The raker teeth, cutting like a plane bit, peel the cut fibers, collect them in the gullets between the cutting teeth and raker teeth, and carry them out of the cut (see figure 6.31). A properly sharpened crosscut saw cuts deep and makes thick shavings. Most importantly, when using a cross-cut saw, make sure these different teeth are at the appropriate levels. The rakers need to be a bit lower than the cutters so that they are not the first to cut into the wood. The U.S. Forest Service publishes a manual about using and caring for crosscut saws, which can be accessed online at www.fs.fed.us.

Few people today know how to properly maintain and use a crosscut saw. The ax, chain saw, and bow saw are more commonly used. Like the ax, the crosscut saw has become somewhat antiquated with the introduction of the chain saw.

Fig. 6.28. Perforated-lance tooth.

Fig. 6.29. Champion tooth.

Fig. 6.30. Plain tooth.

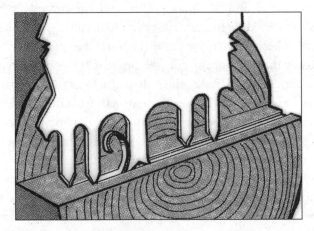

Fig. 6.31. Cutting action of crosscut saw.

Crosscuts do, however, have some advantages over the ax and the chain saw, which make them a good choice for certain projects and applications. They are inexpensive, lightweight, nonpolluting, generally safer to use than an ax, and relatively easy to use. They are often used for performing trail work in wilderness areas where motorized equipment is not allowed. They can be just as effective as a chain saw, especially when the tool must be carried long distances. Sometimes, however, finding someone to properly sharpen a crosscut can be difficult. Small, relatively inexpensive sharpening kits can be obtained, as well as excellent instructions for performing your own crosscut maintenance.

There are a few things about use and safety to keep in mind. When felling timber you should use the same basic technique as outlined for felling with a chain saw or ax (see Chapter 8). When transporting a crosscut, a sheath can be made from a section of old fire hose, slit along its length, and tied or strapped over the teeth. You can also use two strips of plywood held together over the blade with three or four bolts.

 SAFETY TIPS: Be aware of where the wood will roll or shift when it is cut.
SUGGESTED PPE: gloves (especially when handling the blade), eye protection, helmet

Bow Saws and Pruning Saws

Bow saws (see figure 6.32), sometimes known as pulpwood saws, and the smaller, curved-blade pruning saws come in a wide variety of sizes and shapes. Bow saws cut on both a pulling and pushing stroke; pruning saws generally

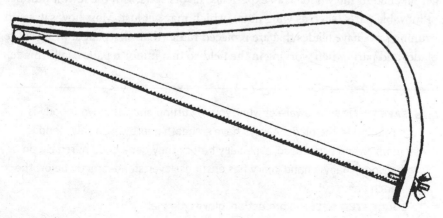

Fig. 6.32. Bow saw.

Fig. 6.33. Pole saw.

cut on a pull stroke only. The choice of saw depends on the size and amount of wood to be cut. Some older bow saws have wooden frames; today, most have steel or aluminum frames with blades ranging in length from 16 to 36 inches. Pruning-saw blades range from 10 to 24 inches in length; some conveniently fold up like a jackknife.

Larger bow saws can be used for cutting moderate-size timber and for removing blowdowns. Smaller bow saws and pruning saws are good for sawing small-diameter timber and clearing trails where saplings or limbs are too large for clippers. They also won't leave undesirable pointed stumps, which sometimes happens when using an ax or brush hook. Some collapsible bows saws are handy for occasional use but are generally too lightweight for continuous, heavy-duty use.

Various types of long-handled pole pruning saws (see figure 6.33) are useful for cutting high limbs when clearing ski touring trails. When using these saws, be sure that moving parts, such as nuts and bolts, are secure and that bow saw blades are at the right tension. Blades that are too loose or too tight can break or get pinched in the wood. Trail experience favors saws with the fewest number of movable parts (such as wing nuts), which may get lost. Most bow saws and pruning saws have blades that are replaced rather than sharpened. Bring spare blades and parts when working in the field so that minor repairs can be made.

 SAFETY TIPS: Be aware of what you're cutting and where your body is in relation to the blade. Always have a sheath nearby. Also saws tend to "jump" when being used, especially before they get a good purchase on the wood. Many a hand injury has ensued. Never stand directly below the branch being cut.

SUGGESTED PPE: eye protection, gloves, helmet

When transporting or storing saws, use a sheath to protect the worker and the blade. Wood, leather, or pieces of garden hose can be used. Many bow saws come with hard plastic sheaths. All unpainted metal parts should be kept lightly oiled to prevent rust.

Lopping Shears, Pole Clippers, and Hand Pruners
Long-handled clippers, pruners, or loppers come in a variety of styles (see figure 6.34). Handles are made of wood, steel, or aluminum. Cutting heads are either the sliding-blade-and-hook type or the anvil type. Some have simple

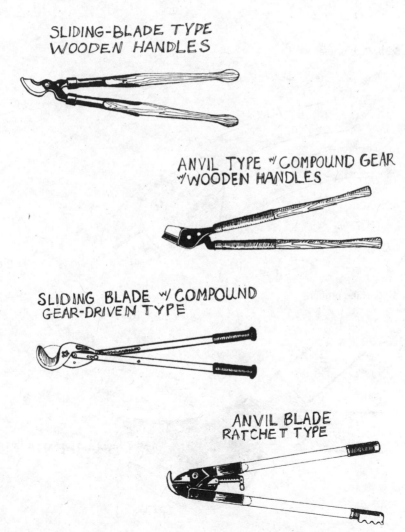

Fig. 6.34. Types of lopping shears.

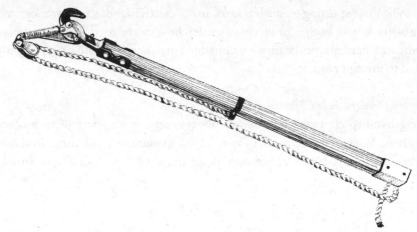

Fig. 6.35. Pole pruner.

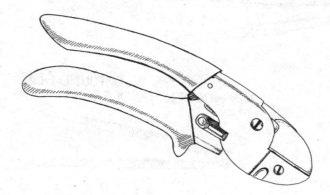

Fig. 6.36. Hand pruner.

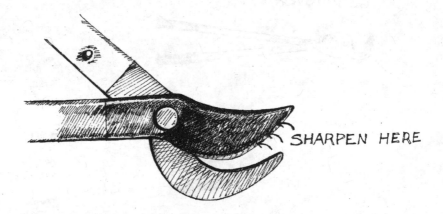

SHARPEN HERE

Fig. 6.37. Sharpen the outside edge of a pruner's cutting blade.

pivot actions, while others have compound or gear-driven actions for increased cutting power. Most cut between 1- and 1¾-inch limbs. Use the "rule of thumb": don't cut anything wider than your thumb, or diameter of the handle.

For specialized work such as clearing ski touring trails, a variety of pole clippers (see figure 6.35) are manufactured for professional tree-trimming work. These are suitable for clipping high limbs up to 1 or 1½ inches in diameter. Generally a 6- to 8-foot handle is sufficient for ski touring trail work. Longer handles can be obtained.

Small hand pruners (see figure 6.36) can sometimes be quite handy for occasional light pruning. These also come in a wide variety of styles.

Since loppers are one of the primary tools of the trail maintainer, it is important to purchase high-quality ones. Look for quality brand-name shears that are built for rugged, professional use and are simple to maintain and repair. The anvil-type loppers are sharpened on both sides of the cutting blade with a stone, like a pocketknife. Care must be taken to sharpen these blades evenly along their length. The soft metal anvils should be adjusted to meet the cutting blade evenly when the lopper is closed.

Clippers should be kept sharp, with all metal parts lightly oiled. A flat file or hand stone works well for sharpening the blade. For sliding-blade pruners, which work like scissors, sharpen only the outside, beveled edge of the cutting blade (see figure 6.37).

 SAFETY TIPS: Keep fingers out of hinges and between blades by transporting with both handles secure. Also beware of grip and branch when cutting above the shoulders.

SUGGESTED PPE: eye protection, gloves, if overhead hazard wear a helmet

---

The Swizzle Stick

The swizzle stick (see figure 6.38) is an important and versatile tool. Also known as a weed whip, it was developed for clearing brush and low growth along hiking trails. Similar tools are commercially available, but they generally lack the strength and durability of the homemade variety. Some have straight edges, while others have serrated blades.

A swizzle stick is used in a swinging motion, like a golf club. One with a double-edged blade (see figure 6.39) enables the worker to cut on the backswing as well. Sharpen a swizzle stick similar to the way an ax is sharpened with a bastard file and stone (see figure 6.40).

Fig. 6.38. Single-bladed swizzle.

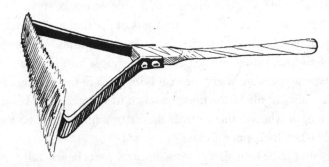

Fig. 6.39. Double-bladed swizzle.

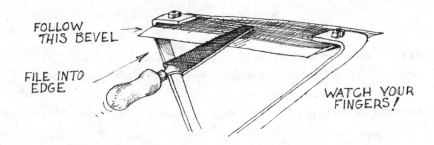

FOLLOW
THIS BEVEL

FILE INTO
EDGE

WATCH YOUR
FINGERS!

Fig. 6.40. Sharpening a swizzle stick is similar to sharpening an ax.

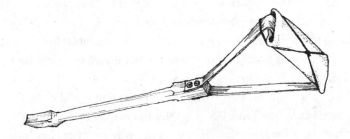

Fig. 6.41. Blade sheath.

A blade sheath should be used when carrying and storing the swizzle (see figure 6.41). Wrap a strip of heavy canvas or old fire hose around the blade and hold it in place with inner-tube rubber shaped in a figure-eight. Adhesive tape can be used in a pinch. A wooden or leather sheath can also be made.

 SAFETY TIPS: Never swing above the waist. Be aware of those around you. The swizzle should always be swung firmly, with both hands on the handle to fully control the swing. A rock or stump may accidentally deflect the tool; therefore, always wear heavy boots when using this tool.
SUGGESTED PPE: eye protection, gloves, possibly shin guards

Safety Ax and Machete
These can be handy, although somewhat more hazardous, supplements to the more classic tools used for trail clearing. They require care, sheathing, and sharpening similar to that described for the ax. All are generally not used for trail work in this region due to the likelihood of injury.

The safety ax (see figure 6.42), also known as a sandvik, as the name implies, is a good choice for most trail workers, because the blade is less exposed than that of a brush hook (see figure 6.43) or machete. If the blade is damaged, it can be replaced. Safety axes are particularly effective on young, springy hardwood growth.

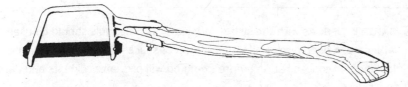

Fig. 6.42. Safety ax.

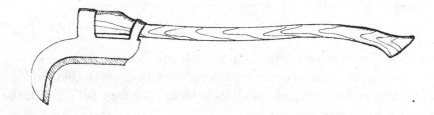

Fig. 6.43. Brush hook.

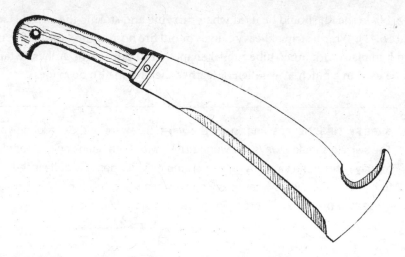

Fig. 6.44. Woodsmen's pal—a type of machete.

The best machete for trail clearing is probably the woodsmen's pal (see figure 6.44). It has some features, such as a cutting hook, that are unavailable on a conventional machete. It is also shorter than the conventional ones, which allows a shorter, more controlled swing.

Because these tools can be hazardous and often leave a sharply pointed stub when limbing or brushing, most trail workers prefer hand saws or clippers for limbing and other brushing, which leave a cleaner, smoother cut and are much safer to use.

 SAFETY TIPS: As with the swizzle stick, all of these tools should be used with care. A good grip at all times, plenty of space between workers, and looking and concentrating before swinging will prevent accidents and damage to the tools.

SUGGESTED PPE: gloves, eye protection, possibly shinguards, helmet (if there's a hazard overhead)

Digging Tools

Virtually all trail reconstruction and maintenance activities require workers to move soil and rock to build steps, water bars, drainage ditches, bridges, and similar projects. Digging tools used to accomplish these tasks include the shovel, mattock, hoe, and rock bar.

Fig. 6.45. Long-handle shovel.

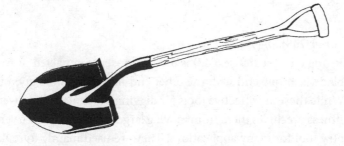

Fig. 6.46. D-handle shovel.

Shovel

The commonly used round-point shovel comes with either a long handle (see figure 6.45) or D-handle (see figure 6.46). The shorter D-handle shovel is more appropriate in congested situations. Some also find lifting with this type of shovel to be easier, since the load is closer to the body. Others favor the long-handle shovel, because it offers a longer reach and usually requires less bending. Do not pry heavily with the shovel or the handle will break. A mattock or rock bar should be used if large rocks impede digging. Some maintainers sharpen the shovel's edge slightly to facilitate cutting roots.

Fire shovels are often well-sharpened and are used to scrape the duff away in the building of a fire line. If a well-sharpened shovel is used in this manner as a trail tool, it should be kept separate and marked from the other shovels to maintain its edges.

 SAFETY TIPS: Be sure to pivot instead of twisting for repeated digging with a shovel.

SUGGESTED PPE: eye protection, gloves, helmet

Fig. 6.47. Digging bar.

Digging Bar or Tamping Bar

A long digging bar (see figure 6.47) is used to loosen compacted or rocky soil. A small blade is at one end with the other end flattened into a good tamping surface. While these are effective tools for digging holes, their light weight and lack of stiffness precludes them from moving large rocks and being a very useful backcountry tool for many applications. They are used mainly to replace sign posts because they help with digging and tamping around the post.

 SAFETY TIPS: Be careful of getting fingers crushed while tamping.
SUGGESTED PPE: eye protection, gloves, helmet

Pick and Cutter Mattock

Two types of mattocks are available, both of which have an adze or a blade set at right angles to the handle for grubbing. They differ by having either a pick or a cutter blade at the other end (see figure 6.48). The pick mattock has become the most important, and favorite, trail tread tool for digging, grubbing, and prying in the White Mountains because of its abundance of rocks and roots. This tool is popular with AMC crews because it doubles as a rock moving tool, which will be discussed in the rock tools section.

Mattocks are heavy, rugged tools that do not break easily. They can be used to chop through roots, loosen compacted soils, and pry out break rock. The cutter mattock may be more effective in areas with deeper soils and more roots than rocks.

To care for your mattock slightly sharpen it periodically to maintain a rudimentary edge capable of effective digging and root cutting. An electric grinding wheel, carefully used to avoid overheating the edge, reduces labor time when

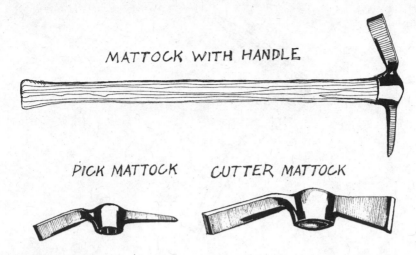

MATTOCK WITH HANDLE

PICK MATTOCK   CUTTER MATTOCK

Fig. 6.48. Mattock.

sharpening. Handles should get a periodic coating of boiled linseed oil; damaged handles should be replaced.

To keep handles from loosening prematurely, screw a ³⁄₁₆-inch-by-1-inch lag bolt into the handle up against the mattock head. Drill a pilot hole first. Do not place it in the side of the handle, because this may cause it to split. This should be done to grub and adze hoes also. However, some workers like having the option to remove the mattock head from the handle for easier transport. To do so, tap the end of the handle on a rock or other hard surface, carefully watching as the head becomes loose and drops down the length of the handle to the ground. To put the head back on, hold the handle upside down and drop the head onto the handle (also upside down). Tamp the entire tool on a rock to secure.

 SAFETY TIPS: Be sure to maintain a well-controlled swing, and stay aware of those around you.

SUGGESTED PPE: eye protection, gloves, helmet

Grub Hoes and Adze Hoes

Hoes of various styles are used in trail construction and maintenance. They are particularly useful for duffing new trail, sidehill grubbing, and building and cleaning drainages. Adze hoes are essentially mattocks without a cutter blade or pick. These hoes are about 3 to 4 inches wide and have a handle like a mattock. Adze hoes are heavy but are preferred where soils are rocky.

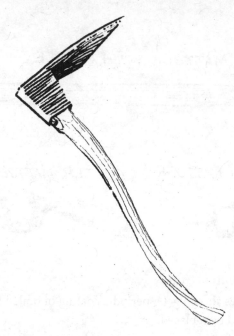

Fig. 6.49. Grub hoe.

A grub hoe (see figure 6.49), or hazel hoe, is lighter and has a wider blade (6 to 8 inches), sharper edge, and curved handle. Where a significant amount of sidehill grubbing has to be done—except where soils are very rocky—the AMC has found this tool to be the most useful. The wider blade moves more soil, the sharper edge cuts roots well, and the curved handle facilitates use.

 SAFETY TIPS: Be aware of shins while swinging.

SUGGESTED PPE: gloves, eye protection, helmet, possibly shin guards

Fire Rakes

Fire rakes (see figure 6.50) are very useful for duffing new trail and are also used to clean drainages primarily clogged with leaves and loose soil.

 SAFETY TIPS: Be sure to set in a safe place, teeth down, when not in use.

SUGGESTED PPE: eye protection, gloves, helmet

Fig. 6.50. Fire rake.

Pick

A pick is rarely necessary in trail work, since its function is adequately served by the pick mattock. However, for loosening compacted earth or chipping rocks, picks may be appropriate. They are particularly helpful for aerating compacted soils while closing and re-vegetating trails.

 SAFETY TIPS: Be sure to maintain a controlled swing.

SUGGESTED PPE: gloves, eye protection, helmet

Rock Tools

Pick Mattock

The pick mattock is one of the most useful and versatile trail hand tools. In addition to its helpfulness when digging, it can also be a highly effective rock moving tool. Using the pick against the rock, the mattock acts as a fulcrum for both lifting and pulling the rock. This technique requires some practice, but when perfected, moving rocks becomes relatively easy.

 SAFETY TIPS: Be aware of your lower back when using the mattock to fulcrum. Also, be ready if the pick slips on the rock . . . it's very easy to end up on the ground.

SUGGESTED PPE: gloves, eye protection, helmet

Rock Bar

The rock bar (see figure 6.51) is an essential tool for moving large and small rocks. Sixteen- to 18-pound hardened-steel rock bars—about 4½ feet long with a beveled tip—are best. Lighter ones tend to bend; shorter ones provide less leverage. The rock bar's length allows for various ways to level and push a rock. Used in conjunction with either a smaller rock or log as a fulcrum, lifting strength is dramatically increased. A rock bar's chisel-shaped tip provides additional mechanical advantage for moving extremely heavy objects. Techniques for using this tool will be further discussed in Chapter 8.

Fig. 6.51. Rock bar.

 SAFETY TIPS: Never have fingers and tools on the rock at the same time; the possibility of crushing a finger with a tool or rock shifting is too great. Always communicate clearly if working with anyone, and make a clear plan. Always lift with your legs, keeping your back straight. Be aware of other hazards that might be encountered while rolling a rock. Never get below a rock while moving it.

SUGGESTED PPE: gloves, eye protection, helmet

Rock Hammers

Rock hammers are used to shape stone; many different kinds of rock hammers are available. Some strike stone directly, some are held against the stone and struck by another hammer, and some only strike other tools. Each type is tempered and hardened for its specific purpose. Using a hammer in a way in which it is not designed can be very dangerous. Hard, brittle metal can chip and crack with incorrect use. Softer tempered metal will tend to mushroom with use. This is natural, so they must be monitored and edges and blades must be ground down to remain safe. Both the hammerhead and the handles should be monitored for cracks or weaknesses before use.

Sledge Hammer. Sledge hammers are used to hit rock directly, as well as for hitting other hammers or chisels. Sledge hammers are also necessary when pounding spikes during certain wood construction projects. Sledge hammers come in different weights. The lighter weights with shorter handles are sometimes called single jacks, while the ones that are six pounds or more and have long handles are called double jacks. Choose one that you feel comfortable swinging repeatedly in a controlled fashion. Sledge hammers from hardware stores are fine. Like all softer metal hammers, be aware that the head may mushroom with extended use. File away metal spurs and mushrooming when necessary.

Hand, or Striking Hammer. This hammer (see figure 6.52) is designed to strike other tools. It is tempered to do so and will last a long time. It should never be used to strike rock directly.

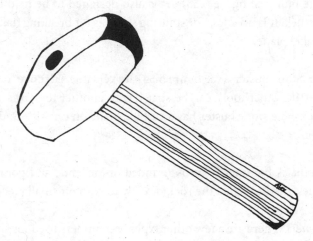

Fig. 6.52. Hand, or striking hammer.

Mash Hammer. A mash hammer, also called a mason's hammer, has both a blade and a flat, square face. The blade is used to break rock into smaller pieces, while the flat side is used to break stone off of edges.

Spalling Hammer. Spalling hammers have a blade on one side and a hammer on the other. Because the metal is soft, it tends to mushroom with use. However, this tool is very versatile, and can be used for chipping, shaping, or scoring rock.

Rifting Hammer. The rifting hammer is used to score rock along a rift line. It is not designed to swing against the rock, but to be held flat against a rock and

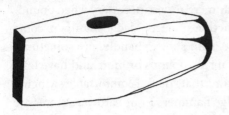

Fig. 6.53. Bull set.

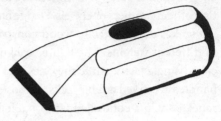

Fig. 6.54. Stone buster.

struck with another hammer while tracing a line. Sometimes rock can be split by this alone, while other times it just makes drilling more precise.

Bull Set. The bull (see figure 6.53) set is also designed to be held against the stone and struck. It is used less for splitting stone as for breaking flakes of stone along a parallel plane.

Stone Buster. Stone busters (see figure 6.54) are versatile, effective tools and can be used to strike other tools, can be struck with another tool, or swung alone to shape rock. The stone buster has a carbide blade on one side and a flat side on the other.

Hammer Point. A hammer point is rounded on one side and pointed on the other. It is designed to strike the rock directly to chip off small pieces of rock.

Other Hammers. There are a few other types of hammers used for shaping and breaking stone. The important thing to remember when using a new hammer is what the metal is tempered to do. It is very important not to swing hammers which are not designed to strike.

 SAFETY TIPS: Be aware of those around you when swinging, especially when hazardous rock shards are flying. Always know what the proper use of each hammer is; never strike metal with a hammer that is not designed to do so. Check handles and hammers for compromised integrity. Always pay close attention to the hitting target and beware of fingers.
SUGGESTED PPE: safety glasses, gloves, possibly dust mask and long sleeves, helmet

---

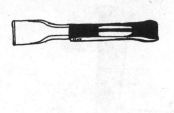

Fig. 6.55. Hand chisels.

Chisels
Many chisels (see figure 6.55) are used in a similar way to their hammer counterparts listed above. However, they are all designed to be struck on the head. Swings should be relatively small and always controlled and sustainable. Some common chisels are the hand point, hand chisel, hand set, and hand tracer. The hand point is generally used to remove high spots or smaller features, the hand set used to remove overhangs or bulges when the surface is flat, the hand tracer for tracing a fracture line for splitting, and the hand chisel for general shaping. Other chisels are available, but these are the most common.

When striking a chisel, make the first hit relatively light to set the chisel into place. Also, when working with a chisel that has a blade, be sure that as much of the blade is contacting the rock as possible.

 SAFETY TIPS: Be aware of the wear and tear on your striking hammer and the striking surface of the chisels. Be sure to grind down any mushrooming when it becomes apparent. Of course, beware of your aim when swinging. **SUGGESTED PPE:** gloves, eye protection, helmet

---

Feathers and Wedges
When splitting rock by drilling—either by hand or with a pneumatic gas or electric drill—use feathers and wedges (see figure 6.56) to actually break the rock. The process will be discussed in Chapter 8. Two feathers and one wedge are in a set. The feathers are placed into the hole with the wedge in the middle. The wedges are pounded down evenly to push the rock apart from the weakness of the drilled holes.

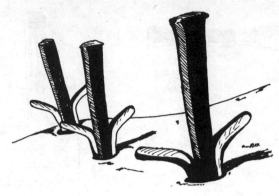

Fig. 6.56. Feathers and wedges.

 SAFETY TIPS: There are plenty of safety concerns when drilling and splitting rock, though those will be discussed in Chapter 8. However, once again, it is important to use the proper hammer and inspect the hammer and wedges for mushrooming and integrity of the metal before striking.
SUGGESTED PPE: gloves, eye protection, helmet, dust mask

Wood Tools

Bark Spud and Draw Knife

In the spring and early summer, when wood is fresh, bark can be easily peeled away with a bark spud (see figure 6.57). The draw knife (see figure 6.58) can also be used for peeling logs, though it is particularly helpful when the wood is less fresh, or late in the season when wood does not peel easily.

Fig. 6.57. Bark spud.

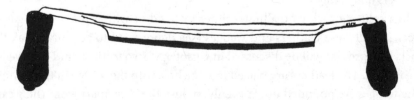

Fig. 6.58. Draw knife.

SAFETY TIPS: When working around felled trees and logs, be aware of where the log could shift, or if anyone else is also working on it. Also, the wood tends to be very slippery when peeled, so be careful when transporting. One way to do this is to brace the log between rocks or other pieces of wood to prevent motion.

SUGGESTED PPE: gloves, eye protection, helmet

Log Carrier

A log carrier (see figure 6.59), or timber tong, consists of a pair of hooks that grip a log and are attached to a handle that extends on both sides (often with the ability to swivel). This allows two people to lift or drag a log without getting underneath it.

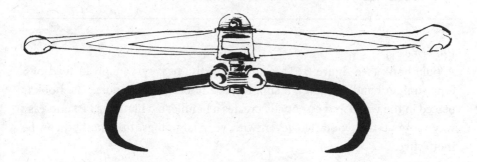

Fig. 6.59. Log carrier.

 SAFETY TIPS: Be sure the tongs are equally well set by lifting the log in unison. Beware of your back while lifting. Communicate closely with others working with you.

SUGGESTED PPE: gloves, eye protection, helmet

Peavey

A peavey (see figure 6.60) is a traditional wood tool used by loggers to roll and manage logs. It has a hook and point and can help rotate and roll logs. The hook serves to bite into the wood, and the handle can then be pulled in the other direction to lever the log.

6
Safety and Preparation

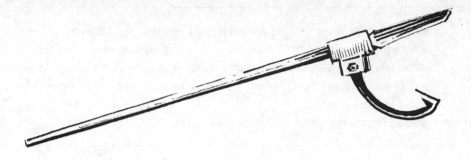

Fig. 6.60. Peavey.

 SAFETY TIPS: Always be careful when working with a pile of logs; assess what can move, where it will go, and who is in the immediate vicinity.
SUGGESTED PPE: gloves, eye protection, helmet

Pulp Hook

A pulp hook (see figure 6.61) is similar to the peavey, though instead of a long straight handle to lever, it simply has a hook with a handle. The hook is placed in the wood and essentially creates a handle, facilitating a fast and easy way to move the wood. However, with very large logs, this method can be ineffective.

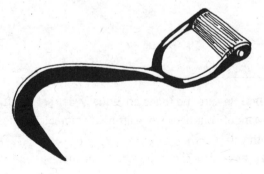

Fig. 6.61. Pulp hook.

 SAFETY TIPS: Be careful while setting the hook and carrying around the wood if the hook loses its bite and the log falls.
SUGGESTED PPE: gloves, eye protection, helmet

Hoisting Tools

Ratchet Winches

A ratchet winch (see figure 6.62) is used to move large rocks or logs. Most are available with varying pull capacities—anywhere from one to four tons. They utilize a single or double cable on a spool.

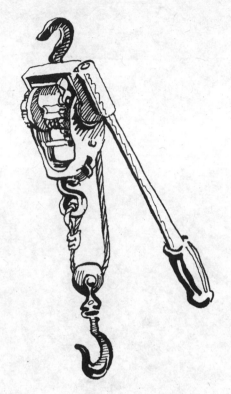

Fig. 6.62. Ratchet winch.

Griphoist

A griphoist (see figure 6.63) is a winch that can feed a cable of varying length, rather than a cable of fixed length, as with a come-along. Griphoists are built with safety mechanisms, which help to make them very powerful trail working tools and systems. However, they can also be very dangerous. Though some basic techniques are discussed in Chapter 8, it is vital to have adequate training before setting up and operating a griphoist system.

 PPE: Leather gloves, helmet, eye protection

Fig. 6.63. Griphoist.

Fig. 6.64. Tripod.

Tripod

When operating a griphoist highline system in an area that lacks natural spars, a metal tripod (see figure 6.64) can be used. Tripods are very helpful, but the operator of the highline system must have adequate knowledge and training. Highline systems are very useful in areas such as alpine zones, where rock construction is necessary, but be sure to protect the ground vegetation and soil.

Power Tools

Though the bulk of trail work is done using hand tools, some occasions call for power tools, because an abundant amount of heavy cutting or specialized work is needed. Information on the chain saw, motorized brush cutter, and rock drill, is given here. Only a broad description of each tool and its specifications is provided; get specific information from manufacturers on the use and care of these instruments.

Chain Saws

When shopping for a chain saw (see figure 6.65), consider the information that manufacturers supply. The opinions of friends and fellow maintainers can also be helpful when comparing the value of different saws. Get recommendations from professional tree-trimming outfits or local logging operators. Chain saws are made by a variety of manufacturers and come in different sizes and types—each suited to a particular job. Each of the major manufacturers of chain saws carries a full line of equipment that ranges in size and power from small, light-duty saws to large machines used by the pulp and paper industry.

Choosing a make, model, and options is a matter of personal taste, like choosing an automobile. First, determine the work you'll be doing, and then find a local dealer who can help you purchase the appropriate saw. Make sure the saw has the best safety features and is easy to operate and maintain in the field. A good dealer who provides prompt and efficient service and safe operating instructions is equally important. Avoid chain saws sold by the large department store outlets.

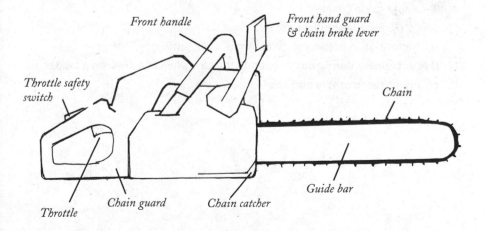

Fig. 6.65. Chain saw.

- **Read your owner's manual and all supplements** thoroughly before operating your saw.
- **Use the personal protective equipment listed on page 108.**
- **Don't use any other fuel** than that recommended in your owner's manual.
- **Refuel in a safe place.** Don't spill fuel or start the saw where you fuel it. Do not refuel a hot saw; allow it to cool off. Be certain the saw has dried thoroughly before starting, if fuel has spilled on the unit.
- **Don't smoke** while fueling or operating the saw.
- **Start your saw without help.** Don't start a saw on your leg or knee. Never operate a chain saw when you are fatigued.
- **Keep all parts** of your body and clothing away from the saw chain when starting or running the engine. Before you start the engine, make sure the saw chain is not in contact with anything.
- **Beware of kickback!** Hold saw firmly with both hands when engine is running; use a firm grip with thumbs and fingers encircling the chain saw handles and watch carefully what you cut. Kickback (saw jumps or jerks up or backward) can be caused by:
  - Striking limbs or other objects accidentally with the tip of the saw while the chain is moving.
  - Striking metal, cement, or other hand material near the wood, or buried in the wood.
  - Running engine slowly at start of or during cut.
  - Dull or loose chain.
  - Cutting above shoulder height.
  - Inattention in holding or guiding saw while cutting.
- **It is extremely dangerous** to operate the saw while **in a tree**, **on a ladder**, or **on any other unstable surface**

- **Be sure of your footing** and pre-plan a safe exit from a falling tree or limbs.
- **When cutting a limb that is under tension** beware of spring back to avoid being struck when the tension is released.
- **Use extreme caution** when cutting small brush and saplings because slender material may catch the saw chain and be whipped toward you or pull you off balance.
- **Vibration.** Avoid prolonged operation of your chain saw and rest periodically. Stop using the saw if your hand or arm starts to have a loss of feeling, swells, or becomes difficult to move.
- **Exhaust fumes.** Do not operate your chain saw in confined or poorly ventilated areas.
- **Observe all local fire-prevention regulations.** It is recommended that you keep a fire extinguisher and shovel close at hand whenever you cut in areas where dry grass, leaves, or other flammable materials are present.
- **Turn off your saw when moving between cuts** and before setting it down. Always carry the chain saw with the engine stopped, the guide bar and saw chain in the rear, and the muffler away from your body.
- **Use wedges to help control felling** and prevent binding the bar and chain in the cut.
- **Don't touch** or try to stop a moving chain with your hand.
- **Keep the chain sharp** and snug on the guide bar.
- **Don't allow dirt, fuel, or sawdust** to build up on the engine or outside of the saw.
- **Keep all screws and fasteners tight.** Never operate a chain saw that is damaged, improperly adjusted, or not completely and securely assembled. Be sure that the saw chain stops moving when the throttle-control trigger is released. Keep the handles dry, clean, and free of oil or fuel mixture.

Fig. 6.66. Use this technique when operating a chain saw.

Smaller saws are the most popular choices for trail work because of their light weight. Larger, more powerful saws are appropriate for heavy cutting, such as the clearing of a trail strewn with fallen tress following a major storm or during timber harvesting. However, these situations occur rarely.

Safe Chain Saw Operation. Constantly stress the importance of safe chain saw operating techniques (see figure 6.66) to all users. Chain saws operate at a fast cutting speed, and the slightest slip or miscalculation can cause serious injury.

 SUGGESTED PPE: gloves, eye protection, ear protection, helmet, chain saw chaps

---

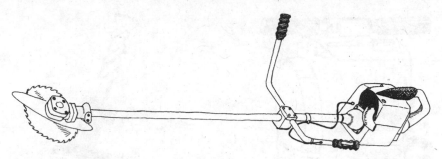

Fig. 6.67. Gas-powerd brush cutter.

Gas-Powered Brush Cutters

Similar to a heavy-duty weed whacker with a metal blade for cutting wood, gas-powered brush cutters (see figure 6.67) are useful for extensive trail clearing through young, heavy growth. Most clearing can be done by hand, and few maintainers find it necessary to invest in this specialized piece of equipment. If one is used, the operator should be experienced and maintain a safe working distance from others.

 SUGGESTED PPE: gloves, eye protection, helmet, ear protection, possibly chain saw chaps

Rock Drills (Pneumatic Hammer Drills)

Referred to as rock drills by many trail workers, pneumatic hammer drills, such as those made by Kango or Punjar or Makita, are used in specific construction applications. They can be used to drill holes in rock for pinning rocks, install metal rungs or ladders, split rock with feathers and wedges, or in a chisel setting with a chisel bit to break rock. Holes drilled in rock can also be used while blasting or using an expanding compound. Both gas-powered and electric drills are available. Gas-powered rock drills (see figure 6.68) are heavier, tend to break more often, and are difficult to find due to a decline in manufacturing caused by stricter emissions standards. Electric rock drills (see figure 6.69) are lighter, but must be powered by a generator. These are advantageous because the generator can be kept far from the work site, which decreases fatigue caused by noise and the operation of a heavy machine; also the exhaust will not be in the vicinity of the operator. With the advent of smaller, lighter generators, electric rock drills have become a more feasible option for backcountry applications.

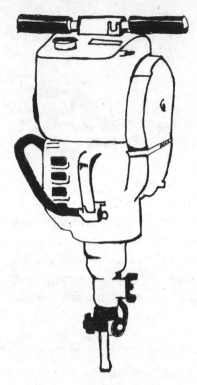

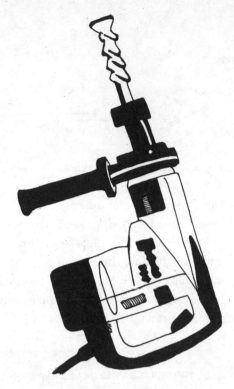

Fig. 6.68. Gas-powered rock drill.　　　**Fig. 6.69.** Electric rock drill.

Special safety concerns when using a rock drill include repetitive impact, vibration, body positioning, and inhalation of particulates. Be sure to take turns drilling so the operator does not become fatigued, and be sure that everyone in the area is wearing OSHA-approved dust masks at all times.

 PPE: eye protection, hearing protection, hard hat, dust mask, gloves

---

Measuring Tools

Measuring Wheel

Measuring wheels (see figure 6.70) are used to measure trail distances for guidebook descriptions. They are also used to locate and index trail features and create work logs to guide work crews. The AMC prefers an inexpensive, rugged, all-steel measuring wheel with an internal cable and counter mechanism on the handle made by Cedarholm. Those with external counters (which sometimes get caught on brush) or bicycle-like wheels (which can get bent easily) do not

Fig. 6.70. Measuring wheel.

work as well. Some enterprising maintainers have made their own measuring tools using a bicycle mileage meter and wheel.

Clinometers

A clinometer is used to measure the slope and grade of the ground. It is best used by two people. First, you must determine the height of the eye of the person measuring. From this, determine where this is in relation to a point on the other person. The person with the clinometer goes to the bottom of the slope, while the other goes to the top. The person at the bottom looks through the viewfinder at the predetermined point; the top person will take a reading from the wheel at that point, indicating the grade or slope.

String Lines

String lines can be used many ways in trail work. They can be used with a tape measure and line level to lay out stairs and determine their desired rise and run. String lines can also be used in the construction process of the stairs or in applications with bridge construction.

FLAGGING

Flagging or marker flags can be used to mark out new trail, possible campsites, potential projects, etc. Pieces tied to trees can be written on in permanent marker with shorthand instructions. However, be sure to remove them when their purpose has been completed, so as not to leave litter in the woods. Decomposing flagging tape is also available, which can be good for trail work, depending on the climate and length of time it needs to be used.

OTHER TOOLS

Wheel barrow (see figure 6.71): This tool can be used for moving rock or soil along a moderate trail. However, wheel barrows are not permitted in wilderness areas.

5 gallon buckets/milk crates (see figure 6.72): These are great for carrying soil or stone for projects such as cribbing, scree walls, turnpiking, or leaves for finishing brush-in of project sites.

Canvas bags (see figure 6.73): Similar to the bucket and crate, canvas bags can be used to move material.

Rakes: These are good for spreading gravel, but must have strong metal tines.

McCloud: Similar to a fire rake with an additional beveled side, it is very useful when breaking new trail, especially on trails with high organic soil.

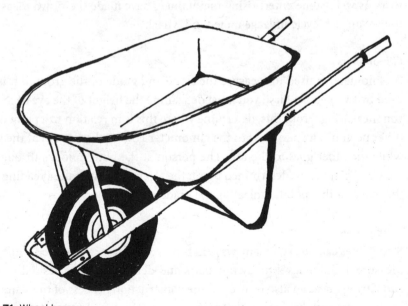

Fig. 6.71. Wheel barrow.

Fig. 6.72. Five-gallon bucket.   **Fig. 6.73.** Canvas bag.

DON'T LOSE YOUR TOOLS

Used wood and metal hand tools quickly become drab and easily blend into trailside brush and woods. Remember where you left them and keep them close by or on the trail. At the end of the work day gather up all the crew's tools and make sure they are accounted for. Keep tools in one stash or cache at camp or near the work site, just out of sight of the trail. To help keep tools from "hiding" in the brush, liberally paint a good portion of the heads and handles with a brightly colored paint like orange or red. Do not paint the cutting or digging edges of the heads or the gripping parts of the handles.

Also, if an extra tarp is available, use a drably colored tarp to keep the tools dry when left in the tool cache at night or through days off. Be sure the sides are tucked in well so as not to collect water, but shed it.

TOOL SOURCES

Tools can be purchased at hardware stores and from catalogs and outlets of forestry, farm, and construction equipment suppliers. Look for inexpensive used tools at garage sales, used tool outlets, and antique shops. Often the best wood-cutting hand tools, like axes and crosscut saws, were made decades ago. See Appendix A for suggestions on where to buy tools.

CHAPTER 7
TRAIL CONSTRUCTION
& EROSION CONTROL

AT-A-GLANCE

By using the proper techniques, you will be able to construct a more sustainable trail and limit erosion.

- **Construction:** Cut the clearing passage, scrape away excess organic material, and create a sustainable treadway.

- **Reconstruction:** Fix problems by fixing old structures and adding new ones where needed.

- **Erosion control:** Address erosion by building drainages, stabilizers, retainers, and hardeners.

Before beginning any trail project, it is always important to take into account the two main reasons we do trail work. First, we strive to reduce human impact to a single path. Second, we aim to make the treadway appealing for hikers, enhancing their outdoor experience. Ultimately, the trail must be stable, supported by structures to prevent erosion, and have a treadway that is safe and inviting for the trail's users—all this without adversely affecting the natural environment that the trail is built on so that people can appreciate and enjoy it. By carefully considering both the surrounding resources and the recreational users, the trail planner can make trail construction and reconstruction decisions that best support the needs of both.

After you have laid out your trail and learned about tool use and safety, you can begin with trail construction and reconstruction. Construction refers to the building of new trails or structures, while reconstruction involves repairing and restoring existing ones. Ideally, a well-laid-out trail, which was discussed in Chapter 4, helps to reduce the need for repairs and, in the worst-case scenario, redesign. However, improper placement of a trail does occur, and many problems may result when relocating the trail, either in entirety or in sections. Often, this may be the best option. In other cases, reconstruction is the best choice. Either way, going back to fix a trail, either by relocation or reconstruction, is expensive and timely.

Construction and reconstruction are ongoing processes since a trail is dynamic and changes over time due to wear from foot travel and erosion from water drainage. Once the trail is "worn in" by use, you'll find there are some places that require construction of more drainage structures due to high water runoff, other places that need a few rock steps up an eroded incline, and some that even require a short reroute.

TRAIL CONSTRUCTION

The initial construction phase is really quite basic, comprised of three parts: cutting the trail clearing passage, tread construction, and marking. To start the construction, pick up the hazel hoes, saws, and other cutting tools and begin creating the clearing passage.

Cutting the Clearing Passage

The very first step of construction is cutting the clearing passage of your trail. If not in a federally designated wilderness area, the most efficient tool is undoubtedly a chain saw wielded by a well-trained and experienced sawyer. Cutting new trail can be dangerous if you're working in a congested forest, so care should be taken regardless of tree size. Before you start cutting, be certain that you have the required permits or other regulatory approval you may need.

Brush and blowdown clearing are nearly identical in the construction phase as in the maintenance phase, except that now you're starting from scratch. (Refer to Chapter 10 for instructions and information on brush clearing.) Avoid cutting out large trees since the stumps are difficult to remove, and those trees left on the side of the trail can serve as natural trail *definers*. Additionally, they add to the aesthetic quality of the trail and serve to stabilize soils.

Be sure that you are cutting according to the flagging placed by the person who initially laid out the proposed trail. Either keep the flagging on center or stay to the right or left, as prescribed by the flagger.

It's necessary to determine whether you're about to cut a softwood tree, such as spruce and fir, which do not sprout from cut stumps, or a hardwood tree, which does sprout. If a stump is a hardwood, it is important to pull the stump out of the ground to prevent re-sprouting. To facilitate this, it is often easier to keep the stump about waist height so that the trunk can be used as leverage for the removal of the lower portion. A commonly used tool for stump removal is a Pulaski, which can be used to both dig around roots and cut them. Rock bars and a griphoist hand winch system can also be helpful for removal of large stumps.

Softwoods should be cut flush to the ground or slightly below *grade*. They will eventually rot, and therefore not sprout into the tread. After major tree removal is complete, the final touches of branch removal can be done using loppers and the guidelines of clearing passage management mentioned in the maintenance section of this book (see Chapter 10).

Tread Construction

Now that the clearing passage has been cut, and you can work safely and easily within this zone, the treadway must be created by clearing organic materials and soil, then shaping the mineral soil into a slightly outsloped walking surface.

Duffing

Once you have cut all trees and shrubs from the designated clearing passage area, you should begin to scrape away any organic materials like leaves, needles, roots, bark (technically termed by soil scientists as the O1 layer, meaning first organic layer, or more informally called duff) and any organic soil (the O2, or second organic layer, comprised of decomposed organic materials). This process is called *duffing*. Ideally, the worker should attempt to scrape down to *mineral soil*, which does not hold as much water as organic soil. Mineral soil is not comprised of decomposed vegetative materials like organic soils, but instead is made up of minute pieces of rocks and minerals. (Upturned trees that have fallen naturally may have mineral soil under their exposed roots.) It percolates (drains) water better than other types of soil and so is the best material for the treadway. Without removal of the duff and with a little bit of use, a trail with lots of organic material becomes a wet and slimy tangle of mud and small roots.

However, if you remove the duff on a completely flat trail, you are essentially digging a trench, which in time will collect water. As we know from trail layout, a flat treadway is not always the best since water has nowhere to drain. If the trail must be flat, you may want to refrain from removing the duff and let the users compact the existing soil. Another commonly used technique is to import mineral soil from a borrow pit, which is a hole dug away from the trail to retrieve soil. Be sure to fill in the pit after use with rocks, soil, branches, etc. and disguise it with leaves and branches.

Fig. 7.1. Scrape away organic materials by duffing.

To duff, use a hazel hoe, mattock, fire rake, or other digging and scraping tool (see figure 7.1). To ensure a uniform tread, mark each side of the treadway to your trail width standard with string or sticks before you start. Begin by scraping and rolling back the duff. Pull it onto the downhill side of the trail, or the uphill side if reserving material. Vegetation can be reserved for replanting areas disturbed in the construction process. Chop out the dense mat of fine roots beneath the duff with a fire rake. Use a root ax for the bigger roots, but only when they present a tripping hazard.

Sidehilling or Cutting a Bench

After removing the duff to expose mineral soil, the treadway must be leveled off. When building a new trail that traverses across a slope, you must create a relatively flat surface for the tread; this process is referred to as sidehilling or cutting a bench. Begin by using a hazel hoe, mattock, or other scraping/digging tool to cut into the bank (see figure 7.2). Here you need to create the three parts of the

Fig. 7.2. Create a flat surface for the treadway by sidehilling.

trail: the upslope, treadway, and *downslope*. The upslope, logically on the uphill side of the trail, should be cut to a grade of 45 degrees or less. If it is steeper, the soil will not be stable on its own and vegetation, which helps to retain the soil, will not likely grow. The treadway, or simply tread, is the main part of the trail. The width of the tread varies from 1.5 feet to about 3 feet depending on the type of trail, topography, and local trail specifications. Though appearing to be flat, the tread should have an outslope of 4 percent to 8 percent so water can drain perpendicular to the trail and not sit on the treadway itself. Remove any piles of debris or soils that collect on the downhill side of the tread in order to allow water to flow freely off the trail. The third part of the trail is the downslope, which, like the upslope, should be of 45 degrees or less. Be sure that you've installed proper *drainage* (discussed below), where water can shed itself easily, and that the downslope is graded well enough to shed water at every outside curve. With the proper grades, curves, and drainage structures installed, it is less likely that your trail will need reconstruction work in the future.

It is very important that the tread, upslope, and downslope are all dug down to mineral soil, with all duff moved far enough downslope or away from the construction zone that it does not inhibit drainage of the trail. For the lowest impact new trail construction, duff and organic material can be transported from the construction site via wheelbarrow or bucket and dispersed away from the trail or used for revegetation.

Final preparation of the treadway will depend upon your standards for the trail and the intended users. If the trail is near a road and used by many families and small children, consider a smoother, higher-standard trail with many of the roots and rocks removed. However, these rocks and roots are seen as part of the backcountry experience and often should be left, as long as they are stable and will not become small ankle-twisting hazards when they loosen themselves after the first few hikers. Once the treadway is completed, you may determine that additional trail structures are needed. These can be installed any time after the initial construction phase.

The final step before the official trail opening involves marking the trail and installing signs as needed. Guidelines for this can be found in Chapter 10.

TRAIL STRUCTURES AND RECONSTRUCTION

Even a well-laid-out and constructed trail needs additional trail structures as it ages. Because trail structures take lot of time and energy to construct, they should be kept to a minimum in the initial trail design. However, in any trail section where the grade is steep enough to warrant concerns about erosion, these structures can be installed either preventively or as erosion issues become apparent. Remember that just by constructing a trail, we remove vegetation and expose bare soils on the trail, allowing minerals and particulates to wash downhill into waterways. If poorly constructed, trail structures can end up stripping the area around the trail of organic soil, which can prohibit growth of trailside vegetation and dirty the local water sources. Our goal as trail builders and maintainers is to reduce this impact as much as possible. Trail structures, such as bridges (see Chapter 9), may also be installed as creative solutions to obstacles on certain routes.

Two factors control the extent of a trail's reconstruction: the number of visitors the area receives and the character of the land. More visitor use means more boots, steps, trekking pole depressions, and thus impact on the trail. Areas that are wet, located on steep slopes, have poor soils, or support fragile vegetation such as an alpine zone require particularly careful—and sometimes costly—reconstruction.

When reconstructing a trail, one should minimize the visual impact of the proposed trail work and avoid undue infringement on the trail's natural and aesthetic qualities. Keep in mind that visitors come to a trail for a specific outdoor experience; often they do not want to visit a highly constructed trail, but rather a more rustic area with close contact to the natural environment. Overconstruction or excessively regular and obvious construction can degrade the trail environment and, consequently, the hiker's experience.

There are three major steps in the reconstruction planning process. The first is to identify the problem. If you are following a trail log, this may be done for you, but the person actually performing the reconstruction should be able to see the problem as well. Often, the actual problem may be caused by a separate source, so the next step is to find and fix the source of the problem. After this, the problem itself can be addressed. For example, with a bootleg trail, the problem is the existence of the trail itself. However, simply trying to close the trail generally does not address the source of the problem, which may be a muddy section in the main trail that the hikers are avoiding. Draining the muddy main trail is an essential component to solving the bootleg trail problem.

In most situations a combination of techniques is necessary to solve both parts of the problem. The most commonly used techniques in trail reconstruction are to "drain and retain," since many tread problems come from lack of drainage, thereby causing erosion of the trail. To fix the source of the problem, install drainage to allow water to flow downhill away from the trail, and also install a retention device to stabilize and retain the existing soils.

EROSION CONTROL STRUCTURES

Preventing erosion is the most difficult task in maintaining trails over steep, mountainous terrain, or through wet and fragile areas. Four categories of structures and techniques are used to prevent and/or control erosion:

- Drainages are probably the most important ally of trail maintainers. Earthen water bars and swales, for example, can be considered a dynamic form of *erosion control*. Set across or along the trail, drainages keep or direct water off the trail. Drainage features must be built into every trail, even the most perfectly planned and laid-out trail. If a trail is properly laid out, constructed, and drained, often no other structures are needed.
- *Stabilizers*, also called retainers, retain the soil that is already present in the trail, stabilizing the tread. They can fill the treadway and retain soil by reducing the steepness of the slope through the creation of terraces. Rock steps are common stabilizers.
- *Hardeners* are used where a trail crosses wet areas that cannot be effectively drained. By keeping the hiker out of the mud, trail hardeners not only make hiking more pleasant, but also protect fragile soils and vegetation. Step stones and bog bridges are examples of hardeners.
- Definers channel hikers onto the established treadway or hardened surface, preventing trail widening and protecting adjacent plants and soil from being trampled. *Scree*, or edge rock, is often used as definers.

While each erosion-control device serves a specific purpose, it is important to note that they may also achieve other goals. For example, scree, set along the edges of a rock staircase not only defines the trail but will also aid in retaining soil along the steps. Bog bridges can also serve as trail definers while performing their principal duty as hardeners.

Drainages

According to almost every trail worker, drainage is the most important feature of any trail. With well-designed and well-constructed drainage, most trails can be very stable. Without adequate drainage, a trail is doomed.

Erosion, due to running water and made worse by hiker traffic, does the greatest damage to a healthy trail. Because of soil compaction and other factors, trails are essentially intermittent stream beds. Even a well-built trail with a proper outslope can develop a small trench in the middle of the tread from soil compaction. Whenever it rains, or during spring snowmelt, the water collects and flows in this small depression. Without proper drainage, the water will continue to wash away treadway soil until a deep gully has formed.

Swales

Swales, or bleeders, ensure that water drains thoroughly from a trail at a natural low spot or obstruction, like a large rock or root, and doesn't pool up or continue down the trail. You can also make swales part of a constructed trail by laying the trail along natural dips in the landscape and digging swales into these low points. This will collect and drain any water accumulating on the trail.

To construct a swale, dig a shallow depression completely across the treadway in the shape of a fan, with the wide edge on the uphill side and the narrow on the downhill edge. The sides of the swale should be very gently sloping. This will allow the low area to drain to the downhill side of the trail, toward the *outflow* ditch that should be dug off the edge of the trail with the same standard of any other outflow ditch. Be sure the sides of the ditch are also gently curved, creating a flat-bottomed, U-shaped cross-section, as opposed to a steeply sided V-shaped cross-section.

Water Bars

Where grades are too steep for simple bleeders or run off too great, water bars should be installed. There are two types of water bars: earthen and reinforced; the latter can be made of either wood or rock.

Effective water bars fit the surrounding topography and trail conditions. On a steep slope where erosion is occurring, water must be removed near the top of the slope before damage can occur. Locate the point on the upslope where the water first comes onto the trail and another point on the downslope to remove it quickly. Look for evidence of seeps or springs, such as leaf litter, soil, and debris deposits showing water movement after spring snowmelt or rainstorms. Check the trail for erosion damage during or just after a rainstorm to see runoff conditions at their worst. With trail reconstruction, areas of gullying are sure signs of needed drainage. At stream crossings, where there is a possibility of the flow jumping the channel and onto the trail, reinforced water bars might be necessary to stabilize and reinforce the lower stream bank.

Ideally, water should be channeled from the trail without its flow being significantly impeded, thereby preventing it from dropping its load of sediment and clogging the water bar. For this reason, natural turns in the trail can be

Trail Construction and Erosion Control

excellent water bar locations (see figure 7.3) because water will be more easily removed and the water bar will be somewhat self-cleaning, an important help in trail maintenance.

The spacing of water bars along a trail depends on the steepness of the slope, the amount of runoff, and the availability of places to divert the water. Poorly laid-out or gullied sections of a trail may offer few good placement choices. Excavating larger and longer outflow ditches may be necessary to ensure that water exits and stays out of a gully or trail running straight down a slope. However, steep trails, such as a fall line trail, may be practically impossible to drain. On grades of 20 percent or more, every place on the trail that can have a water bar should. On lesser slopes water bars can be spaced farther apart.

A combination of steps and water bars is often used on steep slopes (see figure 7.4), though if soils are quite stable and slopes are shallow, then water bars alone may suffice. Creative placement of water bars and steps in a complementary sequence prevents the water bars from clogging, as loose soil is retained by steps. Steps in turn are protected by water bars that remove water from the trail and therefore keep the steps from washing out.

Once a site is chosen, the first step is to dig a trench that will hold the rocks. Be sure the trench, and the wood or rock, extend off both sides of the treadway. Neither water nor people should be able to go around either end of the bar; otherwise, channeling and soil compaction will misdirect water and nullify the water bar's purpose.

In steep-sided gullies where removal of water is difficult, steps may predominate for keeping erosion in check. However, every possible exit for water should have a water bar, even if it requires digging through the walls of the gully.

In order to divert the water efficiently, the water bar and its trench must be at an angle—generally 30 to 50 degrees—to the axis of the treadway. Too shallow an angle will result in the water slowing down and dropping soil and debris that will eventually clog the water bar (see figure 7.5). Too wide an angle, perhaps in excess of 70 degrees, may accelerate runoff, undermining the water bar and increasing erosion damage. In general, the steeper the slope, the greater the angle of the water bar. This ensures that the water will not come to an abrupt stop when it hits the water bar, but instead be redirected off the trail by the presence of the structure. Soil type must also be taken into account when deciding the angle of the water bar. In looser, more granular soils, scouring and eroding of the actual outflow ditch can happen more easily. One solution is to lessen the angle of the drainage. Another solution is to retain the soils in the drainage. This can be done by lining the ditch and outflow with angular rock cobble. However, both of these options can make water bars more difficult to

Fig. 7.3. Install a water bar at a corner to drain a trail easily.

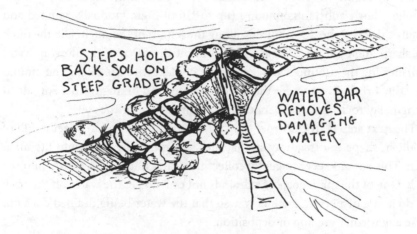

Fig. 7.4. Steep slopes sometimes require steps and water bars.

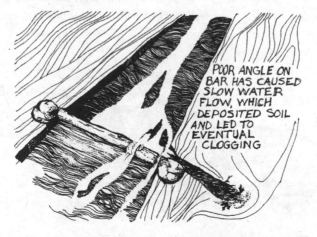

Fig. 7.5. Be sure to install your water bar at the proper angle—30 to 50 degrees.

maintain. A third option is to install a check dam or two in the actual drainage, so water will be slowed and the soil can be reclaimed, if necessary.

Earthen Water Bars. Earthen water bars, also called drainage dips (see figure 7.6), are often used on logging roads and are simple and easy to construct. These water bars are useful where the grade is less than 10 to 12 percent. On unavoidable grades of more than 12 percent, the downhill side of the water bar must be reinforced by either wood or rock.

To make an earthen water bar, dig a very wide, smooth, U-shaped ditch across the trail at an angle. A steep-sided ditch will collapse under hiker traffic and clog the ditch. Extend the ditch across the entire treadway to capture all runoff flowing down the trail. Use the soil you've dug from the ditch as *backfill* to build a fairly substantial mound (up to 1 foot high, gradually ramped and equally thick) on the downhill side along the length of the ditch. Dig the ditch at a sharp angle (45 to 50 degrees) to prevent the force of the flowing water from eroding the mound when it comes in contact with the ditch. The mound can easily break down under the forces of water and hiking traffic. For added strength, lay rocks under the mound as a foundation for the soil.

The next step is to construct the drain. Starting about 4 to 6 feet uphill of the ditch, shape the treadway so that the sides gradually slope into the main ditch. This should serve to gently collect the water and feed it slowly into the ditch. One of the main goals of a drain is not only to get the water off the trail, but do it in a dispersed, gradual way so that the water being drained does not cause any further erosion or deposition.

Add the mineral soil that was excavated and small rocks (do not use any duff, roots, or organic mud) to the backfill mound on the downhill side of the ditch. This needs to be very well packed into a solid, gradual ramp that can

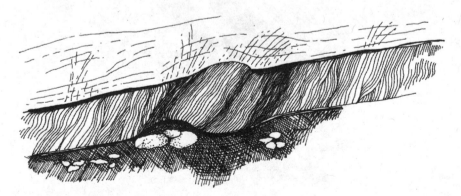

Fig. 7.6. Drainage dip: cross section.

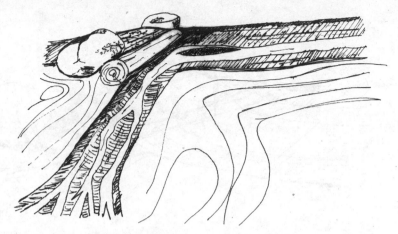

Fig. 7.7. Fan out the end of the outflow ditch to allow water to disperse.

extend as far as 4 feet down the trail. The backfill mound should be slightly higher than the bar, gradually sloped, and about 1 foot high. With traffic it will compact and wear down to the correct size. Once again, for traffic and water to flow through this entire structure without creating excess erosion, all slopes should be very gradual, gently guiding the course of the water.

Finally, an outflow ditch can be dug off the lower end of the water bar to remove the runoff completely from the trail. The outflow ditch should be broad and flat-bottomed (12 inches or more at the bottom), free of roots and obstructing rocks, and with sloped sides. A narrow ditch or one with protruding roots or rocks will clog easily. The length of the outflow ditch depends on the terrain, but it needs to be long enough to ensure that water will leave and not re-enter the trail. Fan out the end of the outflow ditch to allow water to disperse and help prevent it from clogging (see figure 7.7).

If water falls or drops steeply off the edge of the trail, line the outflow ditch with rocks to slow and disperse the water, thus protecting trailside soils from eroding. (This will work much like an object placed at the base of a gutter on a house.) In the alpine zone, where plants are small and easily disturbed, this technique is particularly important.

Reinforced Water Bars. The technique for constructing a reinforced water bar, rock or wood, is much like that of an earthen water bar. Although they take quite a bit more time to install, a well-made, reinforced water bar can last for years. Of the two types, rock water bars, placed solidly and properly, will provide a more durable alternative to log water bars. They are also more appropriate above treeline, where wood is at a premium but rocks can be plentiful. The

Fig. 7.8. Rock water bar, cake method.

basic details on how to construct a wood water bar are nearly identical to those of a rock water bar.

There are two traditional ways to construct a rock water bar. The first is called the cake method (see figure 7.8), which is the preferred technique. Once a site is chosen, the first step is to gather rocks. Use large rocks, at least twelve-inches thick that have at least one flat face to form the face of the bar. Then dig a trench wide enough to hold the chosen rocks. Be sure the trench and the rocks extend off both sides of the treadway. Neither water nor people should be able to go around either end of the bar; otherwise, channeling and soil compaction will misdirect water and nullify the water bar's purpose.

The trench should be deep enough so the top of the rock will be almost flush with the trail on its downhill side. A trench that's too shallow may leave the water bar sticking up too high and increase the danger of it being undermined. Soil and rock excavated from the trench should be heaped on the trail below the water bar to be used later as backfill. Leaf litter, organic mud, and roots will not make for good backfill and should be disposed out of sight of the trail.

Set rocks into the trench one at a time and tightly together, or slightly over-lapping each other, starting at the lower end; each rock should be set slightly forward of the one below it. Much like shingles on a roof, water will flow from one rock down to the next without going between. Rock in the treadway should only protrude 4 inches above the ground. Rocks off to the side may be higher, as they can help to keep hikers from walking around the center of structure. Water bars are meant to be walked over smoothly without the hiker really noticing, which means that they should never act as an obstacle in the trail.

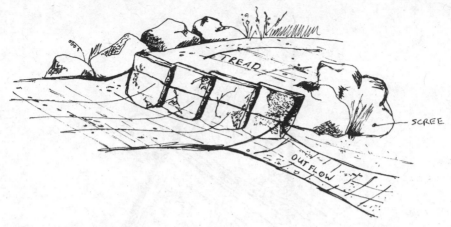

Fig. 7.9. Rock water bar, toast method.

It's important that all rocks are set securely, as flowing water and foot traffic may dislodge them. Test the stability by kicking and jumping on the rock; there should be no movement. If it's not quite set, try to wedge the rock in tighter or reposition it slightly with a pry bar or mattock. Well-packed soil around the rock may also help; be sure that the soil is good mineral soil and will compact solidly when tamped into place. The extra effort it may take to solidly set a rock will ensure that the water bar will work properly and last for decades.

The second way to construct a rock water bar is the toast method—setting thin, flat rocks on edge into a deep and narrow trench (see figure 7.9). Bury the rocks well, set them so they lean back slightly downhill against the backfill, and overlap them in shingle fashion. This technique works fine when only flat, thinner rocks are available, such as in areas with shale or slate. However, a rock on end, especially if not buried completely, has the possibility to give, acting like a lever when stepped on. This method should only be employed when the cake method is not possible.

Any rot-resistant type of wood, such as spruce, fir, or hemlock, can be used for a wood water bar. Avoid using hardwood. The diameter of a water bar log should be at least 8 inches at the log's small end. The length depends on the width of the trail, which in some cases can be more than 10 feet, and it should extend at least 12 inches past both outside edges of the treadway.

Peel the bark off the logs; if left on, the bark can hold water close to the wood and cause accelerated rot, or when it falls off later, it may clog the water bar. Be aware that peeling may be very difficult late in the season. Peeled logs can be very slippery. You may choose to shave the top edge of the logs across

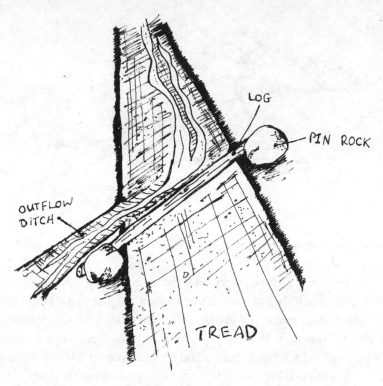

Fig. 7.10. Use pin rocks to anchor a wood water bar.

the treadway with an ax, creating a rough surface for better footing. Be careful not to remove too much of the log; its reduced height may allow water to wash over it.

Dig a trench an appropriate size to accommodate the log. It should be buried with only a few inches showing, using the same guidelines as those used with a rock water bar. The log should fit snugly in the trench with no high point or voids under the log, and when stepped on, it should not see-saw or lift.

A large *pin rock* can be placed on each end of the log to help hold it in place (see figure 7.10). Pin rocks will also serve as barriers to prevent hikers from going around the ends of the bar. Sometimes, with good planning and skillful use of tools, one can wedge the log between existing boulders on the trail.

Once the log is in place, the drain should be built in the same manner as for other types of water bars. The drain should be large and dispersing—a very large, gradual backfill mound (built from the excavated soil) on the downhill side of the structure, and a fan above the bar to direct water into the channel and off the trail.

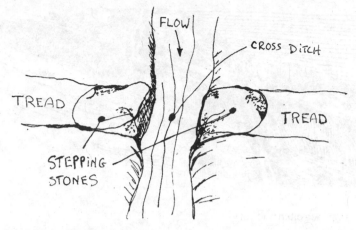

Fig. 7.11. Cross ditch with step stones.

Cross Ditch. A cross ditch ensures that runoff or small streams bisecting a flat section of trail cross cleanly and efficiently, flowing away from the trail (see figure 7.11). Dig a ditch large enough to capture and contain all the runoff. Use soil and rocks excavated from the ditch to build up the banks on both sides. Where flow is high, line the sides of the ditch where it meets the trail with rock as you would in the construction of a rock water bar. To prevent the ditch's banks from being beaten down by hiker traffic, set a large stepping stone into the banks on both sides. To help stabilize the structure, you can also span the ditch with one or more rocks, set flush or below the dirt surface and butted against each stepping stone. This can be quite effective, but difficult to get right. Refer to the section on how to build rock stairs for more information on setting rocks. In either case, make sure the natural water way has an outflow ditch or other exit for the water.

Side Ditch. A drainage ditch along the side of the trail collects water in areas where heavy seepage, springs, or runoff enters a trail and cannot be immediately removed. As water travels downhill toward a trail, a side ditch constructed on the trail's uphill side can catch this water, channeling it alongside but not onto the treadway. Then, after traversing the length of the ditch, it can be carried off by an outflow ditch on the same side, if possible, or across the trail and off the downhill side via a water bar (see figure 7.12). Though helpful in some locations, this drainage structure often needs continual maintenance, and since they are sometimes constructed along the fall line of the slope, they can exacerbate erosion.

Fig. 7.12. Drainage ditch and bar.

Switchback Drainage. One method of draining a switchback is to direct water onto the upper leg of the switchback to its upper side. With the use of a side ditch, the water can then be properly and completely drained out and past the next curve in the switchback. In some cases it may be necessary to drain water off the downhill side of the upper leg of the switchback. If this situation occurs, a second water bar on the lower leg of the switchback may be necessary to remove water completely.

Stabilizers

Stairs

Stairs provide protection from erosion on steep trail grades. The basic purpose of stairs is to provide a stable vertical rise on the trail, which slows water and retains soil. Though highly effective stabilizers, stairs are very costly, time consuming, and labor intensive to install, as well as being unnatural in the landscape. They are necessary on trails with steep slopes, although with proper trail design many can be avoided. Probably less utilized in reconstruction than drainages, stairs are nevertheless an important technique as trail slopes steepen and when erosion damage has already occurred (see figure 7.13).

Place stairs thoughtfully on the trail to ensure that hikers will use them. They should be built in an attractive spot and must not be too tall; otherwise, hikers will bypass them and create a new eroded route. As a general rule, keep the rise to a maximum of 8 to 10 inches. As with any trail structure, standards vary according to users and the character of the trail.

Some hikers avoid even well-placed steps, particularly if they are tired and heading uphill. In order to prevent this, edge the sides of the staircase with scree, a method often used on alpine trails. This is an especially helpful tech-

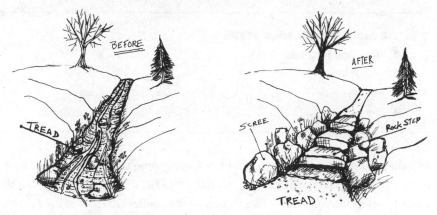

Fig. 7.13. Use rock steps and scree to stabilize a gullied trail.

nique when steps need to be placed in wide gullies, where it is easy for a hiker to get around the steps, with the added benefit of the scree supporting and holding the bank soils in place. (You will learn more about scree later in this chapter.) Brush, logs, and other debris can also be used to prevent hikers from side-stepping the stair structure.

Rock Stairs. Rock stairs are far more desirable than wood stairs, since they last longer and can be built to appear more natural and less intrusive. Over time they will begin to look like part of the trail, especially if they are placed carefully. Even where suitable rock is not readily available, rock stairs are so much more superior to wooden stairs that the additional effort to obtain them is worthwhile. Any shape of rock can be used; however, a large, flat-surfaced rock is much easier to work with and makes a more usable tread. Rocks should weigh at least 100 to 200 pounds, since smaller rocks are more apt to become loose. However, excessively large rocks can result in a trail that feels overbuilt, with structures not fitting into the character of the trail.

Start by laying out the stairs, determining the rise and run of the steps to be installed to reach the desired location.

Always build a staircase from the bottom up. The base step creates a foundation that helps determine the best location for each subsequent step. It should be large and set deep, with the top flush with the treadway. Over time hiker traffic will wear away and compact the soil below the bottom step. If not set deep enough, water will eventually erode the surrounding soil and jeopardize the stability of the stairs above it. Each subsequent stair should be set either resting on the back edge of or sitting behind the stair below, depending on the slope.

Installing Rock Stairs. Find a rock with a flat stepping surface at least 12 by 12 inches, but preferably wide enough to fill the treadway. Use the side that has the flattest surface as your tread. Dig a cone-shaped hole—narrow at the bottom, wider at the top—so that the bottom of the rock will contact the *sides*, not the bottom, of the hole (see figure 7.14). The hole needs to be deep enough for the top of the rock to be at the desired height. The rock should fit in the hole so its perimeter rests on the sloping sides of the hole and not on the bottom, or it will rock back and forth. Avoid a straight-sided hole, or the rock will fall to the bottom when placed in the hole. It should sit like a scoop of ice cream in a cone. Three solid and widely-spaced points of contact are ideal and will keep the step from rocking. Remove all roots from holes for the longest life on your staircase. Also remove all medium or small stones, which will only work themselves loose and cause problems when trying to set the rock in place.

Once the hole is dug, maneuver the rock so it can be lowered, flipped, or slid into the hole. Try to get it right the first time: once a large rock is dropped into place it may be very difficult to pull it out and reset it, especially if the trail is muddy or if the soils are loose or sandy. Use brains, ingenuity, pick mattocks, and pry bars (sometimes with fulcrums—other rocks work great) to position the rock. Rock steps should not shift at any point, even slightly. Jump on it; if the rock moves at all, try repositioning it. Tightly packing or tamping good mineral soil around it may help keep it in place. Do not shim above the ground

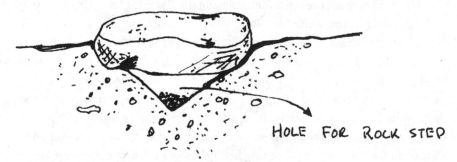

Fig. 7.14. Use a cone-shaped hole to securely set a rock step.

Supplies

Tape Measure, Line Level, Line (Parachute cord or smaller), 2 or 3 people

Step 1: Measure the rise and run.

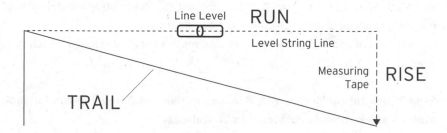

1. With one person at the top of slope and one at the bottom, run a string line with a level across the top of project. Be sure to have the top end at grade and the bottom end directly above the proposed site of the base step. Now, make sure the string line is level, with the line level in the middle of the string line. You may need an additional person to look at the level.
2. Now measure the height from the ground (at middle of base step). This is your RISE.
3. Then measure the length of string being used. This is your RUN.

Now you have the amount of elevation (rise) you need to gain, as well as the length (run) you have to gain it in.

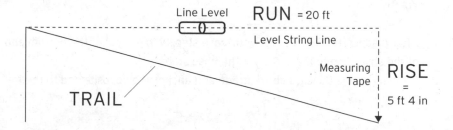

Step 2: Use the measured rise and run of the slope to calculate the rise and run needed for each stair.

So, in this example, you have 5 feet, 4 inches (64 inches) to gain over 20 feet (240 inches).

The optimal rise of each stair would be between 8 and 10 inches. Using 8 inches as a starting point, then 5 feet, 4 inches (64 inches) broken up into increments of 8 inches would be 8 steps (64/8=8), a nice round number.

If these 8 steps are spread out evenly over the entire 20-foot run, each step would have a 2.5-foot run (20/8=2.5).

Step 3: Use this guideline, with 8 inches of rise and 2.5 feet of run for each stair as an example, to construct your staircase.

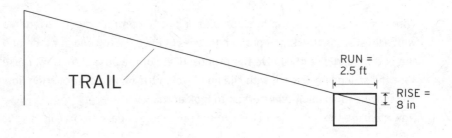

Start with a string line as a guide. Given that equal rise should occur throughout the entire staircase, the outer edge of each rock stair should form an even and consistent slope over the entire staircase.

Setting the string line up involves, 1 line and 2 people (or 1 person with anchoring creativity).

1. After placing the first rock for your base step, hold or anchor the bottom end of the string line to the middle of the base step.
2. Stretch the line 8 inches above grade and anchor the opposite end to the top of your slope.

3. Be sure to hold this line taut to get the most exact reading.
4. The outer edge of each stair should touch the string line. This may be difficult to see in the midst of construction, since leaving the string line in place is often not practical. But it's a relatively easy device to set up, so you can check your work as you proceed with the construction. Once again, another pair of eyes can be helpful.

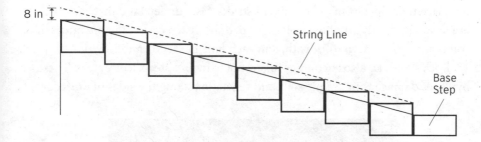

8 in

String Line

Base Step

This technique is particularly helpful when you have a predetermined amount of rise to gain, such as in a very severely eroded/gullied section of trail. By using the string line and gaining height consistently, you can avoid tunneling into the ground (not getting enough rise), a pier-style staircase (getting too much rise too soon), or inconsistent rise (which is uncomfortable and can be tough on the knees).

A string line is a useful guide to help builders stay on track. If your stair ends up being above or below the string line, the rise of the next stair will have to be lowered or raised accordingly. If this happens, the angle of the string line will be changed. You can get around this by setting the line up next to the other con-structed stairs, as opposed to directly over them, and eyeballing the stair height from there.

Yes, you are building with native rock, and no, it is not exact. However, with a little bit of planning, not only can certain disasters be avoided (i.e., tearing out work), but the finished product can be functional, professional, and generally good trail work.

with rocks; they can work themselves loose with seasonal freezing and thawing. Occasionally a rock can be stabilized by pinning it with a large adjacent building rock, although both must be solid when finished. Sometimes a stubborn rock needs to be removed after you've placed it, so you can improve the hole or find a better rock to fit in that location. Proper rock stair placement requires skill, experience, and lots of hard work and patience.

For aesthetic reasons, and in some cases to allow for better drainage, it is best to avoid building perfectly straight staircases up a slope. Nature is unruly, so put some twists and bends in the staircase to mimic this trait (see figure 7.15). You can offset some stairs rather than keep them in a direct line, and make sure that the placement doesn't impede a hiker's stride. Also, understand that each rock is a lesson in creative problem solving. Not only is each rock different, but each soil type is different to work with, and each hole has its own difficulties.

Rock stairs can also encourage hikers not to bypass steep, ledgy areas. These bypasses damage thin, fragile soils and vegetation along the sides of the ledge.

Fig. 7.15. Rock steps with scree.

Although more difficult than setting steps in soil, secure and attractive footing can be built to help hikers gain a short ledge. However, in these areas there is often little or no soil to set the rocks into. This often leaves the builder with just two choices, setting the rock stairs on the exposed bedrock or creating a bed of gravel to set the rocks in. Called dry setting, setting rock on top of rock is the most challenging type of stair placement, and much more precision is needed than for setting rock stairs in soil. Often this type of setting is easier if protruding knobs of rock can be broken off, though this is also time-consuming. Another technique for working without soil involves creating a *gravel*, or crushed rock bed, to set the rocks in; this is called gravel setting or crush-and-fill setting. The first rock must be solidly installed with absolutely no movement or shifting. Behind the first rock lay a bed of gravel, into which you'll shape a shallow cone to set your next rock; then install scree rock on the sides to hold in the gravel. Though still challenging and time consuming, this method is very helpful in places that lack soil.

As with the entire trail, rock steps need drainage. Without it, even the largest, most stable steps will eventually work loose as the soil around them washes away. Ice will move steps, too. Drainage, preferably rock water bars, should be installed above a series of steps. Plan for and install rock water bars in the middle of long staircases, taking advantage of turns if possible.

Wood Stairs. Wood or log stairs are often much more simple to construct, but they have a fatal flaw—wood always rots. The traditional design of log stairs only provides a short term fix to a long-term problem, and its use is discouraged. Unless laid out in the same manner as rock stairs, log stairs act as check dams, retaining soil, but they also encourage the washing away of that soil.

The construction of wood stairs is similar to building wood water bars, except that steps are installed perpendicular to the trail, not on an angle. Also, backfill is moved not to the downhill side of the log, but to the unditched uphill side.

Like wood water bars, spruce and fir are the usual choices for wood stairs; the diameter should be between 6 and 12 inches. On steeper slopes a larger-diameter log gives more vertical rise. With small-diameter stock, stairs have to be closer together and more numerous to provide the desired vertical rise. Peel the bark off the logs if possible.

Wood stairs should be longer than the width of the trail. When placed in a gully, the ends of the logs should extend into the banks. Too short a stair will allow water and people to go around, and will not adequately retain the soil.

Fig. 7.16. Log steps.

To build a wood stair, dig a trench at a depth roughly one-third the diameter of the log. Save the excavated soil for backfill. Then set the log into the trench and secure it with pin rocks (see figure 7.16).

Once the log stair is secure, backfill the uphill side with the soil removed from the trench. When steps are placed in a series, the bottom of the upper log should be just a bit higher than the top of the lower log, with the soil in between sloped slightly downhill. This will prevent puddling behind the step. For a final touch, flatten the top of the log slightly with an ax to make a firm, flat tread.

A much more stable design for wood stairs involves tying all the stairs together with runners. These can be either dimensional or native timber, and they can be connected using many different types of wood joinery, depending on the type of building materials. There can be many variations to this design, but essentially all the wooden steps become platforms of well-drained soil, boxed in on all sides to prevent the soil from spilling out.

Crib Stairs. Check stairs, also called crib stairs or terrace stairs, are boxes made of wood or large rocks, filled with smaller rocks and capped with mineral soil. This type of stair-building technique works well where livestock live and also intermingles with regular rock stairs in areas that are less steep but still need stabilization.

Before building your rock check staircase, determine the amount of rise and run you'll need in the given space. Then choose large, heavy rocks that will be sunk in the ground to serve as the support for the cribs. Dig a hole and set the first front rock. If there is any possibility of the soil around the sunken rock washing out and undermining the stair, sink the first rock flush with the ground, as you would for a traditional rock staircase.

Next, set rocks to serve as sides of the proposed step, ensuring good, high contact points with the front rock. Once these are set, proceed with setting the front rock of the next stair. Make sure that over half of this rock is buried, with the bottom at least one-quarter of its height below the top of the first stair; you don't want to have to ramp the soil tread of the first stair to adjust for a second stair that is too high. If the soil in the first stair is properly retained, there is no way the second stair can be undermined.

Now fill the box you've just made with small rocks, decreasing the size of your stone as you fill, and ending with crushed gravel; then top it off with several inches of well-drained mineral soil. Continue with additional steps until you reach the top of your planned run.

Wood check steps can be made in a similar manner. For more information about working with wood, refer to the section on turnpikes.

Special Techniques

Where more traditional reconstruction methods fail or are not possible, such as in very steep locations or on bare ledges, more complex structures such as log ladders, metal rungs, or pinned steps may be necessary.

Log Ladders. Log ladders (see figure 7.17) allow hikers to safely, comfortably, and responsibly ascend or descend a difficult ledge. Without it hikers may risk injury or bypass the difficult ledge, damaging adjacent soils and vegetation and further exposing the ledge. There are many variations of log ladders to suit the steepness and characteristics of each ledge. A basic design is described below, but the main components of a ladder are the two long uprights, known as *stringers*, and the steps, known as *rungs* (the log rungs are fastened in between the two stringers).

First measure the ledge to determine the length needed for the two stringers. Make sure the stringers are a few feet taller than the ledge so hikers have something to hang on to when standing on the top rung. Cut, limb, and peel a matching pair of stringers from straight, sound trees 8 to 12 inches in diameter. Put stringers into place with larger, butt ends down, leaving about 18 to 24 inches between them. If there isn't a good, solid foundation for the butt ends, a base log should be used to support the stringers. Use a log equal or larger in diameter than the butt of the stringers, and at least a couple of feet longer than the distance between the outer edges of the stringers. Base logs may be cut

Fig. 7.17. Log ladders.

longer to fit securely into particular features at the base of the ladder. Set the base log into a trench dug in the earth or fitted into gaps or cracks in the ledge. Cut a shallow, flat notch on top of the base log into which the bottoms of the stringer can be set. Then spike them into place. Shave the top of the base log to act as the first step.

Lay out the placement of the notches for the rungs along the inside of the stringers so the spacing from the top of one to the next is the same (about 12 to 16 inches). The notches should be 4-inch-deep and 4-inch-wide dadoes, or three-side notches, with the top and bottom sides flat, level, and parallel to each other. Be sure the notches on the left are level with those on the right. Saw the top and bottom sides first, then saw a few relief cuts in between and chisel out the remaining wood. Once a pair of notches is complete, a rung can be cut and shaped to fit.

Cut rungs from 6-to-8-inch-diameter logs and top them to provide a stepping surface. Remove no more than one-quarter to one-third of the log. Measure the distance between the insides of the pair of notches and cut the rung to

⚲ **THE RIGHT TOOLS: LOG LADDERS**
- ax
- crosscut saw, bow saw, or chain saw
- large chisel and mallet
- hatchet (for shaping the log)
- tape measure, small level, crayon
- mattock and shovel
- sledgehammer (for driving spikes)
- 10–12, 3/8-inch-diameter spikes

that length. Cut the bottom and top of the rung ends to form a tongue 4 inches wide and a little more than 4 inches long to fit into the notches. Fine-tune as needed to achieve a good, snug fit. Position the rung in the notches and drive a spike through the outside edge of the stringers and into the ends of the rung. It's best to do one step at a time, starting at the bottom.

Crib Ladder. On steeper slopes, another stabilizer to consider is the *crib ladder* (see figure 7.18), or a combination of cribbing and stepping. This technique is useful on very steep slopes or those with thin soil or bedrock near the surface of the ground, which would normally make it difficult to secure regular steps.

Fig. 7.18. Crib ladder. Rungs fit into notches and are spiked. Steps are backfilled with rock and scree.

Here you build a log ladder, lay it into or up against the slope, then backfill each step with soil and small rocks to help secure the ladder and the slope. Do not leave gaps behind the rungs, as people might inadvertently step into them.

Pinned Stairs. Local U.S. Forest Service staff has used wooden *pinned stairs* (see figure 7.19) to climb and traverse difficult ledges that do not provide adequate foot- and handholds and that cannot be avoided through relocation. Pressure-treated wooden steps 2 feet long are produced by ripping 6-by-8-inch stock diagonally across the long axis from end to end. They are attached to the ledge with foot-long steel bars set partially into the rock, using a pneumatic rock drill to drill the holes. A drill can also be used to cut steps into a ledge. Most managers agree that these techniques should be utilized only as a last resort to more-conventional work or relocation due to expense and difficulty, as well as aesthetics.

It may also be necessary to use pins when building rock stairs on a ledge. Once again, this is not only difficult, but it also changes the character of the area itself by introducing a permanent, non-native piece of metal into the ledge. The decision to pin should be taken seriously, as it is a complicated and labor-

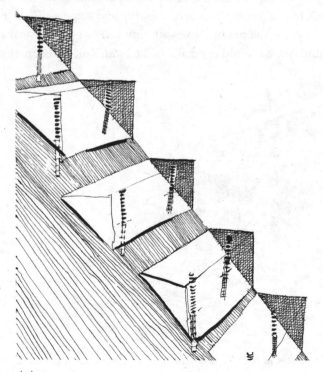

Fig. 7.19. Pinned steps.

intensive process. Also, the resulting stairs will be a permanent part of the trail, and some hikers may feel that it is not fitting with a backcountry aesthetic. However, when it becomes the only option, it can create tread where it may seem impossible otherwise.

Proceed cautiously and take your time, as mistakes are irreversible and will create a permanent mark on the ledge. Though further training and preparatory practice for this work is greatly encouraged, the main steps are as follows.

Place the rock you want to pin exactly where it is to sit. The ledge should be free of organic debris. The rock must be of good quality and its placement must be solid enough, with two good contact points below, where you will drill the holes. (Pinning does not stabilize the rock; it only keeps it from sliding along the ledge.) Next mark these spots on the bottom of the rock. Then drill your holes into the ledge at the desired locations, using necessary precautions and a trained drill operator. Be sure to keep the drill bit perpendicular to the rock to ensure that the drilled hole will line up with the marks on the underside of the step. Before drilling the holes in the step, place the pins in the cleaned ledge holes and line them up with the markings on the rock, a difficult but necessary step. After drilling the stair holes, seal all four holes around the steel pins with either epoxy or tamped lead wool, using necessary precautions. Your rock has now become a semi-permanent feature on the ledge.

Steel Rungs and Ladders. These are also pinned into the ledge itself, so many of the same precautions should be taken when building steel rungs and ladders. Be sure to receive proper training and practice before attempting this on the trail worksite. As with pinned steps, holes are drilled in the ledge, but in this case, two holes are drilled to receive a ½- to ¾-inch staple-shaped metal rung (often galvanized steel, or sometimes rebar). Each set of holes must be drilled at the same slight uphill angle, to ensure the rungs will fit properly. Drilling the holes slightly wider than the distance between the rung's legs will insure a tight fit. Steel rungs are made solid when they are hammered into the holes. Three to 4 inches of the rungs should be left protruding from the ledge to serve as hand and footholds. This can vary slightly to match the steepness of the terrain, but more than this can leave a dangerous gap where hikers' toes and children's feet may become stuck. After the rungs are securely pounded in, the holes must be sealed with either epoxy or tamped lead wool. Fabricated steel ladders are installed in much the same way.

Check Dams. Check dams can be effective soil-retaining structures for trails that are severely gullied. A series of check dams can be built to slow erosion in steps.

They are constructed similarly to water bars, but they are built perpendicular to the trail instead of at an angle. While water bars channel water off the trail, check dams serve to drain water in sheets across the ground surface, while retaining soil behind the dam. These structures are used as stopgap measures, not intended to last but to help the gully fill in and hold soil. Therefore, wood is an acceptable material to use.

Rock and Log Cribbing. Rock and log *cribbing*, sometimes called retaining walls, are structures that can be used to support a treadway along gullied sections of trail or on steep side slopes. They are also useful in work zones that need to be built up to a usable height. Some types of retaining walls are also often necessary when building switchbacks.

Steps and water bars can help to retain soils, but in especially deep and wide gullies that are difficult to drain, erosion may still occur. In this case, it may be better to support the trail with cribbing, allowing regular drainage to occur. On steep sidehill cuts, cribbing stabilizes the upper or lower slopes along the trail.

Rock cribbing, the most aesthetically pleasing and durable technique, is used to either retain the trail or slope, or even to create the tread for the trail itself. On steep sidehill locations the low side of a treadway must sometimes be built up as a rock wall. Though there are many different kinds of retaining walls, they may be split up into two categories: traditional laid rock retaining walls and *rubble* retaining walls.

Traditional laid rock retaining walls are perhaps the most difficult rock structures that can be built on a trail. They require intense effort and patience, strong wall-building skills, and many rocks of relatively uniform size and shape.

This kind of rock wall is built in tiers. The first tier serves as the base of the wall and is laid with an inward lean, and the rocks at least halfway below grade. The inslope of the base rocks guides the batter, or overall slope of the rock wall. The greater the batter, the stronger the wall. Each subsequently laid layer exerts a strong downward force on the layer beneath. It is important to determine how much batter is needed in the wall before you begin to build in order to determine how far out the first tier needs to be laid. Behind these large face rocks, which are laid first, is the core rock, which provides much of the strength of the wall. It consists of smaller rocks of varying sizes, also laid in tiers, fitting tightly, with all the gaps between filled with even smaller rocks. The core rock extends back into the soil. In this fashion the wall is built: first the face rocks, slightly insloped, moving into the slope with each tier, backed by a layer of core rock. Each of these rocks are set and fitted into place so they have optimal, solid contact and do not create any lever points.

As the tiers progress, it is also very important that the side contact points between the rocks, known as the joints, do not line up. Doing this properly is referred to as "breaking the joints." It is very important to create overall stability of the wall. Anywhere that joints line up creates a potential instability in the wall. Another factor of stability involves the orientation of the face rocks. Rocks that extend into the wall and core rock are called headers. They create a very strong wall, tying the core rock together with the face rocks. Spreaders are face rocks that are orientated the length of the wall. They cover more area, and therefore are more efficient, though not as strong overall. So, a healthy mix of headers and spreaders should be used for the face rocks throughout the wall, taking into account the strength needs of the wall.

The last rocks set in the wall are called cap rocks and are often larger than the face rocks below. These are less supported by the weight of neighboring rocks, so their mass helps to hold them.

To finish the wall, cap the tread with well-crowned mineral soil. This can be separated from the core rock with filter fabric, where possible, to keep the soil from filtering into the wall itself.

Of course this type of wall is most easily built with more uniform rock, though variations can be built with almost any type of rock. This technique is best suited for larger projects where the trail surface is no longer existent and a bench simply can't be built due to lack of soil.

Another variation on this is called a *rubble wall* (see figure 7.20). It is best used for unstable banks where there is still enough soil present for the tread. A rubble wall consists mainly of large rocks set into the bank; make sure they are stable and touching each other to retain the slope. These walls can either be a looser retaining wall without core rock, or simply rocks set into the bank. Many variations between a rubble wall and a more labor-intensive laid rock wall can work in different locations and can stabilize the bank well enough. However, areas with severe erosion or heavier traffic may require a more aggressive retainment technique.

Log cribbing, sometimes referred to as a log or wood retaining wall, has the same applications and follows some of the same building principles as rock retaining walls. The logs should be at least 10 inches in diameter and peeled. Length depends on the area, but generally long, heavy logs are best. The weight helps to hold the cribbing in place. The logs should be very secure, as they must support large amounts of soil and rock along with the weight of passing hikers. Logs can be secured by large stakes or rocks, or butted up against rocks or trees. On multi-tiered walls, logs are notched together using a preferred wood joinery method. Breaking the joints, using headers, and the batter of the wall

Fig. 7.20. Rubble walls retain banks.

are as important with log walls as with rock walls. Logs set perpendicular to the trail, like a wood step, and notched and spiked into the crib logs can be used as combination steps, spacers, and retainers, as well as acting as headers.

Fill any gaps in the cribbing and build a treadway above with excavated rock and soil. The treadway should remain gently sloped to the outside or downhill side to ensure drainage. No cribbing should inhibit this drainage, nor should the treadway be flat or sloped toward the inside or uphill side of the treadway. Otherwise, water will puddle on or flow along the tread.

Hardeners

Hikers on trails in flat, low-lying, wet terrain frequently cause destruction of bordering plants and surface soil. Wet, slippery, muddy spots develop very quickly on these soils. When water accumulates on the treadway, hikers walk to the side of the tread to keep their feet clean and dry. This causes a growing problem of soil breakdown and trail widening. There are a number of techniques that harden the treadway and help to stabilize the damaged soils, allowing trailside plant life to recover.

Step stones, bog bridges, or built-up treadways are the most frequently used solutions in these situations. Keep in mind that they are labor intensive and impact the environment through their construction. Before these techniques are used, drainage and relocation techniques should be considered first.

Wet, muddy locations frequently develop on trails because the treadway is usually lower than surrounding terrain. Water draining laterally through trail soils becomes trapped on the lower and compacted surfaces of the treadway. Often, what initially appears to be a low, flat section of trail may actually have a very moderate slope, allowing an imperceptible flow of water. Rather than installing a bridge or step-stone trails in these situations, a better long-term solution may be to drain the wet area in question—especially if it is small and has a low end that, once ditched, would permit water to flow off the trail. Drain small, flowing, wet spots such as this with water bars and drainage ditches. While installing drainages may not completely dry up the trail, it can reduce the amount of hardening needed.

If an area cannot be drained (or if for environmental reasons it should not be drained) and if relocation is not feasible, then use trail-hardening techniques. These techniques offer dry passage for hikers and contain traffic on a hardened surface, allowing adjacent soils and plant life to reestablish themselves.

Stone Hardeners

Step Stones. These are rocks set into the mud so that a stable, dry, and easily traversed treadway is formed. They can also be used to cross slow-moving streams. *Step stones* (see figure 7.21) should have a flat stepping surface at least twelve inches across, and they should be thick enough to sit above the mud. Larger and flatter rocks will be easier to set and are less prone to unwanted movement than smaller, rounded ones. Present the flattest surface for walking by setting

Fig. 7.21. Step stones help hikers pass across a muddy section of trail.

the stone in cone-shaped holes, like setting a rock for a staircase. Space them in line along the trail so a hiker with a heavy pack can easily stride from one to the next. Step stones should be stable and must not protrude too high above the ground or be so low as to be inundated with mud and water; otherwise, people are likely to avoid them. Even when constructed in a seemingly inviting manner, they are the most circumvented trail structure. For this reason, even though stones last much longer than wood, bog bridging can sometimes be the more effective option, when choosing between the two.

Rock Treadway. Also called a rock patio, a *rock treadway* is simply a more intensive use of rock than step stones. Many step-stone-sized rocks are set side by side, covering the whole treadway, providing for a rock-paved section of trail. Gaps between rocks can be filled with crushed stone to create a continuous walking surface. This structure is not all that different from a back-yard patio made of flat rocks. Be sure to use large rocks to ensure stability and keep rock surfaces level with adjacent rocks. Because it is made of rock, water seepage from uphill can percolate through the rocks and to the other side of the treadway without swamping it.

Turnpikes. Where an ample supply of good soil is available, rock or log boxes can be filled with small rocks then capped with soil—much like when making crib steps—in order to create a *turnpike* (see figure 7.22). The rocks must be stable and adequately dug into the ground, with high contact points between the rocks to prevent soil from spilling out. When using native logs, be sure they are large enough to provide enough height when set into the ground. Different techniques of joinery can be used, though one of the easiest is a lap joint, which is then spiked into place. Alternatively, re-bar can be used to pin the logs to the ground, though holes must be pre-drilled in the logs.

Fig. 7.22. Wooden turnpick before mineral soil capping.

To begin, dig ditches along the perimeter of the wet area on the treadway. Make sure rocks or logs are buried to a depth of at least half their height to ensure stability. When rocks or logs have been secured, fill the interior of the box with rocks of decreasing size, starting with larger, softball-sized rocks at the bottom and working up to gravel. Top this with well-drained mineral soil, crowned in the middle to allow for water run-off to the sides. Turnpikes provide a nice walking surface and last for a long time, even well after the wood box has decomposed, though the construction process is very time-consuming. Long stretches of turnpike can be broken in smaller 10- to 20-foot sections with a cross drain in between. In very wet areas it is also wise to dig drainage ditches on one or both sides of the turnpike.

Bog Bridges. In areas where mud is soft and deep, which is often the case in boggy locations, *bog bridges*, constructed of either milled lumber or native timber, serve to elevate the tread surface.

These bridges can also be used to ford small streams and gullies. In either case they provide a dry, stable treadway. Such bridges usually last 10 to 15 years, or more, depending on species of tree, diameter and quality of wood used, and wetness of location. Softwoods such as cedar, hemlock, spruce, and fir are the easiest to work with and last the longest.

A bog bridge is generally made up of two 8- to 12-foot-long, flat-topped logs (stringers), which form the walking surface. The stringers are supported near their ends on two base logs securely set into the surface of the mud. The stringers are fitted into notches in the base logs and spiked into place (see figure 7.23).

Trail Construction and Erosion Control   7

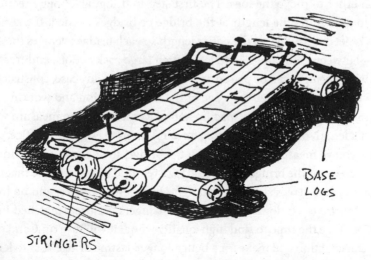

BASE LOGS

STRINGERS

Fig. 7.23. Bog bridge.

Native bog bridges are relatively simple to construct, requiring only a few hand tools (although a chain saw can help speed up the process). However, dimensional bog bridges, which are made of milled 8- or 10-inch-wide stringers and pre-cut base logs, are even easier and faster to install. Getting the materials on site may be difficult, so time and cost of transport should be factored into construction considerations. Often milled stringers can be used with native base logs, limiting the number of trees that need to be cut on site.

Building Bog Bridges. A sharp ax is the one tool necessary to construct a native bog bridge. A crosscut saw may be helpful, and a small chain saw can make the work easier and faster. A peeler or bark spud facilitates peeling, and an adze can be used for topping. For driving spikes a sledgehammer is best, but the back of a root ax will do. Digging tools such as a mattock, shovel, and root ax are used for placing base logs.

Two stringers are needed side-by-side to provide a treadway of adequate width. Stringers should be 8 to 10 inches in width or diameter and 8 to 12 feet long; longer lengths tend to be springy and may even break under a hiker's weight. The base logs should be 3 to 4 feet long and 8 to 12 inches in diameter. Where it is extremely wet and mud is soft and deep, larger and longer base logs may be necessary for stability and better flotation. If the mud and water is particularly deep, a crib box of logs may be needed to make up the height difference and keep the surface above water; refer to Chapter 9 on bridges for more information. Logs should be peeled to retard rot. Building a bog bridge is best done in pairs, one person working on each end of the bridge and helping each other to move the logs. The first step in bridging a boggy section of trail is to determine the length of the bridge or bridges needed. If a series of bridges is needed, divide up the entire length so each bridge averages the same length—between eight and twelve feet. Often large rocks, roots, and trees will dictate where bridges can be placed and their lengths. In any case, construct one bridge at a time, starting at one edge of the muddy section and working your way across to achieve proper spacing and placement. A tape measure works best, but a length of rope or counting ax handle lengths will also suffice.

Once you've measured the length of the bridge, the next step is to find appropriate trees for the bridge parts. Don't waste wood by using a tree that is too long for a bridge. Trees should be straight, have few branches, and be free of defects. Be sure to cut logs so each pair of stringers is closely matched in size and shape. Take the time to find high-quality wood; it will save time and effort during construction and make for a better, longer-lasting bridge. Cut to length, limb, and peel logs away from the trail so the debris stays out of sight.

To provide a good, safe walking surface the stringers should be topped flat, level, and even with each other, which is most often done using both a saw and an ax. Remove only one-quarter to one-third of the log's diameter; this will still be wide enough for walking without decreasing the log's strength. It is helpful to make a mark on the stringer to guide this cut; a chalk line is easiest, but a rope or string can be used with a lumber crayon. When cutting, brace the stringers between other logs, rocks or branches to prevent rolling. First, saw relief cuts at 4- to 6-inch intervals with a crosscut or chain saw, and then chip out the sections with an ax or adze. Be sure to clean up the chips and scatter them off the trail.

If you have not already done so, now you can carry the two base logs and pair of stringers to the trail. Position and set the base logs in place. To gauge their placement, lay out one stringer along the center of the treadway on the surface of the mud. Make sure it is no more than 6 inches from solid treadway, step stone, or another bridge. Position the base logs so that they are perpendicular to the stringer and so the stringers overhang the base logs at their centers by no more than 6 inches. Too much overhang can break off the end or tip up the bridge when stepped on. This is the most common cause of failure, aside from rot. Move the stringer aside and dig a trench to fit each of the base logs. The trenches should be as wide and long as the base logs and about as deep as one-half their diameter. The base logs need to be level and secure; check this by stomping on both ends. It may be necessary to remove roots and small rocks to properly place the base logs. Make sure that they do not rock from side to side; a slight rocking back and forth in the direction of the stringers will be remedied when the bridge is secured.

The next step is to lay out the two stringers on the base logs. Alternate the thicker butt ends to achieve a uniform width. For greater strength, rotate the stringers so any slight crown or curve is up, higher in the center than the ends. Position the pair so they fit closely together along their entire length but with a small gap still remaining for drainage. This gap should be no more than 1 to 2 inches so a foot cannot slip between them.

With the stringers in position, the placement of the notches in the base logs can now be marked. Draw a line with a pencil, lumber crayon, or ax on the top of the base log parallel to and straight down along both sides of the stringers. Move the stringers to the side and chop or saw out a 90-degree, V-shaped notch between the lines. Be careful not to make the notches too large at first; they can always be made larger but never smaller. Check the fit and fine-tune them as needed. The sides of the stringers should fit neatly along the sides of the notches and not rest on the bottom. To get the tops of two stringers at the same level,

7

Trail Construction and Erosion Control

widen the notch of the higher or larger stringer to set it lower. The stringers should not rock when walked upon, though small movements will disappear when they are secured to the base logs with nails.

When constructing a dimensional bog bridge (see figure 7.24), base logs are set as described above. The difference is that the lumbered stringers can sit flush upon the base logs. You may need to slightly flatten the tops of the base logs with an ax to remove irregularities and knots.

Fig. 7.24. An AMC trail builder spiking a dimensional bog bridge.

Fig. 7.25. Cross section of stringers secured to a base log with spikes.

The final step is to spike the stringers to the base logs (see figure 7.25). Use 10- to 12-inch-long, ⅜-inch spikes. Ten-inch spikes are best for dimensional lumber stringers, while 12-inch spikes are better for native material. Drive them in with a sledgehammer or the back side of a root ax, and strike them squarely. A bent-over spike is extremely difficult to remove. Slightly angle the spikes so they pass through the stringers and into the side of the notch. Angle the spikes in opposite directions at each end to provide tension to hold the stringers more securely in place.

Bog Bridge Construction Reminders

- For a bog bridge to be effective it must be used by the hiker. Make sure that the treadway width is sufficient to make walking on it easy. In the case of particularly thin logs, three stringers in parallel may be used. Sometimes three stringers are used every four or six bog bridges as a passing area for hikers.

- The treadway should not be tilted or angled to one side, nor should the bridge be unstable, rocking, or very springy. For stringers that are more than 8- to 10-feet long or that are very springy, use three or more base logs for support. It is probably best to keep bridges short and therefore stable. Shorter bridges are also easier to work with.

- The height of the bridge surface should not be greater than 8 to 10 inches from the ground. It's hard to step up onto or off of a high bridge, and it can be difficult to traverse for those uncomfortable with heights. Dig in the base logs if the unit will be too high or if it is unstable.

- Hikers should find stable, rocky, or dry soil or a step stone at the end of a bridge, not mud or slippery roots. When bridges are placed end to end, a space of no more than 6 inches should separate them.

- A step stone can be used at the end of a bog bridge or between adjacent bridges to span a large gap.
- Caution should be exercised when building bridges on pond shores or in any areas that are prone to flooding in wet seasons. If water levels rise substantially, bridges will float and drift off the trail. This might happen, for instance, along a pond shore that has beaver activity. Trails in these situations might best be relocated rather than bridged.
- If relocation is not possible in areas with seasonal flooding, it may be necessary to place large rocks on the bridge's base logs or to pin them down to help prevent rising or floating.

Definers

Over time many hikers using the same shortcuts create bootleg trails. People tend to seek the path of least resistance. To save time and effort hikers will cut corners at switchbacks, walk on the smooth carpet of alpine vegetation, or go around rock steps. Hikers who stray off a trail will quickly trample vegetation, compact soils, and hasten trailside erosion. Even a well-marked and maintained trail may need further defining. Place definers to make walking off the trail difficult, thus containing traffic to a single stabilized treadway.

However, in many ways, a number of the structures mentioned above serve as definers. Often, if people see the best option for foot travel, such as a bog bridge, they will choose that option as the obviously intended route, as well as the best route of travel. There are certain structures that serve the sole purpose of defining the trail, when normal definition is not effective enough.

Scree Walls

Low, simple rows of small rocks, called scree walls, lining the edges of a trail clearly show the boundaries and act as an impediment to straying hikers. Scree walls are often needed alongside heavily used trails in open alpine zones. Always line rock steps with scree walls; bypassed edges of steps will soon erode and threaten the stability of the steps and the entire slope. Scree is also used to block the shortcutting of switchbacks and to keep hikers from going around water bars or into drainage ditches.

Use small- to medium-sized rocks that can be carried by one person. Set scree so it can't be kicked or knocked out by someone walking on it. Toppled walls and loose rocks in the trail are hazards, not a help. Securely set scree is particularly important along rock steps because scree also serves to stabilize the soil. Scree walls should only be as large as they need to be, though more substantial walls are needed where hikers regularly walk off the trail. The main-

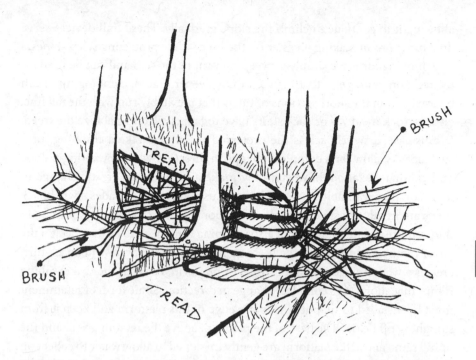

Fig. 7.26. Use dead brush and logs to keep hikers on a trail, discouraging short cutting.

tainer should recognize that scree walls can greatly infringe on the primitive qualities of the trail environment. Strive to blend these scree walls into the natural environment, making them as unobtrusive as possible.

Rubble

To help widened sections of trail outside the scree wall recover from damage, scatter rubble over the area. Walking on a jumble of small, loose stones is no fun and should keep people on the trail. Rubble is also an effective way to close a bootleg trail.

Brush

In scrubby and wooded areas, dead brush and logs (see figure 7.26) are useful for narrowing trails, protecting switchbacks, and closing unwanted trails. Remember that this brush will eventually rot away, but it will allow time for plants and trees to start growing.

Switchbacks and Climbing Turns

Even on a very well-laid-out trail, in order to gain elevation, either switchbacks or climbing turns must often be constructed. They introduce turns in the trail, allowing it to continue to climb the slope gradually. These trail devices serve dual functions of making it easier on the hiker while protecting steep slopes.

Climbing turns are simply a sweeping turn in the trail and can be used effectively on grades of 7 to 10 percent. On steeper grades, climbing turns can be used, but in the short sections of turns that inevitably run with the fall line, either a rock treadway or rock stairs have to be installed to stabilize the tread. In this case, a switchback is the preferred technique. Like a climbing turn, switchbacks allow for a complete change in direction while traversing a slope and gaining elevation; however, they make a much more drastic change in direction than a climbing turn and can be used on steeper grades. Switchback turns are highly effective, though very labor intensive to install. Not only do they require careful shaping, but also retaining walls need to be installed on the lower ramp and supporting the turning platform. Basically, a switchback turn creates a well-drained transition zone, or platform, between the two climbing ramps that allows for a complete change in direction. Some form of retainment must be installed to support the lower edge of this platform and keep it from sloughing off below. The base of the platform above the retaining wall and the uphill ramp above the platform are gently in-sloped to allow water to collect on the inside of the trail. This feeds the water above the turning platform, where it is drained off the side before it has a chance to cut down the trail. Refer to Chapter 4, which addresses switchbacks. Another important component of a well-constructed switchback is to include an anchor point for the trail to switchback around. It can be an existing feature, such as a tree, or a large rock that is moved into place specifically for that purpose. It creates either a physical or visual barrier so the switchback will not be shortcut by hikers.

CLEANUP

After the trail work is completed, it is important to make the area look as natural and untouched as possible. The land will repair itself with a little care, both in the material extraction and construction, but also in the site cleanup. Many heavily-worked trails will look muddy or raw immediately after construction but will wear in over the course of a year or two. In this respect, rock work has an advantage over wood, since well-constructed rock work fits into the landscape.

It is also very important to cover the raw, worked soil with leaf litter or pine needles. This helps with revegetation by keeping the soil moist, which provides resident native seeds with the right conditions for germination. Plus, it's more aesthetically appealing. Brush can then be placed over this to close in the clearing passage and help hold down the leaf litter. Don't forget to fill in and naturalize your quarry holes and borrow bits where you excavated rocks and soil. As always, try to make this process fit into the surrounding landscape as much as possible. When construction is complete, the ideal trail work is practically invisible to the ordinary hiker.

WHEN TO RELOCATE OR REPAIR A DAMAGED TRAIL

Heavily damaged trail sections need to be carefully examined when deciding whether to reconstruct the old path or relocate the section entirely. Eroded gullies, difficult ledges, or wide muddy areas on trails can be circumnavigated with a relocated section of trail or they can be hardened and stabilized. To decide, ask the following questions:

- Will the new section of trail have the same kind of terrain as the damaged section? Often the answer is yes. If so, it is often best to repair the trail in the old location rather than open up a new trail that will deteriorate in the same fashion. However, if a bypass can cross the same terrain in a less damaging way—e.g., if the trail will cross the slope rather than climb directly up it—then the relocation is worth considering.
- Will the current section of the trail be too difficult to close and restore?

If the section of trail under consideration is the most obvious route in a given landscape (for example, on a pond shore or on a pronounced ridge), hikers naturally tend to use the trail even after a relocation is built and the damaged section has been closed. In this case, it is best to stick to the current location. Sometimes a relocation can actually hasten environmental degradation when hikers confuse it with the old location and begin using both routes interchangeably. When this happens there can be many problems with both locations; unplanned crossover trails may also develop because of hikers' confusion.

Long relocations should only be used when they result in a substantial improvement in the overall environmental conditions. Short relocations around a wet area or eroded section may be appropriate, but the best long-term solution is usually either to close and relocate a long trail section or to reconstruct it. Depending on terrain and management of the area, reconstruction is usually the best alternative.

CHAPTER 8
BUILDING MATERIALS FOR TRAIL RECONSTRUCTION

Once you decide whether to use wood or rock on your trail, use different techniques to remove your material and move it to the trail.

- **Moving, shaping, and breaking rock:** Use the correct tools and proper lifting techniques to move rocks. Break and shape them with hammers, chisels, drills, and wedges.

- **Felling trees:** Assess the tree and its surroundings before bringing down trees with an ax, saw, or chain saw.

- **Hoist systems:** Use griphoists to move rock efficiently and in tricky situations.

Now that you have learned about trail construction and reconstruction techniques, it is time to start thinking about field planning. Once problems are identified and the project planned, think about the materials that will be chosen for construction.

In front country trail reconstruction sites, having materials delivered to a building site can be more time and cost efficient. However, due to the terrain of most trail projects, that is impossible. Instead, native materials must be found near the trail and moved to the treadway. This laborious process should be undertaken carefully to ensure safety, minimize damage to the trail environment, and maximize the efficiency and quality of reconstruction.

The materials—usually rock, wood, or soil—are either found on the surface or are dug/cut from sites near the trail, but preferably out of sight from it. This is very important—reconstruction material and its source should blend into the local environment. In addition, be sure to limit your impact on the surrounding areas as much as possible. Even with care, the extraction process will impact the land. With diligence, trail crews can minimize their impact during the construction process, ensuring that their work has a net positive impact on the environment. Remember you may be killing a small number of trees to save the forest, but take only what you need and clean up after yourself.

WOOD VS. ROCK

When constructing and reconstructing trails, choose natural materials to preserve the aesthetic quality and natural character of the landscape. These materials are usually native rock or wood. On rare occasions, metal is used for trail structures, but due to the non-native and semipermanent nature of this material, it is used rarely. For example, when replacing bog bridging the old spikes can be removed to prevent non-native materials from littering the woods. So, aside from the occasional use of metal for fasteners, pinning, or staples, the majority of trail structures are made from either wood or rock.

Because many structures could be made with either rock or wood, a decision must be made on which is most appropriate. There are definitely pros and cons to building with either, though often the final decision is based on proximity and availability.

Long before rock was used to build trail structures, wood was the dominant material. It is lighter, easier to transport, can be shaped and moved in larger pieces, and is abundant at lower elevations. Various species of trees can be used, and woodworking tools are relatively light. However, wood has one final and fatal flaw—it rots. Regardless of how well-built a structure is, wood (especially wood which is in contact with the ground) will always rot.

The other option, rock, is heavy and difficult to move. Because of this, positioning rock correctly and building with it can be problematic. Moving and working with rock takes much more time to learn than working with wood. Rock can be shaped, but this is also laborious and sometimes inefficient. Finding good rocks can be challenging since they are often hidden under moss or inches of soil. However, well-placed rock on a well-planned trail structure has the potential to last until the next glaciation.

The problem of whether to choose wood or rock as a building material is not easily solved simply by considering longevity. The decision will also depend on the situation. Many managers prefer rock due to its long life and because they think it blends more easily with the character of the trail, while others like the ease and efficiency of working with wood. Regardless, the first consideration is availability. If the project is above treeline, working with native timber may not be an option. Either rock must be harvested locally, or non-native material must be used. In some areas the rock or tree size and species is not as suitable or as available as it is in other places, or can simply be nonexistent. Remember, longevity must be balanced with availability and maintaining the character of the trail.

ROCK

Rocks of many sizes are used for trail definition and marking, erosion control and drainage, trail hardening, and other purposes. First, you will need to determine the amount, size, and shape of rock needed for a project. Then, find a quarry of suitable rock. The quarry should be out of sight of the trail and uphill, as gravity and slope will help you move rock to the trail. Usually rock can be found on the surface, but in some cases rock may be partially buried under duff or leaf litter, requiring some excavation.

Moving Rocks to Trail

The most important rule to remember when moving rocks is that you should not lift anything unnecessarily. First try to slide or roll the material. Most rocks used for trail structures are impossible to lift by hand, and many require two people to roll or slide. However, smaller rocks, like those used for scree or cairns, can be carried to the trail by one person. Remember to lift correctly to protect your back, and watch your step while walking over uneven terrain.

Fig. 8.1. Use a rock bar to move heavy objects.

Larger rocks needed for steps, rock water bars, and other uses will require additional effort. Sometimes one person can maneuver a rock to the trail using a rock bar (see figure 8.1) or muscle power by rolling, flipping, and sliding the rock along.

Occasionally several people will need to work together to move rock, with some using rock bars and pick mattocks and others pushing with arms or legs. Two people with rock bars can also move rocks more easily over greater distances. This is often called "double barring" a rock. It requires extra safety precautions and clear communication. One person places the bar firmly below the rock and holds the bar as parallel to the ground as possible and lifts as far as the bar placement, safety, and strength allow. Once this has been accomplished, the first person communicates with the second person that he or she is ready. The second person then plants the other bar firmly below the rock, at the same level as the first bar. This firm placement is called a "bite." Both people then lift, until the first person begins to lose the bite. This is where communication is most critical; it is essential to be sure the second person can hold the weight of the rock while the first person gets a better bite that will allow him or her to lift further. Repeat this process until the rock flips or rolls.

- ■ Choose a good route, clear of obstacles.
- ■ Always quarry uphill of project.
- ■ Never get below the rock or on the downhill side.
- ■ Lift with your legs and do not twist.
- ■ Learn how a particular shape of rock moves.
- ■ Anticipate and prepare each move to save energy.
- ■ Use logs as runners to avoid low spots, muddy sections, or holes along a quarry path.
- ■ Build large, sturdy barricades to avoid losing rocks.
- ■ Always choose the lowest impact route to move materials.

In locations with boggy areas between rock sources and the trail, crews can make a skidway by placing dead logs side-by-side on the mud on which to slide the rock across. Rolling rocks through the mud, with its strong suction power and slipperiness, can be extremely difficult.

Joint efforts must be carefully coordinated to prevent accidents, particularly pinched or crushed fingers. As a general rule, use either tools or hands when moving a rock with two people. Often, the mixing of the two can cause fingers to be crushed between steel tools and hard rock as objects shift with movement.

Safety

Avoid working below a person moving rocks. Everyone should wear hard hats. Limiting the number of people working on a particular slope is also wise; it is possible to have too many people and too much activity in one location.

In some cases it may be best to either close a trail to hikers during construction or post someone to direct traffic. Hikers sometimes stand in a particularly hazardous location and observe the work in progress, so watch for such bystanders, know where your coworkers are, and let everyone know when you are attempting a difficult maneuver. Losing a rock is not only very dangerous, but also a waste of energy, so be sure not to get too over zealous. If a rock does roll out of control, shout a warning of "ROCK!"

Barricades

While working on steep slopes, crews build simple log-and-debris barricades (see figure 8.2) next to the trail and below where they are quarrying rock to

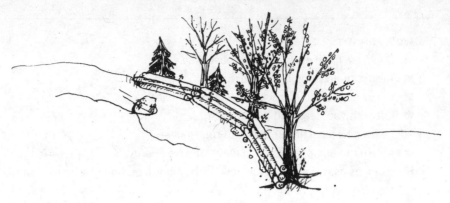

Fig. 8.2. Build a barricade to stop rocks from rolling down a slope.

prevent rocks from rolling down the slope. Stack solid dead logs and a few freshly cut ones between trees or boulders to create a backstop into which rocks can be rolled. In some cases barricades are built just in case a rock may be lost when it's being maneuvered to the trail, while in other areas they can be necessary for the safety of coworkers and hikers. Spending a lot of time and sweat moving a rock, only to see it slip away and roll down a slope, can be very frustrating and dangerous.

Shaping and Breaking Rock

A special, more advanced technique when working with rock is using hammers and chisels to shape or break rock. This can remove bumps, protrusions, overhangs, or other irregularities that make a particular rock difficult to work with. Examples include a rock with an overhang that causes it to be off-balance and difficult to stabilize or set, or a bulge on the rock surface that would be easier to set if it were smoother.

In deciding where to break the rock, or if the break in the desired location is possible, examine the rock to find places of weakness or fracture planes that run through the rock. Once these are determined rock shaping can be done with a variety of specialty hammers and chisels, each designed to be used in slightly different applications. By either hitting the chisel or swinging the hammer with a blow in the desired location, a shock wave is sent through the rock. The energy will be released through the path of least resistance. If the strike is along an existing weakness, the energy will travel down this plane of least resistance and weaken the bonds between the particles in the rock. Shaping rock can often save time and energy if done by an experienced stone worker, though for the less experienced it can prove to be a waste of time. Before picking up a hammer, be sure that you have weighed your options and then decide whether breaking the rock in question is the most efficient option. As a general rule, if a rock does not break after a few well-aimed, precise blows, that approach is inefficient and the plan should be reconsidered.

Because rocks types all break differently, it is very important to have the experience to read the rock and anticipate how it will break to avoid wasting time, energy, and materials. This evaluation takes experience and training, and even a bit of knowledge about local and general geology can be very helpful.

Splitting Rock

Sometimes a trail is located far away from appropriate-sized rock. If so, bedrock or large boulders can be split into manageable pieces. To improve the chance of a controlled, clear fracture, use a stone hammer and score a line to weaken the rock. As with shaping and breaking rock, the break is more likely to be successful if done along a fracture plane. Be exact and consistent with each swing. If a break is difficult, more scoring may be necessary to insure success.

Drilling. Drill a line of holes along the score line, which is where you want the rock to split. This can either be done by hand, or with a pneumatic hammer-drill, known as a rock drill. The distance between the holes will vary according to the difficulty of breaking the rock in the desired location. This will depend on the rock type and fracture planes in the rock. Drill holes that are deep enough to insert the feathers and wedges properly, as shown in Chapter 6. With a small sledgehammer, pound the wedges alternately. As the rock starts to be wedged apart, the pitch of each wedge will change as it is hit with the hammer. In order to get an even break, hit each wedge until they all reach a similarly high pitch. They can then be left to sit while the rock is slowly wedged apart. If this does not happen, repeat the pounding process, or drill additional holes and insert wedges until the rock splits.

Successfully splitting rock can be difficult, or almost impossible with certain types of rock. It can also be complex, and further training in the subject is highly suggested for success. Even with the advent of powered drills, the process of breaking rock is very time consuming and the question of need should be highly scrutinized. Training is highly recommended and help can be found occasionally through the American Trails website or Professional Trail Builders.

WOOD MATERIALS

Native wood, cut from trees in the vicinity of the trail, is an essential reconstruction material and is used to build stream bridges, bog bridges, ladders, water bars, and cribbing. If a large amount of wood is needed, cut down trees over a large area to minimize the impact on the environment.

Find trees appropriate in size and length located uphill and hidden from the trail. Usually the trail worker has to use what is readily available. If you have the luxury of a choice, spruce and hemlock are ideal in the Northeast, since they are usually straight, lack large branches, can be cut and peeled easily, and are relatively lightweight. Hardwood, such as locust and oak, can also be a good choice, but in the large dimensions required for good water bars, they are difficult to carry. Conifers such as hemlock, fir, spruce, and cedar are much more resistant to rot than common hardwoods such as beech or birch. Get to know your local tree species, and find out which local species are resistant to rot.

Trees should be felled, limbed, peeled, and cut to the appropriate length on-site (away from the trail) to prevent bark, wood chips, and other waste products from littering the trail. A freshly-peeled log can be slippery, so some trail workers peel the log at the trail and remove the debris afterward or, if time allows, wait for the log to dry.

Once prepared, logs can be hand carried, dragged, flipped, or slid down to the trail by one or more people. Large and heavy logs can be dragged to the trail or lowered down a steep slope with the aid of a griphoist.

Felling a Tree with Hand Tools

Trail builders can improve their tree cutting skills even after years of experience. The inexperienced feller should learn on small-diameter trees, guided by an experienced feller. With practice, the novice can graduate to larger-diameter trees and more complex felling situations. The directions given in this section are simply an introduction to felling and do not contain all the information needed to safely fell a tree, which is learned through training and practice with an experienced feller. It is highly recommended to learn safe felling and bucking techniques from a certified trainer.

First, be sure to choose a tree that fits the project's needs. Proximity to the trail and project site should be taken into consideration, as well as the species of tree, and the amount of usable wood the tree will provide. Once the tree is chosen, many factors must be considered in assessing the tree and creating a felling plan.

Assessing the Tree and Surroundings

Health of the Tree. Look for signs of rot, insect or animal sign, basal scars, signs of fire weakening, splits or any other irregularities. Rot can sometimes

THE RIGHT TOOLS: TREE FELLING

For hand tool felling:

- hard hat
- ax
- plastic wedges
- sledgehammer

For chain saw felling:

- hard hat; ear, eye, and face protection
- chaps
- gloves
- wedges and sledgehammer
- felling lever
- gas mix and bar oil
- chain saw
- scrench, files, and gauges

---

be found by taking the butt end of an ax and thumping the tree. Often rotted trees will emit a dull thud. A tree with rot is a hazard tree and takes special consideration in felling due to the increased unpredictability and will most likely not provide good building material. Never fell a hazard tree that is above your felling ability.

The Lean of the Tree. The lean is the deviation of tree trunk from completely vertical. There is often a lean in two directions: both must be taken into consideration. It is easiest to fell a tree in the general direction it is leaning. With advanced felling techniques a tree can sometimes be made to fall in any direction. However, when using basic hand tools it's easiest to bring a tree down toward the direction it's already heading.

Weight Distribution of the Tree. With big trees, particularly hardwoods, it can be difficult to determine how the weight of the limbs is distributed. The feller has to study the tree carefully to determine how the weights of the major limbs, multiple tops, snow and leaf loads, and bends in the trunk will affect the balance of the tree. At this time, it is also important to become aware of any dead branches in the tree that could be hazardous in the felling process.

The Direction and Strength of the Wind. Wind speed and direction can be inconsistent. If a strong wind is present, it may make sense to wait until weather conditions improve to fell.

Clear Felling Zone. When choosing the direction for felling, remember that space should be available for the tree to fall to the ground. If a tree gets hung up on another tree, it can be very troublesome and hazardous when the feller tries to get it down, and can damage the needed wood and surrounding trees. Look for additional hazards, such as standing dead trees in the area, debris, rocks, uneven ground, or downed logs in the felling area. Once the tree has been assessed and a safe fall zone has been established, examine the work area. Look for people, dead trees or branches that could be disturbed in the felling process, structures, or other additional hazards. The zone of safety should be at least two tree lengths away from the stump.

Now, you are ready to establish your escape route and alternate escape route, reassess the felling plan, and begin to cut, after following these safety procedures:

- Clear the area around the base of the tree so the feller will not be restricted, confined, or have his or her concentration disturbed during the cut.
- Clear an escape route and alternate route and rehearse exiting several times so the feller can quickly move away from the danger area. The escape route should be out of the 180-degree fall zone, but not directly behind the desired felling location. Be sure to walk the route and clear it of debris and tripping hazards.
- Before felling, clear everyone two tree lengths away. If the tree could fall near a trail, post one or two people on the trail to halt traffic until the tree is safely down.
- Once the tree starts to fall, the feller should move away from the butt of the tree. The danger of kickback, the butt jumping back off the stump, is always a potential hazard.

Front Cut and Back Cut

The first cut to make in a tree to be felled is the front cut, which is done on the side of the trunk in the direction of the planned fall line. Proper preparation of the front cut ensures a predictable fall line. The front cut depth should be about one-third the diameter of the trunk.

The front cut consists of a face cut and undercut. The front cut should be an open V-shaped notch of more than 45 degrees. Because cutting out this

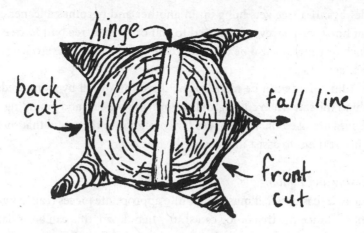

Fig. 8.3. Top view of a proper ax cut, showing a hinge.

wood creates an area that is unsupported, the weight of the tree should go in the desired direction when it falls. It is imperative that all wood is cleared where the face cut and undercut meet to provide for safe and controlled directional felling. Any wood chips left will tend to wedge the tree off the planned fall line. If done properly the fall line will be exactly at a right angle to the back of the front cut.

After completing the front cut, the feller will make the back cut. Before beginning, check to make sure no coworkers are near the fall line. Check escape routes one final time before proceeding. Those in the area should be made aware of the progress of the cut.

The back cut should be about 2 to 4 inches higher than where the face cuts meet, and parallel to the ground. This is most accurately done with a saw. At this point the only thing holding the tree is the wood remaining in the back, so when the right amount of wood is removed, the weight of the tree can no longer be supported by the back wood, and the tree will fall, closing the face cut as it reaches the ground. The wood left over between the front cut and the back when the tree eventually falls is called the hinge, or holding wood (see figure 8.3). The hinge will vary from tree to tree, but should not generally be less than 2 inches and should never be cut through. Be very, very aware at this stage in the felling process; once you start the back cut, do not leave the felling site. As the feller finishes the back cut he or she should watch for the first, almost imperceptible movement of the tree, and then quickly and carefully escape the stump.

As soon as the fall begins, the feller should immediately leave the spot via one of the preplanned escape routes; tree butts frequently jump backward or sideways. If a tree gets hung up in another and becomes a leaner, a rock bar, cant hook, or peavey can be used to roll or twist a tree butt to free the top. A winch or rope can also be used. Extreme care should be exercised when doing these activities.

Adjustments can be made to the direction of fall by using wedges, either behind the saw when cutting, or by removing the saw and pounding the wedge. Wedges are used once the saw is far enough into the wood that there is room to insert them to assist in levering the tree over.

Bucking and Limbing

Once a tree is down, it must be cut into appropriate pieces (called bucking) and limbed. Since the tree or log can shift when down, this can be as dangerous as felling, so stay aware.

Tension and Compression

When working with wood of any length, one must consider the two forces being exerted on the wood before making a cut. These are tension and compression. In short, because a tree's fibers are flexible, it bends under its own weight. This causes the wood fibers on one side of the tree to be compressed and the fibers on the other side to be stretched. The stretched side is said to be under tension, and the other under compression. Before cutting, determine where the tree or wood is compressed or under tension. If the side under compression is sawed into, the saw will most likely bind, as the wood continues to compress. If there is a lot of tension and compression on wood and the tension is released quickly, the saw will not bind, but it will not be a controlled cut and is more likely to break quickly and split the wood before the cut is complete. Spring poles (see Chapter 10) are the most extreme cases of tension and compression, and can be very dangerous.

Be sure to determine tension and compression before making a cut. Assess what will happen in each instance before releasing the tension or compression. Down trees and logs can be very dangerous if they are not assessed properly. As with felling, determine an escape route and be aware of the tree, as the tree will shift as limbs and wood are cut.

Chain Saws

Chain saws are very common tools for working with wood on trails, though adequate training is necessary. The main principles of assessing a tree for felling, limbing, and bucking do not change if using a chain saw or a non-motorized saw or ax, but for the experienced sawyer there are more options for accurate directional felling techniques. These all involve the face-cut, but how the back-cut and hinge wood are released is how techniques are varied. The two most widely accepted and respected chain saw certifications are from Game of Logging and Missoula Technology and Development Center. Courses for these certifications can be found around the United States through the Forest Service, Park Service, Bureau of Land Management, or many certified agency or private trainers.

OTHER MATERIALS

Dimensional wood is also commonly used in front country trail reconstruction. Even in the backcountry, the ease of installation can prove to make it more cost efficient to transport materials to the site rather than shape and process native wood. Pressure treated wood is also an option that is used by some land managers, but be sure to use proper safety procedures and gear when working with pressure treated wood.

Soil

Aside from rock and wood, soil is a material that is part of most trail projects. Occasionally a soil pit needs to be dug to provide soil for fill work along the trail. Though such pits can be dug near the trail, they should be out of direct view, and after they are no longer needed should be filled with debris and hidden. Soil for trail projects needs to be inorganic and well draining, and can be transported to the work site in sacks, buckets, or if possible, with a wheelbarrow.

HOISTING EQUIPMENT

Moving rocks with winches and hoisting equipment has the potential to be very dangerous if not done properly. Be sure to get the appropriate training before using any hoists or winch. Trainings can be found through Trail Services, Inc., the AMC, or others through Professional Trail Builders Association or American Trails.

Griphoist

The griphoist is the most commonly used trail hoisting mechanism. Though come-alongs or winches are usually easily available, the griphoist has more safety features and versatility. The number of safety features depends on the model of griphoist. One feature is the mechanism by which it pulls or releases the wire rope. It has two clamps, one which is always clamped around the wire

Griphoists and winches may prove valuable and even necessary to move rock easily and safely. Moving very heavy or large amounts of rock over long distances may be effectively done only with the help of a winch. Griphoists are used to control the lowering of rock down a steep slope and are also capable of pulling rock uphill or out of a hole. Large rocks can also be positioned, rotated, and flipped with such equipment.

Trail crews have found a griphoist with one- or two-ton capacity superior to the spool-and-ratchet-type winch. The griphoist is a closed-cased device that grabs and pulls, or releases, a wire rope straight through itself. This has the advantage of ease of operation and the ability to use wire rope of unlimited length. Chain falls, chain winches, and some winches with enclosed casings sometimes do not work well, since dirt and debris get into the mechanisms, jamming them and requiring frequent maintenance. Whichever winch or hoisting device you use, make sure it is rated for the job and be sure to read, understand, and follow safety procedures and operation and maintenance instructions. Use of hard hats and leather gloves is encouraged when working with winches and wire rope, which may develop very sharp splinters.

Never use "cheater" bars on a winch. Safety handles supplied with most winches are generally designed to bend or shear pins will break after a certain load limit is exceeded. Do not overstrain the winch, or its cable or rigging. Snapping cables and rigging can cause serious injury.

Chain-saw-powered "donkey" winches may prove practical for moving rock or logs in some cases. Horses, oxen, or machinery might be feasible, even necessary, to move large volumes of material at times. Generally they are not needed and may not be appropriate for trail work due to the damage they may do to the treadway.

Griphoist with anchor and rock sling.

rope; so if one were to fail, the other should hold the system. Many griphoists also have a safety feature that does not allow the griphoist to be put into "neutral" while there is tension on the system. Another major safety feature is a shear pin that prevents the machine from going beyond its load capacity. For this reason, be sure to carry extra shear pins, since they can break from wear and tear.

Griphoists are built in many different sizes, but those used for trail work have a working capacity of one or two tons. Most importantly, know your machine and all of the safety ratings for the equipment in the system. Be sure that the hardware matches the size of wire rope and griphoist model being used. Once again, be sure to receive adequate training before using a griphoist system. Included here are only the basics; this chapter does not contain all the safety information needed to use a griphoist system safely and effectively.

Rigging

A variety of rigging equipment is needed to accompany a griphoist. Be sure to use rigging that is load rated for the task. To ensure adequate safety, all rigging should be able to bear five times more weight than expected; this ratio is called the safety factor, while the weight an item can bear is the safety rating or safe working load. The safe working load of each rigging component will vary depending on how they are set up and used. Inspect rigging regularly for wear and damage; retire any that is questionable. The following items are common rigging used for griphoist systems.

Nylon Slings. A common example is the 3-inch-wide eye and eye, 4-to-10 feet long sling for griphoist and skyline anchors, suspension points, and guy lines. There are also endless loops, 4 to 12 feet long, for choke-hitching rocks to be lifted, extending anchors, or guy lines. Newer, thinner, lighter slings are now available as well. Be sure to know the difference in safety ratings for the two.

Rock Basket. A custom-made nylon webbing basket for wrapping large rocks for winching, the rock basket is especially good for rocks expected to roll and tumble as they're moved.

Snatch Block. This is a pulley, usually with a hook, whose side opens to insert wire rope.

Shackle. A U-shaped steel piece closed with a heavy pin, it is used for connecting slings, chain, and wire rope.

Building Materials for Trail Reconstruction

Fig. 8.4. A saurman/mule.

Rock Box. This is a 3-foot-square, 6-inch-deep homemade box for carrying scree and rubble along a skyline.

Steel Tripods (for treeless areas). These 10-foot-high tripods are made of 2-inch-square steel tubing with ⅛-inch-thick walls and are attached at the tops with threaded rod.

Saurman/Mule. This hardware is used to create a point of attachment on the hookless end of the wire rope (see figure 8.4).

Basic Single-Line Pull
Griphoists are used mostly to simply pull or lower a rock by dragging it or controlling its descent down to the work site on the trail. Anchor the griphoist to a large tree by looping a sling around the base of the trunk. A 3-inch-wide eye and eye sling around the tree in basket fashion will help avoid chafing the bark and damaging the tree. Securely wrap the rock to be moved with a two-inch endless loop sling. Encircle the rock, taking advantage of indentations and projections on the rock's surface. The easiest, self-tightening way to secure the rock with a sling is to put one end of the loop through the other, creating a girth-hitch. A rock bar or mattock is often necessary to lift a rock to allow the sling to be slipped under and around it. A rock basket greatly facilitates securing a rock and will hold the rock if it tumbles and rolls.

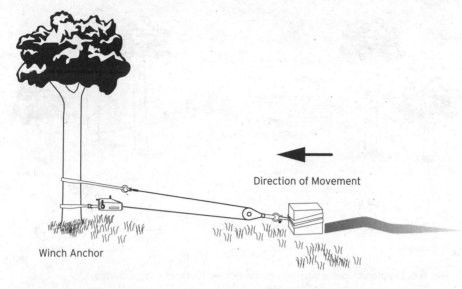

Fig. 8.5. Use this technique to gain a 2:1 mechanical advantage. (Courtesy Julian Wiggins.)

Always have someone stationed at the griphoist and at the loading site. When pulling a rock across the ground, never let the griphoist alone do the work. Have someone raise the leading edge of the rock and un-snag it with a rock bar or mattock when it gets caught or digs into the ground. On a slope the rock handler should avoid the area below the rock in case it slips from the webbing.

A 2:1 mechanical advantage can be achieved by hooking a snatch block to the load and running the wire rope through the pulley and hooking the end to another anchor near the winch's anchor (see figure 8.5). If this is used, be sure to have the appropriately sized snatch block to correspond with the diameter of wire rope, so as not to create a kink in the wire rope. Also, be aware of the excess force that is now being exerted on the system.

The Skyline

The skyline is a more advanced griphoist technique (see figure 8.6). This technique allows rocks to be lifted and transported above the ground from quarry to trail along a tensioned wire rope. A skyline can also be used to transport buckets of soil or gravel or boxes and baskets of small rocks for scree walls. Rocks can be lowered, traversed across a slope, and even pulled up slight inclines. Wire rope is suspended above the ground by trees or, in treeless areas, by 10-foot-high steel tripods (see figure 8.7). Items can be transport distances of 200 feet or more with a skyline. Although a skyline requires additional equipment and

Building Materials for Trail Reconstruction

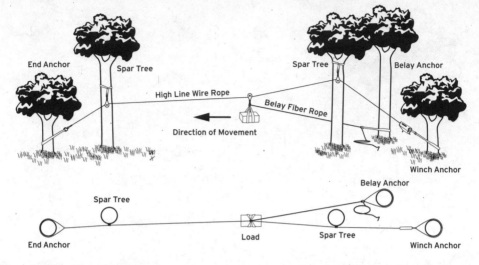

Fig. 8.6. Simple one cable belayed skyline system. (Courtesy Julian Wiggins.)

setup time, it is an efficient way to move large quantities of rock. One of its greatest advantages is that it does not drag rock over the ground, which protects soils, vegetation, and fragile alpine environments. It is particularly effective when a large quantity of rock in the same area is a certain distance from the trail. A skyline can be used to transport this rock either up hill, over a gully, or can be a controlled way to bring rock across a steep side slope.

Skyline Setup. If trees are in the area, the first step is to find two appropriately placed large trees (called spar trees) and two anchor points, which can be either large trees or boulders. Ideally, the quarry and the project site on the trail should be between and in line with the two spar trees. The two anchor points should also be in line and far enough beyond the trees so that the wire rope is suspended at a 45-degree (or less) angle from the suspension point in the spar trees.

Place the two suspension snatch blocks high enough in the spar trees to prevent the rock hanging under the wire rope from touching the ground. Skillful and protected tree climbing techniques or a ladder will help. Choker the trunk of the tree above a limb or bulge to keep it from slipping down. Do this with a 3-inch-wide, 3- or 4-foot-long eye and eye sling, and hook a snatch block to the free eye. Anchor the griphoist close to the ground so it can be easily operated, and hook the end of the wire rope to the anchor on the far end. Put the wire rope in the snatch blocks and feed it into the griphoist, leaving enough slack in the line to reach the load. Put the third, traveling snatch block on the slack line. Finally, tie a belay rope (one that is long enough to pull, or lower, the load

Fig. 8.7. In treeless areas, use a tripod to set up skylines.

along the skyline) to this snatch block. Now, first fully tension the system and be sure everything is in line. Then test the system with a small rock, watching the entire system to be sure everything is still in place. Now you're ready to sling, lift, and move a load.

Sling a rock so it can be lifted straight up and be held securely while it's suspended. Hook the traveling snatch block to the sling. Keep one person stationed to operate the griphoist and one near the load to watch and coordinate its progress. The person near the load should be in charge of the whole operation and communicate with the griphoist operator with simple commands such as, "tension," "slack," and "hold," which mean, respectively, to take wire rope in, let wire rope out, or pause until further direction.

The griphoist can increase the tension of wire rope and lift the rock. As the wire rope approaches horizontal, its tension will greatly increase. Check all equipment and anchors to ensure they are working properly and holding securely. Once the load is suspended from the taut skyline—high enough to clear the ground during transit—it can be pulled, or lowered, to the work site. To aid in pulling the load, anchor one end of the belay rope and run it through a pulley attached to the traveling snatch block to increase the mechanical advantage. To control lowering, belay the load by wrapping the rope around a tree a few times.

- Beware of the byte (any place where the wire rope changes direction).
- Keep fingers away from the snatch blocks.
- Keep an eye on your system; visually inspect entire system many times a day.
- Make sure there is only one person giving clear direction.
- Always use a belay rope when moving rocks down hill.
- Stay uphill of rock at all times
- Wear all appropriate PPE, and limit the number of people around the system.
- Be aware of damage to anchors or spars.
- Check to see that webbing is in good condition and in the appropriate place.
- Make sure all hardware is pulling in line and nothing has shifted.
- Be aware of damage to anchors or spars.

Once the rock is over the work site continue to hold the belay rope, or tie it off. Release the tension of the skyline with the griphoist and lower the rock to the ground. Completely slack the skyline before unhooking the load.

A skyline system is quite versatile and adaptable. The setup and operation just described is the most basic and may have limitations due to the terrain, availability of convenient trees, and distance between quarry and trail. To overcome these real-world factors it's a good idea to have extra gear on hand. A selection of slings of various lengths and types, shackles, extra rope, and snatch blocks will allow for greater flexibility of setup. Overall skyline length can be increased by using a longer griphoist wire rope or by having a long auxiliary wire rope for the skyline which is tensioned by the griphoist and its wire rope.

Griphoists can be very useful, effective, and efficient tools when used safely and wisely. Be sure to get adequate training before using a griphoist or skyline system. Information, training, supplies and resources can be found through Trail Services Inc.

WORKING IN THE ALPINE ZONE

Special considerations for working in the alpine zone must be taken. Because it is so fragile, use extra care to avoid disturbing fragile plants and soils. Because of this, materials can be difficult to gather. As mentioned earlier, tripods are practically indispensable in alpine zone rock projects. Smaller rocks bucket and crates can be helpful, especially for rocks for scree walls, which are commonly needed in popular alpine zones. When rocks are gathered, try to disturb as little soil as possible. If possible, remove rocks from the windward side of slopes, where less vegetation grows due to its exposure.

Also, especially due to the openness of the alpine terrain, those areas are perfect for airlifting non-native materials, if it is desirable and the funds are available. Though the building materials would not be local, it still serves to preserve the resource in the fragile alpine zone.

CLEANUP

After the quarrying is completed brush in evidence of excavation and "skidder trails" and fill holes with debris, deadwood, and leaf litter, especially near the trail.

Not only should quarry holes be filled, but any areas were materials were removed should be filled with debris, and corridors where materials were transported should be brushed in well. This will physically prevent curious hikers from adventuring into an area that is revegetating, and should look natural enough so as to escape the notice of anyone who is not looking for the disturbance. If brushed in, the area should revegetate and blend into the surrounding forest in little time.

8

Building Materials for Trail Reconstruction

CHAPTER 9
BRIDGES

AT-A-GLANCE

When a trail crosses a body of water, trail builders must determine the best way to handle that situation.

- **Decide whether to build a bridge:** Consider the likely users of the trail, its location, and alternative routes before you conclude that a bridge is necessary.
- **Architecture:** Design a bridge based on aesthetics, its size, and the experience of the designer and builders.
- **Construction:** Use the right size lumber for the span and decking of single-span bridges; build supports if necessary.
- **Alternatives to single-span bridges:** Build elaborate bridges or cableways where needed.

Almost all trails cross one or more waterways somewhere on their route. Proper recreation management planning plays an important role in users' experience of a trail. On a front country urban trail, users often expect that they will have a safe and dry route across water. On such trails, even minor stream crossings may be candidates for bridges. On the other hand, in a Federally Designated Wilderness, the opposite may hold true. On backcountry trails in wilderness areas, bridges are usually constructed only if there is a consistent hazard to hikers. It is important, therefore, to determine as part of the management plan to what degree trails or areas need to be managed.

IS A BRIDGE NEEDED?

Urban, or front country, trails almost always have bridges installed over waterways for user convenience, as well as for user safety. This type of trail demands good accessibility for all types of users and as few challenges as possible; these trails are typically used by individuals with little or no hiking experience, wearing street shoes. During the design phase it is recommended, and in some cases required, that you consider constructing your bridge to broad accessibility standards.

On the other hand, backcountry trails are often managed to challenge the visitor and provide a more natural experience. The choice to install a bridge is usually dependent on a variety of environmental considerations and management goals: Is it important to preserve the natural look of a river? What are the potential impacts of bridge construction? Should the site be limited to a seasonal crossing to increase off-season challenges and maintain a more natural feel on a low-use trail? Management sometimes allows for a bridge to be installed only if it is determined that there is an absolute need. Examples include spanning a watercourse that cannot be easily forded or allowing passage across a steep or hazardous natural feature, such as canyon walls.

The first step is to determine if a bridge crossing is absolutely necessary. Careful planning and site reconnaissance should be conducted to explore all options before the design and construction phases begin. Often, by changing a trail's path, the need for a bridge can be eliminated, thus limiting the cost and the potential environmental impact. For instance, by carefully choosing an area along a stream that allows for a natural crossing, such as a rock hop, bridge building can be avoided altogether.

Knowing the characteristics of the stream and the area's use patterns also helps to determine if a bridge is necessary. Bridge width and design requirements for summer and winter recreation needs are generally different. A trail crossing that does not require a bridge in the summer may need one installed for use in other seasons. Often a stream is easily crossed in dry summertime conditions but may be nearly impossible or, at best, dangerous to cross during spring runoff or in a flash flood situation.

Once it has been decided that a bridge is necessary to span a waterway, consider the correct alignment of the bridge in relation to the trail. The bridge's location should not create an abrupt or awkward turn onto the structure that could be difficult to maneuver or potentially cause injury. Avoid any sharp turns in the approach to the bridge, especially on a multiuse trail or one that allows wheeled or motorized use.

For small stream crossings of ten to fifteen feet in width, a simple log puncheon or bog bridge (see Chapter 7) may suffice. Use a bridge with double stringers (long, heavy horizontal timbers used as supports or connectors) to provide better footing. Build a handrail for bridges 3 feet or higher above the stream or for any bridges over a fast current.

AESTHETICS

Aesthetics should also play a role in your bridge design. It is important for the bridge to suit the surroundings, both in terms of landscape and type of recreational use. For instance, a bridge in a remote wilderness should have a more rustic look. However, it may not always be possible to use natural or natural-looking materials. The bridge's intended uses may require stronger or more long-lasting materials. On other projects, such as those in urban or front country areas, a bridge could be considered the signature feature of the entire project. Often, a bridge defines the trail because of its appearance and setting in the landscape. Bridges can be places where users, especially those in front country locations, pause to reflect or take in the surrounding scenery. However, the aesthetic requirements need to be balanced with the structural needs of the project.

DESIGN AND CONSTRUCTION CONSIDERATIONS

Bridges with long span lengths (typically, more than 35 feet) or those over challenging terrain or unstable soils often require professional engineering design —for instance, a bridge needing to span a steep canyon with bedrock on either side. Professional engineers will evaluate flood-level data and the load-bearing abilities of the soils, as well as prepare and submit permits, estimate total project costs, and design a bridge that meets the owner's aesthetic requirements. Large bridges often require the use of heavy equipment during construction; therefore, access considerations must be anticipated. Today, lightweight composite materials can be used in place of standard wood or steel components. These composite bridges (see figure 9.1) are excellent choices when access is difficult.

Even if you choose not to employ the design services of a professional, you must determine annual flood levels in order to establish how high the bridge must be during high-water events. For smaller or less costly bridges it is common practice to look for evidence of the high-water mark in the form of scraped bark on trees lining the bank and deposits of debris, such as sticks and leaves. It may be possible to obtain hydrological data from local, state, or federal government agencies to determine flood levels for your particular stream. Often, asking local individuals who have knowledge of the river is invaluable.

Depending on their location, bridges greater than certain lengths and heights may require a permit from the local jurisdiction. Most activities involving soil disturbance in a stream bed or along its banks require obtaining wetlands permits. Check with local and state governments before starting any project.

The type of labor you employ will also influence the design and construction of the bridge. A project that is easily done by skilled professionals may be too difficult to complete using inexperienced volunteers. For example, a multi-stringer bridge over a large waterway would likely require professional help, while simple bog bridges or log puncheon bridges would be suitable for those

Fig. 9.1. Composite bridge.

with limited experience. While volunteers can help with bridge construction, bridges should be planned and the construction overseen by experienced trail maintainers. Considerations such as load capacity of the materials, potential flood levels, and permits need to be taken into account by someone experienced with the process.

BUILDING SINGLE-SPAN STRINGER BRIDGES

Single-span wooden bridges of native materials or milled timber are the most common large bridges on trails. If both streambanks are high enough to keep the stringers well above the flood level, extensive support is not necessary. A crib box—a box-like structure typically made of timber filled with rocks that acts as an elevated base for the stringers while allowing controlled water drainage—may be needed when the watercourse is subject to drastic changes in seasonal levels. Secure the stringers to a single base log, sill (a flat stone or ledge), or crib box on each end (see figure 9.2), using 10- or 12-inch spikes or large bolts. (Place the base log on a sill to prevent rot; the base log should not directly contact soil if at all possible.) Drift pins can be used to hold the base log in place on the rock if the weight of the bridge itself is not sufficient. In some situations crib boxes will need to be placed directly in the water. Keep in mind that this will reduce the overall longevity of the bridge.

Fig. 9.2. Two stringer with rail and crib boxes.

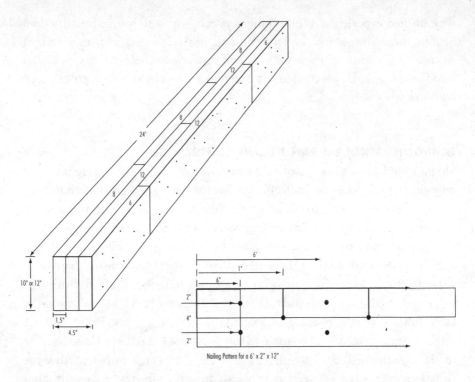

Fig. 9.3. Laminate 2-by-12s as shown to create stringer. Be certain all joints are at least 2 feet apart along the bridge's length. Laminate with construction adhesive and 16d galvanized nails as shown.

Dimensional, pressure-treated lumber can be used to build simple and durable triple-laminated bridge stringers. Spans up to 12 feet long can be bridged using 2-by-10-inch lumber lengths. For spans between 12 and 24 feet, laminated stringers are created by joining sections of 2-by-12-inch lumber together in three layers to form one solid beam. Before laminating, each 2-by-12-inch section should be checked for bows; bowed sections should be positioned crown up to take advantage of the bow's strength. Laminate the 2-by-12s together using both galvanized nails (see figure 9.3) and construction adhesive for maximum strength. Joints between laminated sections should never be closer than 2 feet apart.

For bridges made of native materials, use rot-resistant wood such as hemlock, locust, spruce, larch, or Douglas fir for the entire bridge, including the base logs. Remove all bark to retard rot. If you think the bridge should be treated further, use pressure-treated wood or treat the native wood with borax. Use liquid wood treatments with extreme caution; while they can lengthen the life of the bridge, their ingredients are often toxic and may leach into the stream.

Should you use such a treatment, dry the logs before application and apply the treatment on dry ground to keep the liquid preservative out of the stream.

Where access is easy and the use of non-native material is appropriate (for example, on a high-use trail close to a road), pressure-treated telephone poles can be used as stringers. However, keep in mind that the chemicals used to treat the lumber may be hazardous to the environment, especially water bodies.

Crib Boxes

When one streambank is lower than the other, a crib box can be used to elevate the low end so that the bridge is level. In other locations, crib boxes (see figure 9.4), or piers, may be necessary at both ends. Piers can also be made of stone, and though they are more durable than the log version, stone piers require a great deal of effort and the skill of a mason; they may also be out of place in some settings. Gabions, wire cages filled with stones, can be used instead of piers, but they are not aesthetically appealing. Abutments (see figure 9.5), usually made of large square stones to elevate the ends or secure the center of the bridge, can be constructed. Log cribs are most commonly used.

To make log crib boxes, cut 8- to 10-inch diameter logs to the length needed, depending on the width of your bridge. A small, 16-inch-wide bog bridge will need only a 3-foot-wide crib box, while a much wider bridge will require a bigger box. Construct the boxes by laying two logs parallel to each other to form the base of two sides of the box. Then overlay two sections perpendicular to

Fig. 9.4. Crib box with overflow extensions.

these to form the other two box sides, like a log cabin. Cut notches with an ax or chain saw on the underside of each log to help them fit together. Use drift pins or 10- to 12-inch-long, ⅜-inch-diameter spikes to hold the logs together. Add as many layers of wood to the box as needed to elevate your bridge.

To add mass and strength, fill the crib box with rock gathered nearby or from the stream. Be aware that removing stones from the stream channel may change water flow, and such work almost always requires a permit. Larger rocks can be pushed or pulled to either side of the stream and placed along the bases of the cribs, particularly on the upstream side, for added protection during high-water events. Use a taught string or squared-off, milled lumber and a builder's level to get the adjacent cribs the same height. In the field, trail builders often use a half-filled water bottle to determine levelness of structures.

After the crib has been built high enough, secure the stringer to it using large spikes or galvanized bolts. The size of the stringer will depend upon the type of wood and length of the span.

Due to their length and weight, stringers are hard to carry and maneuver into position. Timber carriers, hand winches with extra lengths of cable or chain, and crowbars can greatly facilitate the task. Place small lengths of log underneath stringers to act as rollers. Horses or small tractors might be used

Fig. 9.5. Stone abutments under a bridge.

in easily accessible locations. When you get the stringer to the site, place it across the stream, with the ends beside each sill or crib, and then lift it into place. Ramps made of logs and placed against the side of a crib can help get the stringer up on top. Again, check the bridge's length and width with the carpenter's level.

Decking

Decking, made from small-diameter (4- to 6-inch) logs, larger logs split in half, or rough-cut timber 2 inches thick, is installed next (see figure 9.6). It is possible to have two or more stringers, *hewn* or *adzed* flat on the top for good footing, to provide an adequate treadway if the stringers are close together. However, decking is generally best. Small spaces, ¼ to ¾ inches wide, should be left between deck pieces to allow for drainage. Before putting decking on, place tar paper or aluminum flashing over the top of the stringers for drainage and to help prevent rot. If the bridge is over a fast current or is 3 feet or more above the stream, add a secure railing to one or both sides. In some cases, steps or a small ladder might be required on each end due to the height of the cribs. Pressure-treated lumber can also be used for the decking and railings. However, avoid pressure-treated wood for a foot surface on sloped bridges or in areas that stay damp—it

Fig. 9.6. A bridge with decking.

is extremely slippery when wet. If there is no alternative, use a surface treatment such as anti-slip paint or wire mesh lath to enhance traction.

To prevent the complete loss of the bridge during floods, cable one end of the stringers to a large tree, boulder, or other anchor upstream. If washed loose, one end will float free and the bridge will end up against the streambank more or less intact. Later, the bridge can be put back, or at least taken apart and reassembled in place. If you cable both sides, the bridge may stay in place but collect debris and eventually succumb completely to the force of the flood. Do not underestimate the power of a flooding stream.

OTHER DESIGNS

The load capacity of fixed stringers generally limits bridge spans to 40 feet or less. A longer distance can be bridged using a midstream center crib and two spans on either side. This is recommended only where flood levels are low and flow is slow; otherwise, the center crib may be destroyed.

Most stream crossings of 40 feet or more require specially designed bridges such as a laminated timber bridge (10 to 60 feet), a prefabricated steel bridge (20 to 168 feet), a web joist bridge (about 100 feet), or a timber suspension bridge

Fig. 9.7. A timber suspension bridge.

(up to 200 feet) (see figure 9.7). These are all extremely expensive, ranging in total cost from \$20,000 to \$150,000, and they require the expertise of engineers and experienced builders to install them.

Where stream crossings are wide and unavoidable, requiring an expensive bridge, check to see if a nearby trail or road bridge could be used instead. Sometimes it is best to consider relocating a trail rather than tackle such a large, expensive project.

SPECIAL STREAM-CROSSING DEVICES

Cableways can be used for stream crossings as an alternative to bridging. The simplest design involves two cables suspended across the stream width, one above the other, a few feet apart. With feet on the lower cable and hands on the upper cable, the hikers slide-step across. A more advanced design employs a small cable car capable of carrying one person. The hiker climbs in, grabs a secondary cable, and pulls herself or himself across. The next hiker pulls the car back and repeats the process. Neither system is easy to use for most people, especially if they are carrying large packs or are accompanied by young children and pets.

Where large bodies of water must be crossed, bridges built on pilings may be the answer. Floating bridges, much like life rafts and docks, can be constructed using foam blocks, but they will need to be removed during the winter. Anchor cables should be placed to keep such bridges stable and in position. Use rot-resistant wood and make sure all hardware is galvanized or plated. Consult a local dock builder for advice on pilings and Styrofoam.

PLANNING FOR OTHER USES

If your trail is only for hiking, build your bridge accordingly to prevent prohibited uses such as snowmobiling or trail biking. Build narrow bridges or place barricades at each end of the bridge to prevent undesirable use. Gates or stiles may also be used to prevent access to the bridge; they are particularly effective for keeping out farm animals. If the bridge is in fact to be used by motor vehicles or animals, be certain to plan the load-bearing capacity of the bridge and its structure with this amount of weight in mind.

Suspension bridges that are easily accessible or located near the roadside need extra considerations, given their visibility and thus the potential for vandalism or mischief. For example, groups of children might jump on or hang from the bridge to try to make the structure flex up and down and from side to side. Anti-sway cables attached to each side will make the bridge more stable. Also, while it may sometimes be advantageous to have a high-visibility bridge, well-designed landscaping and plantings can be used to hide the bridge if vandalism is feared.

ASSISTANCE

The U.S. Forest Service has a great deal of experience with and information on various trail bridge designs. The National Park Service and state parks departments may also be able to provide advice. Local engineers, contractors, and utility companies might offer guidance or provide hardware and cable. Sometimes local National Guard units are willing to take on public service projects and can offer labor and technical help. Check with trail clubs and trail bike and snowmobile organizations for information and contacts. The Professional Trailbuilders Association has information on their website, www.trailbuilders.org, about working with and locating trail bridge designers and fabricators. American Trails, www.americantrails.org, provides links to consultants and contractors as well as private and governmental funding sources for trail projects.

MAINTENANCE

Remember to inspect all bridges and stream crossings annually, since bridges that are not maintained can be dangerous to hikers. Perform regular maintenance and replace materials as needed. Check all wood for soundness, paint or treat with preservative if required (while taking particular care to protect the water below), and fix loose decking and railings. Have a qualified engineer perform annual inspections of suspension or engineered bridges or any bridge that would likely cause serious injury should it fail. Paint any cables, steel beams, or hardware with rust-resistant paint. Keep a blueprint and photos of each structure on file to aid repair work. Try to inspect bridges after flood events and before and after high traffic times. At that time, take special note of changes to the riverbanks adjacent to the bridge abutments. Look for modifications in river course since the last visit based on loss of riverbank soil, stone, and vegetation. Sometimes, bridges and water crossings may need to be relocated due to unforeseen streambank erosion.

CHAPTER 10
TRAIL MAINTENANCE

AT-A-GLANCE

Once a trail has been constructed, you will need to take care of it. Basic maintenance involves four tasks, listed here in order of priority. All should be done annually or as needed.

- **Cleaning drainages:** Clear debris from drainages to ensure that water runs away from—and not down—trails so that they will not erode away.
- **Clearing blowdowns:** Remove trees and branches from trails to provide a clear path for hikers.
- **Brushing:** Prevent trails from becoming overgrown with vegetation to keep them well-defined.
- **Blazing or marking:** Mark trees or construct cairns so hikers won't get confused or lost.

Just like a car, garden, or house, trails require regular maintenance. If this maintenance is left undone, small issues will arise, which over time can snowball into bigger and more serious problems. Just as a failure to clean the gutters on your house could lead to expensive water damage, failure to maintain drainages on a trail could lead to severe erosion (see figure 10.1). In both cases, your initial investment (in money and hours of labor) has been wasted. Constructing a drainage takes a lot of time and effort: rocks have to be located, excavated, moved, and installed; trees have to be felled, limbed, peeled, bucked, moved, and buried; and there is always lots of digging involved. Cleaning drainages helps ensure a good return on a trail crew's initial investment of building a trail.

Basic maintenance helps to keep a trail usable and prevents damage to the delicate areas around it. The main goals of this work are to concentrate impact on the trail clearing passage—the swath of land designated for hiker travel—and to get water off the trail. With these goals properly achieved, you prevent severe damage to the resources around the trail.

CLEANING DRAINAGES

Clean drainages prevent large-scale soil erosion and the costly reconstruction that could follow. Soil is something that cannot be easily replaced on a trail. Keeping drainages clear goes beyond mere maintenance. It involves the pro-

Fig. 10.1. Erosion on trails can to lead to significant soil loss.

tection of the trail and surrounding environment, and thus it is the work of a conservationist. While clearing blowdowns, brushing, and marking the trail do protect resources, their main purpose is to ease hiker passage and keep a physical trail clearing passage open. A maintainer can always return to blaze or cut brush. But if a maintainer does not clean a trail's drainage in a timely fashion, the results could be cumulatively disastrous for the trail.

If you are not familiar with the various aspects of drainage, see Chapter 7, which examines drainage and its construction in far greater detail. This section describes only the cleaning of existing drainage structures.

The physics involved in drainages are simple. Trails are a perfect place for water to continue its endless journey downhill. Water seeks the path of least resistance, and it finds much less resistance moving down a trail than it does moving down the same slope in the woods. There is less duff, fewer roots and rocks to impede its journey, and once it gets on a trail, water is going to stay there unless the terrain or a well-constructed drainage moves it off.

As it moves down a trail, water gathers speed. As it picks up speed, more water joins in from the side of the trail. Soon a destructive torrent is formed that washes soil away from the trail. Erosion can be just as devastating to a trail over many years as it can be during a flash flood. Exemplary trail maintenance involves the continual cleaning, maintenance, and protection of all drainages on a trail. In fact, the best time to clean a drainage is during or after a rain event so that you can notice exactly where the water travels.

Drainages that have not been cleaned regularly will often be difficult to find. The accumulation of topsoil, rocks, and leaf litter can obscure drainages from sight. However, you can recover these lost drainages, particularly if they are water bars made of rock or earthen drainage dips. Log water bars buried for long periods of time may be rotten and in need of replacement. Search for lost drainages on a trail by looking for random *pin rocks*, *outflow* ditches off the trail, or even the tops of rocks or logs protruding from the trail in a telltale diagonal line.

A problem in the East, with its large amount of annual leaf litter and high precipitation, is that drainages become clogged with organic debris. Drainages must receive proper maintenance to be consistently effective. Once a drainage has been located, clean it and restore it to optimal working condition. Do not simply kick the leaves or dirt out of the drainage (a task often recommended to hikers by land managers). Kicking away loose debris works well enough for assessing the state of the drainage, but tools will be needed thereafter.

One effective type of drainage is a wide, flat-bottomed ditch, 12 to 18 inches wide and 6 to 8 inches deep. Adequate width is critical, for small twigs and a

The tools needed to clean a drainage depend on the type of soil and the extent of debris in the drainage:

- Use a pick mattock with rocky soil and drainages that are heavily clogged. A grub hoe also works.
- For fully clogged drainages, use a pair of loppers to cut small, tough roots that have grown in.
- For more neglected drainages, use a root ax.
- Use shovels or grub hoes for final shaping, or for touching up drainages that just need light cleaning.
- Use clippers or loppers to remove vegetation that is growing or leaning into drainage.

few leaves will clog a narrow ditch very quickly. The ditch's sides should slope gently up and out; vertical walls crumble or slough off into the drainage, decrease overall width, and contribute to clogging.

Begin cleaning at the uphill edge of the drainage ditch and work down. Typically this is done with a hazel hoe or a pick mattock (see figure 10.2). Scatter all organic matter pulled from the ditch (leaves, roots, and organic soil) well off-trail and downslope, where it won't wash back into the drainage. Use *mineral soil* pulled from the ditch as *backfill* on the downhill trail section of a water bar or drainage dip. Continue to move down the ditch, clipping and removing any roots and digging out all rocks. Smooth and pack the sides and bottom of the ditch, and tamp excess mineral soil onto the downhill slope with a shovel or your feet. An ideal drainage has a U-shaped cross section and, when used in conjunction with a rock or wood water bar, rises above and behind this downhill structure to protect it. A properly made drainage is the first defense in getting water off the trail; the actual water bar serves to reinforce the trail and hold back soil.

Simply clearing the loose debris and breaking up the compacted sediments in the drainage on the trail is not enough; you still must clean the outflow section of the ditch. The outflow ditch, which typically extends 4 feet or more off the trail, and the drainage ditch should be considered one unit. Therefore, debris, rocks, and roots should be removed from the entire structure. However, the outflow will often be the most clogged section of a drainage and will likely require more work to clear. The outflow ditch permanently removes water from the trail and assures it won't find its way back. This section of the drainage

Fig. 10.2. Start uphill and work your way down when cleaning drainage.

is critical, and it is often much longer than the portion that crosses the trail. Length will vary depending upon trail alignment; a trail moving straight down a very gradual or almost imperceptible slope requires an outflow ditch of at least 15 feet as water can more easily find its way back to the trail on a gradual slope, while a trail that follows a contour on a steep hill needs only a 3- or 4-foot outflow to remove the water.

Drainage will not be fully effective unless the outflow ditch is wide and clear. The outflow ditch should be constructed straight, never curved, to allow water to get far from the treadway and not return. Widen the outflow ditch gradually as it moves away from the trail, so it ends in a flat flare allowing water to disperse and saturate the ground rather than create an erosive, consolidated stream.

It usually takes several different drainage methods to assure proper water removal on a section of trail. Side ditches, rock crossovers, and bleeders are some other styles of drainage that will require cleaning as well. For further details, see Chapter 7 on the construction of and applications for these and other styles of drainage.

Once you have met the standards described above, move on to the next drainage with confidence, knowing that the one you just finished will effectively protect the treadway and the trail for years to come.

CLEARING BLOWDOWNS

Patrolling trails to clear blowdowns—trees or large branches that have fallen onto or across the trails—is one of a trail maintainer's first springtime tasks. While blowdowns are more common in winter due to heavy snow, ice, and wind, downed woody debris can be a problem at any time of the year. Clearing blowdowns:

- eases passage for the hiker.
- protects resources because hikers tend to create bootleg trails around un-cleared blowdowns.
- opens trails for early season hiking use.
- reduces complaints.
- offers an opportunity to assess the upcoming season's work needs.

AMC crews complete a trail condition report (see Chapter 3) after each trip, detailing the conditions they find on the trail. Patrollers should carry, in addition to their axes, bow saws, crosscuts or chain saws, a hazel hoe, pulaski, or small mattock to clean water bars and other drainage. For clearing blowdowns, the AMC's staff trail crew prefers the ax for its light weight, ready availability, low cost, and ease of maintenance. Also, because its blade cannot get pinched as a saw's blade can, many maintainers find an ax easier to use (see figure 10.3).

Fig. 10.3. Using an ax to remove a blowdown across a trail.

With proper training and practice, an ax can be very effective and safe. For information on tool training and safety, see Chapter 6.

Patrollers clearing trails should work in pairs, leapfrogging from blowdown to blowdown. This technique allows patrollers to cover significant distances in a day—anywhere from 5 to 10 miles depending on the number of blowdowns encountered, the number of drainages to be cleaned, and the difficulty of the terrain. Pairing up also provides a measure of safety in case of accidents or other issues. Remember to stay far away from your partner's flying ax!

In the most common situation a blowdown lies across the trail within 6 feet of the ground. Taking a minute to assess the situation can conserve energy, save time, and prevent unnecessary cutting. It might be possible to just lift or drag the tree off the trail. Partnering up with others may take less time and be safer than making a cut. If the tree or limb is too heavy or complicated to drag away and has a small diameter, one cut can be made and the top section of the tree completely removed from the trail. If the tree is too large, two cuts are required—one on each side of the trail (see figure 10.4). Remove the center piece and discard it off the trail. When moving large pieces of tree, bend your knees and lift your head to ensure a straight back. Enlist the help of a partner if needed. Move all debris off the trail. Be sure not to place debris in a drainage structure or natural drainage feature.

Fig. 10.4. Two cuts are needed to remove a blowdown.

Trees sometimes fall entirely across the trail or their tops break off and hang down onto the trail. Removing these blowdowns is time-consuming and best done with a partner—the tree has to be cut into manageable pieces that can be rolled or carried off the trail. Again, move debris well away from the trail, and completely clear all drainages of blowdown debris.

Leaning or hanging trees are called "widow makers," as their limbs or tops can snap off without warning and potentially injure or kill anyone underneath. Exercise extreme care when dealing with these trees. If a tree is not impeding a passage or in the designated clearing passage, leave it alone. Even if it is a leaner or hanger impeding a passage, consider very carefully the danger involved in cutting it, keeping the option of leaving it in your deliberations. Mother Nature will likely bring the tree or its branches down safely in the next windstorm or significant weather event. Spring poles are another hazard caused by blowdowns. Spring poles are small trees or branches that have been bent into an arch or bow by a blowdown or other heavy object exerting downward pressure. The spring pole, therefore, is under a great deal of tension and, if handled improperly, can spring back with immense force when released, possibly causing serious injury. One way to relieve stress on a spring pole is to make small cuts on the inside of the bend, allowing the tree or branch to slowly release pressure. The same caution should be applied for tree butts with roots still anchored in the soil; they may snap back to a vertical position when cut.

If a very large blowdown crosses the treadway, cut a notch or steps into the tree to allow passage. Some blowdowns are considered helpful and can be left in place to serve as barriers to unwanted vehicle traffic, as long as hikers can negotiate passage over or around them. Remove them if there is no clear passage for hikers, or if hikers will widen the trail to bypass them. Each land management area may have special regulations concerning trail clearing passage maintenance; contact your land manager for specific regulations regarding blowdown removal.

BRUSHING

A well-brushed trail is one on which a large hiker with a big pack can walk without touching limbs, trees, or brush. Footing is clear and the trail is easy to follow because the line of sight is open and unobstructed. Branches of trailside shrubs, even if weighted down by rain or snow, should not obscure the trail or soak passing hikers.

Brushing out, sometimes called brushing or standardizing, means clearing vegetation from established trails. Without regular brushing, even frequently used trails can be overgrown in just two to three years. In addition to vegetation lining the treadway, the area overhead should be "standardized" as well, depending on established clearing passage dimensions. Brushing in, on the other hand, is a term used when a decommissioned trail, visitor-created trail or campsite (also known as a bootlegs), or wide section of trail needs to be closed to traffic or made smaller. In this case, downed branches and small trees can be put haphazardly in the trail, thus closing the trail to hikers while attempting to mimic the natural state of the forest floor.

THE RIGHT TOOLS: BRUSHING
- loppers
- bow saw
- hand pruners
- pole saw (for ski trails)

The Door Technique

To brush a trail, we recommend the door technique: while hiking down the trail with clippers in hand, imagine you are carrying a door vertically, like a shield. The door's outline marks the trail standard for brushing, though width and height will vary with the terrain. Everything that falls within the door's outline should be removed.

Look for branches, shrubs, and brush that touch the door. Limbs or branches should not be cut flush with the tree as this can damage the trunk or stem. Leave a small amount of the stem to prevent this, but not enough to form a stub or stump (see figure 10.5). Stubs are unsightly, can detract from a hiker's aesthetic experience, and can create bothersome and sometimes dangerous snags for packs and clothing. If all branches along one side of a small tree need to be removed, it is advisable to remove the entire tree instead. Low shrubs and young trees should be cut as close to the ground as possible for aesthetic reasons, to avoid tripping, and to keep the stumps from sprouting. Do not leave pointed stumps. Remove low growth back to the outside edge of the cleared trail.

Machetes and brush hooks should not be used for woody growth, as they leave pointed stumps and stubs that can be a danger to hikers. Where there is heavy growth on a long section of trail, a gasoline-powered brush cutter or clearing saw will save time. They are not allowed in every area, however, so local regulations should be checked before proceeding. When using a mechanical brush cutter, be certain the operator is trained and knows how to use the equip-

10

Trail Maintenance

Fig. 10.5. Cut limbs close to the trunk, but be careful not to damage the trunk itself.

ment properly; as always, safety should be the paramount concern. Keep all other workers a safe distance away from power equipment when it is in use.

Leave annual growth of grasses, herbaceous plants, and ferns. If annual growth is particularly thick and aggravating, use swizzle sticks to cut it. Swizzle sticks should be used with caution and an acute awareness of your foot placement and the location of other people. When removing vegetation, think ahead. Remove entire branches of plants that, if left unattended, will continue to grow into the trail in subsequent years.

Pay special attention to small softwoods and the lateral branches of larger softwoods extending into the trail clearing passage. Their needles collect moisture on a misty mountain day and can create a car-wash effect: hikers brushing by them get wet quickly and surprisingly.

Width

The proper width for a cleared trail varies with terrain and vegetation. A 4- to 6-foot clearance suffices in most situations. In thick growth or in very remote

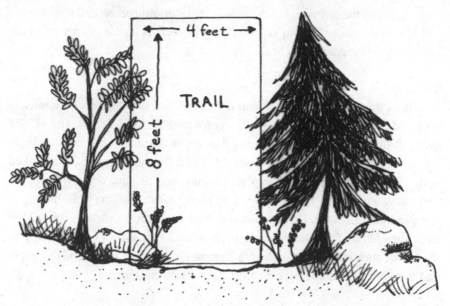

Fig. 10.6. The door technique helps to visualize the standard hiking trail height and width.

areas a 3-foot clearance may be the most practical and even desirable, if it adds to a feeling of remoteness. In high-use areas and on steep slopes with thin, unstable soils, a narrow trail may be desirable to limit hiker impact on the surrounding terrain and vegetation. The nearby roots of trailside trees, shrubs, and other plants stabilize soils. However, a narrow trail is not always the solution; heavy user pressure on steep, sloping trails will cause unstable soils to deteriorate regardless of trail width. The best solution may be to reroute the trail and close the existing section.

Height

Normally a trail is cleared to a height of 8 feet, or as high as one can reach (see figure 10.6). On slopes, stand uphill from your work to reach high branches more easily. If tree branches are higher than 8 feet, leaving this canopy over the trail to dampen the growth of shrubs, weeds, and grasses is desirable. Conversely, if more trailside vegetation is desired, encourage the growth of wildflowers, grasses, and shrubs by clearing back the canopy to let in sunlight. Be careful: you can easily achieve a scorched-earth effect and make the trail clearing passage look like an interstate roadway by mistake. Leave some of the most attractive trees and shrubs standing.

If a trail is popular in winter, the maintainer should clear it to 12 feet high to enable easier travel when snow depths reach 3 or 4 feet deep. Do this high clearing at any time of year, but remember that standing on several feet of snow will bring you closer to your target. Use tools such as a pole pruner or a pole saw for those hard-to-reach branches.

Cleanup

Your brushing job is not complete until all branches and debris are completely removed from the trail. Pick up all trees, branches, and debris, and scatter them off the trail. Avoid piles because they are noticeable to the hiker and also a potential fire hazard. In some cases the trail treadway may need to be raked with a lawn rake to ensure complete cleanup and unobstructed footing. To conceal downed trees from hikers, drag them away butt-first until the top is completely off the trail. Large limbs and small trees can be thrown clear of the trail, provided that they do not hang in the branches of shrubs and trees next to the trail or stick up butt-first. Most importantly, remember to clear all drainages and their outflow ditches of brushing and blowdown debris.

TRAIL MARKING SYSTEMS

Good trail markings will effortlessly guide the hiker along the route without intruding on the natural experience. The marks must be easily understandable, systematic, and vandal-resistant. The most often used types of marking include paint blazes; metal or plastic markers; signs; and, for treeless areas, posts or cairns. Marking should be tailored to each specific trail type. For example, a short trail within a state park that is heavily used by inexperienced hikers might be extensively marked. On the other hand, it may be desirable to have sparse marking on a trail through private land in an urban area to prevent heavy or undesirable use. Light marking in remote backcountry areas preserves the wild character of the area. Note that standards for markings in federally designated wilderness areas may be more stringent or not allowed at all.

Installing a Marking System

For the installation of a new trail system or when freshly marking an older trail, develop a standard system. Color, frequency, placement, and form of markings should be carefully thought out before installation so that changes do not have to be made later. Plot out the color scheme of your marking system on a map of the area, especially if there are a lot of loop trails close together. Blue, red, yellow, white, and orange are good choices; they are visible yet not offensive. Natural colors like brown, gray, and green blend into the surroundings and are not good choices for marking in the Northeast. Think carefully about how your trail will be used and choose the color accordingly. For example, white is not a good color to use on a ski trail, and red or orange are not good for a trail through a maple grove. One may wish to use one color for the main trail in a system and mark all side trails with a second color. This is the procedure used along the Appalachian Trail; the main route is marked in white with side trails in blue. Use care when the trail is located next to boundary lines; property boundaries are usually marked with paint, and if the trail blazes are of the same color confusion can result.

Place markers in both forward and rearward directions, alongside the trail, to indicate the route of travel both ways. They should be placed on trees that are plainly visible along the trail. A large tree is preferable to a small one, and a marker on a live tree will likely last longer than one on a dead tree. Using a live tree decreases the risk of the tree falling and the marker being lost. If using a light-colored marker, search out darker-colored trees—and vice versa—to increase contrast.

To ensure adequate and consistent spacing, treat marking as a separate job for each direction; blazes should be painted in one direction at a time. Where possible, avoid placing blazes on either side of the same tree since the loss of one tree will result in a twofold loss of marking. It will take more time, but your marking will last longer and have the same quality and character in each direction.

To determine the best place to locate your next blaze, face down the trail ahead. Quickly note a tree that stands out at a suitable distance. Walk to it, and if it is alongside the trail, place the next marker on it. On a straight, wide, or well-cleared trail this may be far ahead. Do not limit yourself to marking only one side of the trail. If there are a lot of turns or curves, the side with the best visibility or line of sight will vary. Put the marker at an easily visible height. The usual height for marking is 5 to 6 feet, which is at or just above eye level for many hikers. If a trail is to be used in winter, the markers should be slightly higher than this.

The frequency of markers will be determined by the character of the trail. A good rule of thumb is that a hiker should never have to walk more than a hundred paces without being able to see a marker either ahead or behind. On narrow woods trails with an obvious tread and trail clearing passage and with little opportunity for the hiker to stray off track, markers can be widely spaced, perhaps every 100 to 200 feet. On the other hand, a trail without an obvious treadway through an open hardwood forest should be closely marked, possibly every 30 to 50 feet. This is particularly true if the trail is used in winter. Where trails follow well-worn roads, markers may be spread farther apart. However, if there are many opportunities for the hiker to turn off the road onto other roads or trails, marking should be more frequent.

Do not fail to mark the trail because you think no one could possibly get lost in that area. New trail or road construction, timber harvesting, or blowdowns resulting from storms may unexpectedly change conditions. Bear in mind that trail marking is for the benefit of those who are unfamiliar with the trail and terrain. Even if you know it well, many other hikers, some with little hiking experience, will walk that trail. They will rely on your blazes to guide them. Marking or blazing should be consistent along a trail's entire length; interrupting or changing frequency of blazes can confuse hikers.

Immediately beyond any road crossing, brook, or trail, there must be a trail marker, even though there may also be a direction sign. Place a second marker nearby, perhaps 20 to 50 feet from the crossing, in case the first marker disappears.

At important changes in the route, such as if the trail becomes a less well-defined track or road, some maintainers and clubs use the double blaze or marker, consisting of two disconnected blazes or markers of the prescribed size, one two inches above the other. This double marker serves as a warning to the hiker: "Stop. Look!" This marking does not indicate a turn, such as is often denoted by two markers placed one atop the other. Some trail maintainers will use offset double markers to indicate direction, the top marker being slightly offset in the direction of the turn.

When a trail is relocated, all blazes or markers on the abandoned section should be obliterated or removed. It is not sufficient to eliminate those at each end, since persons straying onto the old route may see the markers in between and assume they are on the correct trail. This could cause the hiker to become confused and lost.

Paint Blazes

Paint blazes of oil-based paint are the most effective, durable, and commonly used markers on hiking trails. Water-based paints such as latex are the easiest to handle and apply, and they also dry quickly, but they do not last as long. Durability, universal availability, low cost, and ease of application also make paint the most practical solution for marking most hiking trails. Blazes should be neat and well-placed (see figure 10.7)

Oil-based enamels, paints, or inks developed especially for boundary marking last the longest and are best to use. The AMC has had good success with a brushable boundary-marking ink from the American Coding & Marking Ink

Company. (For other firms manufacturing such paints and inks, see a list of tool suppliers in Appendix A.) It is fast drying, easy to apply, and rated to last for five to eight years. Boundaries marked with such inks are often visible for ten to fifteen years or more. Enamels or highway paints can be more durable on some surfaces.

The standard blaze on the Appalachian Trail is a white 2-by-6-inch mark placed on trees. For more than half a century, the shape and color of this blaze—approximately the size of a dollar bill—has proven to be visible and effective.

As with any paint job, preparation of the surface is at least half the work. On trees with smooth, thin bark, a wire brush or nylon scrub pad works well to scrape off dirt and lichen. On trees with rough bark, such as hemlock or oak, use a paint scraper to scrape a flat, fairly smooth surface the size of a paint blaze. Do not scrape through the bark on any tree, as it will cause resin to ooze out and discolor the blaze. Try to avoid blazing during rainy or damp weather, as the paint may run or fail to adhere to your surface.

Fig. 10.7. Blazes should be painted with a visible color and well placed.

When painting a blaze, keep the edges neat and don't let the paint drip on the ground or the tree. A 1-inch brush works well, and a 2-inch brush can be used with a very light touch and can also serve as a size guide.

A plastic pail is a convenient way to keep all your blazing supplies within easy reach. You can make carrying the pail more comfortable by taping the handle or splitting open a segment of old garden hose lengthwise and wrapping it around the handle. Pouring small quantities of paint into a paper cup make painting easier and, if spilled, it will not make a huge mess. To aid in painting the blaze the correct size, make a 2-by-6-inch stencil out of hose, rubber inner tube, or similar material.

Occasionally it becomes necessary to remove paint blazes. This may happen when you relocate a section of trail or standardize the marking of a trail section that has been improperly marked. Other changes, such as recent growth that has obstructed the view of a blaze or the occasional curveball from Mother Nature (such as your blazed tree being blown down), may also necessitate the removal or renewal of blazes. When renewing blazes, portions of old blazes that have been widened by tree growth need to be removed. To eliminate all or a portion of a blaze, scrape it off the tree with a paint scraper or wire brush, or use a brown, gray, or custom-mixed paint matched to the surface being covered. When covering a blaze, use oil-based enamel paint.

Plastic or Metal Markers

Plastic and metal markers nailed to trees and posts are also effective for guiding hikers. A benefit to using plastic or metal markers is they are most helpful when a directional marker is needed, or when a marker requires text or a logo to

Fig. 10.8. Plastic and metal markers are available in a variety of shapes, sizes, and designs.

identify or publicize the trail (see figure 10.8). Plastic and metal markers range from simple, unpainted tin-can tops to custom-designed and -manufactured plastic or aluminum markers. These come in various shapes, colors, and sizes. While these markers are easy to install, they also run the risk of being removed by souvenir seekers and other vandals. Markers can also be expensive, and any color and lettering may fade after several years.

Markers must be carefully installed so they will last. The nails used for installation should be made of soft metal, like aluminum, so they will not damage a chain saw should the tree need to be cut. Copper nails should never be used, as copper is toxic to a living tree and will kill it. When installing markers, drive the nail into both the marker and the tree, but leave an inch between the marker and the head of the nail (see figure 10.9). This allows the tree to grow out along the nail without bending or growing around the marker.

Fig. 10.9. Leave 1-inch gap between the marker and the tree for tree growth.

Making Trail Signs

Signs are an essential component of any trail; they are usually located at trail-heads, junctions, road crossings, and trail features. They can indicate the trail name, direction, highlights, facilities, and distances (see figure 10.10). Some also have a symbol or abbreviation of the land manager and maintaining organization(s). In addition to trail signs, some trails have plastic or metal markers that refer to a special designation or point out that the trail is part of a specific trail system. These markers are usually placed at trailheads or hung at intervals along the trail.

Wooden Routed Signs

The most common trail signs are made of wood, with the lettering cut into the sign using a router. Because the lettering is actually incised into the wood, the sign will be legible even after the weather has worn off all paint or stain.

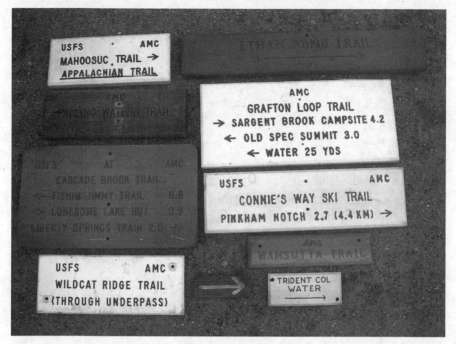

Fig. 10.10. Trail signs can be designed to meet the needs and character of the trail.

Type of Wood

Take into account workability, durability, and strength, as well as availability and cost. The best woods are clear heartwood from Ponderosa pine, yellow pine, white pine, western fir, redwood, or basswood. In the southeastern United States, cypress and locust are often used. Use high-quality stock, straight and free of knots, checks, and warps. Also consider what is abundant and available locally—standard kiln-dried spruce and fir works well. Routing signs on plywood is strongly discouraged and may cause irreparable damage to the router bit because of the hard glue used to join layers of plywood.

Size of Signboard

Smoothly planed boards 1½ inches thick are appropriate for most routed wooden signs. At trailheads, where large descriptive signs are needed, 2-inch or larger stock may be best. The length and width of the sign varies with the length of the message, the size of letters, and the sign's importance. For most of your sign needs, consider using standard dimensional lumber that is readily available. This will tend to be more cost effective, as well as speed up production time. Signs used along the trail can be made from standard 2-by-6-inch to

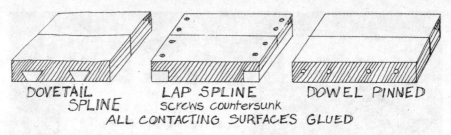

DOVETAIL SPLINE   LAP SPLINE   DOWEL PINNED
screws countersunk
ALL CONTACTING SURFACES GLUED

Fig. 10.11. Some different joints for 2-inch sign stock.

2-by-12-inch milled lumber. Roadside trailhead signs may be as large as 2-by-3 feet. Because hikers stand directly in front of a trail sign, it is not necessary to make it large, except for the sign at the roadside. Large signs can be made from several boards joined together with biscuit joints, dowels and glue, threaded rods, cleats, or similar equipment (see figure 10.11).

Size of Lettering
Most trail signs will not need lettering larger than 1½ inches in height. Larger lettering can be used for the name of a trail so it will stand out. The text of a sign should be 1 inch or ¾ inch in height.

Routing
A sharp, high-quality bit is essential for good lettering. A dull bit will burn the wood and leave feathers that make painting difficult and have to be sanded out. Use a U-shaped or V-shaped, carbide-tipped veining or grooving bit. Carbide steel, though more expensive than plain steel, is extremely hard, will last much longer, and do a better job if used properly. For 1¼- to 1-inch-tall letters, use a ¼-inch bit, and for ¾-inch letters use a ⅛-inch bit. Larger letters will require an appropriately larger-size bit. Set the depth of the bit based on the desired look of the letters. It is advisable to test out different bit depth settings on scrap wood to see how the letters will look. When routing letters taller than 2 inches, first set the router to cut half the depth of the letter, then go over it again, cutting at full depth; this saves wear and tear on the router. Repair mistakes with small amounts of plastic wood filler. This information about routing and bit size applies to routing by hand as well as using a commercial sign machine.

Freehand Routing
Because routing machines are expensive and bulky, some people prefer to hand rout their signs (see figure 10.12). While hand-routing can be a time-consuming process that requires skill and patience, an artistic person can make

Fig. 10.12. With a little practice, hand routing trail signs can be very effective.

Fig. 10.13. Stenciling a sign before using a router.

professional-looking signs with a small hand router and other proper equipment. Use letter stencils to lay out the text of a sign (see figure 10.13). Letter style should be simple and all capitals. Many stationery or art supply stores sell various sizes of inexpensive paper or plastic stencils for tracing letters. Higher-quality plastic or metal stencils can be obtained from a sign manufacturer, but they may be fairly expensive. Some trail maintainers, rather than lay out letters again and again, lay out the text on high-quality drafting paper. This can be placed over the signboard with carbon paper in between and the text traced, producing a carbon outline on the signboard. The text can then be filed away for future use. Such reusable texts can also save time when making multiple copies of one sign or where certain words like "trail" and "path" or lines of text are repeated. Before routing text laid out on a sign, practice on scrap wood. Considerable skill is needed to achieve professional results. Use a relaxed, smooth, and steady motion while following the stenciled letters with the router. Practice will make perfect.

Machine Routing

Several types of commercial sign machines with letter templates are available, but they are expensive. However, the efficiency of production and exactness of the routing can be worth the initial expense.

Fig. 10.14. Using a sign routing machine can provide a quick and effective way to make consistent signs.

There are several styles of sign machines commercially available. A common design is a sign machine with a router mounted on a movable arm (see figure 10.14). The arm is attached to the machine's work surface, which accepts a wide range of lumber sizes and letter templates. A pin at the operator end tracks the letter templates up the arm of the machine. This system allows the sign maker to lay out text for signs several lines at a time, all with proper spacing and alignment. The only limitation is the inability to accept larger signs for trailheads.

The machine router's letter templates are different from those used for hand routing. The templates for machine routing are available in a variety of sizes and fonts. While the templates are designed to track the pin of the sign machine, moving the router across the sign, a steady and careful hand is still needed to create clean letters. Logos and designs are also easily transferred to sign machine templates, allowing the sign maker to consistently place logos on signs.

Following the same guidelines outlined in the routing section, a variety of signs can be made with ease and consistency. A sign machine can be particularly useful if there is a need to make a large number of signs each year or for making signs with four to six lines of text.

Painting and Staining

Many signs are not painted or stained at all. For instance, signs in federally designated wilderness areas are unpainted to retain a more rustic appearance. However, many others signs should get painted or stained (see figure 10.15). Two colors are generally used for painting or staining a sign, one for the background and one for the lettering. Some simply stain the entire sign or treat it with a clear wood preservative. Others stain first and then paint the lettering with enamel. The entire sign can also be painted, with the background in one color and the lettering in another. For contrast and better visibility, use a light-colored background with dark letters or vice versa. Use a good-quality enamel or latex paint over a compatible primer coat. After the background paint dries, patiently paint the letters. Use a small brush, squeeze bottle, or syringe to neatly fill the routed letters with paint. Then with a small brush, nail, or painted stick direct the paint so it covers the entire inside surface of the routed letters. Wipe away any mistakes before they dry, and touch up as needed.

Here's a trick to facilitate letter painting while hand routing: Stencil the sign text on the pre-painted board, cover the face of the sign with contact paper, and then rout through it. Quickly brush paint into the lettering, and pull off the contact paper. Generally, some touch up will be needed, and the contact paper and paint do tend to dull the router bit more quickly.

Fig. 10.15. Painting trail signs provides a weather-tight seal as well as contrast and visibility.

Hanging the Sign

The most attractive and effective method of hanging signs is to use a signpost. Trees are not always available or in the right location. Also, posts do not damage trees. It's best to use a 6- to 10-inch-diameter post, buried to a depth of 3 feet. To make a natural post, use a rot-resistant tree such as cedar, locust, or hemlock, since they will last the longest. Peel off the bark to discourage insects and prevent moisture retention. If you can't get a natural post, use a squared pressure-treated post from a lumberyard.

Bolt the sign to a flattened edge of the post. Bevel the upper end of the post with an ax or saw to shed rain and to give a slightly more rustic appearance. To prevent turning or removal of the post, drive either one length or two crossed lengths of threaded rod, rebar, or large metal spike through the bottom of the post before it is buried. Alternatively, you can nail one or two pieces of wood to the bottom of the post. Above treeline or on ledge, use the lengths of rebar or wood to anchor posts inside stone cairns.

To protect your signs from vandals, be sure to hang them securely. Maintainers use many different techniques to prevent vandalism and theft. Signs that are often stolen can be mounted using special nuts and bolts, such as Vandlgard or Tufnut brands, or you can countersink bolts and cover the tops with wooden plugs or wood putty. If you can, place the sign high and out of reach. Fixing the

Fig. 10.16. Bolting a sign to a tree.

signs to a tree or post with two lag bolts (see figure 10.16) works particularly well for signs thicker than 1 inch; thinner signs tend to crack with these bolts.

Another vandal-resistant (but more expensive) technique to consider is to mount ¾-inch-thick signs on a backboard of the same size cut from 1½-inch stock. First, lag-bolt the backboard to a tree or post through at least two pre-drilled and countersunk holes. Then bolt the sign to the backboard. Fasten small signs to the backboard with two bolts. These bolts should be offset in opposite corners so as not to split the sign along the grain. Larger signs need four bolts. Using backboards provides more secure mounting and, when bolted to a tree, also helps protect the sign from splitting due to tree growth. All bolts, washers, and nails should be galvanized or at least zinc plated. Standard ones will rust, leaving an unsightly stain on the sign. Be careful not to over-tighten the bolts. This can cause the sign to crack and the paint to chip, allowing water to degrade the sign more quickly.

Master Sign List

Develop a master sign list for your trail system. This list documents each sign's location, the text, its condition, and the date and time it was last checked. The list facilitates maintenance, repair, and replacement. Number signs and key them to your master list.

Fig. 10.17. Temporary signs are far better for hikers than no signs.

Temporary Signs

If permanent signs are not ready when a trail is to be opened, or if an important sign is stolen, you will need a temporary sign (see figure 10.17). While they are no substitute for the real thing, decent temporary signs can be made by writing on heavy posterboard with permanent, weatherproof ink, such as a Sharpie. Laminate the temporary sign to weatherproof it, staple and glue it to plywood, and hang it on a tree or post. A painted piece of plywood marked on with a Sharpie will also work. Such signs should easily last one to two years. Check it for defacing and animal damage if it must serve longer. Use a dark-colored ink; red and light colors tend to fade quickly. Temporary blank signs are available from Voss signs in Manlius, New York.

Other Signs

Some maintainers make signs simply by using a stencil and painting outlined letters on a board (see figure 10.18). This can be tedious to make and, when left out in the woods, can have a shorter lifespan; the text can become illegible as the paint is worn away by the elements. Some signs are fashioned from plate steel, with letters made with a bead of brazing or stenciled and cut out with a torch.

Fig. 10.18. Sign with painted-only text.   **Fig. 10.19.** Sign text routed into post.

This technique is costly, and such signs are generally not aesthetically pleasing in a backwoods setting. However, they may be desirable for vandal-prone areas. Some also use the posts themselves as signs; text is vertically routed or cast into wooden or concrete posts (see figure 10.19). Since these can be securely buried and tend to be very long and heavy, theft is less of a problem.

Retired Signs

As part of the annual maintenance of the trails, an assessment is made of the condition of every trail sign. Each year several signs will need to be replaced due to damage from animals, fallen trees, or simply weathering. The lifespan of a trail sign depends greatly upon the materials used, weatherproofing, and the location of the sign. When you replace an old sign, don't discard it. Trail signs can have a life beyond the trail.

Give retired trail signs as recognition to individuals that have helped in the construction or maintenance of that trail—they're wonderful gifts. Retired trail signs can be auctioned off to benefit trail maintenance efforts in future years. Before giving retired signs away, consider assigning them a unique identification number, different from the standard location identification number on a master sign list. This unique identification number will prove that a sign was legally acquired rather than stolen.

ALPINE TRAIL MAINTENANCE

Different techniques of trail maintenance should be utilized if the treadway crosses through environments such as boreal forest, desert, slab rock, or alpine areas. In northern New England we have a number of trails that are classified as "alpine," which simply means of or relating to the mountains. More specifically, it describes high-elevation ecosystems, above treeline, which are marked by short summers and long, harsh winters (see figure 10.20). The alpine environment is home to a number of unique and rare plants, many of which live nowhere else. Alpine trails are typically rocky and exposed.

Drainage Cleaning

Similar to lower elevation trails, erosion control is the trail maintainer's primary task. The loose soils of alpine trails are easily eroded by the lack of drainage structures or just poorly maintained ones. In this environment drainages quickly clog up with loose sand and gravel. Removing this material and reshaping the

Fig. 10.20. Cairn construction on the Alpine Garden Trail, Mount Washington, NH.

drainages in the alpine zone can be a lot of work. In some instances heavier tools such as pick mattocks may be needed to loosen and remove compacted soils.

Even though digging in the soils above treeline may seem counterintuitive to protecting this fragile ecosystem, a trail without proper water drainage can cause much more damage through erosion. Just as on trails in other environments, a well-maintained and flared outflow is just as important as a well-maintained drainage ditch in the alpine zone. Once the water is carried off the trail it is important to prevent further erosion in the outflow of the drainage.

Brushing

Trails through alpine areas require special treatment when it comes to brushing. Use judgment and temperance when clearing trails near or above treeline, where the climate is severe and growth rates are very slow. Krummholz accounts for the majority of plant life as you approach treeline in the alpine zone. Krummholz is composed of old and dense dwarf trees that have been contorted from years of exposure to the elements; trees 3 to 4 feet tall can be 60 or 70 years old. Removing one tree in a patch of krummholz can jeopardize the other trees in the patch that join roots and branches in protection against wind and cold. Trees below treeline focus much of their growth vertically, but krummholz plants grow horizontally and close to ground level to avoid the wind, which is much stronger just 3 or 4 feet above the ground.

In lower elevation areas the standard clearing passage for a hiking trail should be 4 feet wide by 8 feet high. However, trails in the alpine zone that travel through krummholz do not need to be as wide. The old and gnarled trees are very slow growers and need only minimal cutting to maintain an open clearing passage for several years. Making proper cuts, as described in the brushing section earlier in this chapter, is very important to foster quick healing. In the alpine zone, maintain a clearing passage that is passable through the krummholz while minimizing any cutting.

Stay on top of your alpine brushing. If you don't, the krummholz can slowly but insidiously spread across the ground, obscure the treadway, and force hikers onto fragile vegetation. The resulting widening of the tread will be difficult to repair, to say nothing of the damage caused to those delicate and rare plants. Be vigilant, but remember that what you cut will not grow back as quickly as it will down in the valley.

Trail Definition

As trails pass through alpine environments trail definition is critical to the survival of fragile trailside plants. A successful technique used to define the

Fig. 10.21. Scree walls help to define the trail and keep hikers from trampling fragile alpine plants.

treadway through alpine zones is the use of scree walls, which help to concentrate users onto a single track through open alpine environments and provide a buffer for fragile plant life (see figure 10.21). These walls can be small and sporadic, providing a reminder of the treadway, or they can be larger and more consistent, lining both sides of the trail for long distances. The degree of trail use, amount of plant life, and type of user will determine the size of the scree wall needed.

Scree walls also serve to stabilize soils along the sides of the trail that may have been loosened by visitor use and erosion. In areas where the trail has become very wide and has begun to impact the alpine vegetation, use scree walls to narrow the trail's treadway. Then install rubble (see figure 10.22), a collection of smaller rocks placed in impacted areas, to discourage hikers from walking in the area, help stabilize soils, and encourage revegetation behind scree walls. Care should be taken when constructing scree walls to only choose rocks which are not already protecting alpine vegetation or holding back soil.

Fig. 10.22. Rubble placed on a section of trail helps to keep hikers off and allow for re-growth of vegetation.

Trail Marking

In treeless areas, trails are marked with the conspicuous rock piles known as cairns. (In the absence of rock, you can use posts.) Constructed from alpine rocks, cairns make attractive trail markers. They are effective year-round because of their visibility even under snow and ice conditions. Well-placed and well-built cairns also help protect the fragile soils of alpine areas by keeping hikers on a single trail. Cairns are especially important when weary travelers must find their way in the poor visibility of an alpine storm.

Cairns should be placed along trails that have been laid out in a fairly direct fashion. People will shortcut sharp turns; therefore, it is best to keep the trail curving with the land in gentle undulations. Such trails take the easiest route and represent the most likely choice of travel for the average hiker.

For maximum visibility in marginal conditions, place cairns between 50 and 100 feet apart at conspicuous locations: a knoll is obviously a better location than a hollow. The cairn has greater visibility if placed on a ledge or mound.

Occasionally light-colored rocks can be found and used for the top of the cairn, making it more visible. Some maintainers paint the uppermost rock. Painted blazes are also used in conjunction with cairns to mark the route, especially in areas where rock for building cairns is scarce, or where the blaze's color is needed to identify the trail. Though it is not recommended, if needed, blazes can be painted on visible rocks to mark the trail. Keep in mind that any blaze painted near the ground may be covered with snow and/or ice in winter. While large cairns are sometimes used to mark junctions, they do not resist wind and lightning well and should be avoided because of their obtrusive appearance and frequent need for rebuilding.

For all alpine trail maintenance needs, be sure to collect rocks that are well away from the trail and not stuck in the soil or serving to hold back soil. Look for rocks that are sitting on top of other rocks or that are wedged between other rocks. Trail maintainers are working toward preserving all soil in the alpine environment; careful rock selection will play a critical role in this effort. It is also wise to educate hikers on the importance of staying on the trail.

Basic maintenance is crucial to the health of any trail, but there is one last thing to remember: take care of drainages first. Before you build cairns, freshen up the marking, or clear the brush on that last quarter-mile of trail, be sure the drainages are clear, wide, and free. While you can always go back and cut brush, paint blazes, or clear a blowdown, you can't replace the soil that makes up your treadway.

CHAPTER 11
SKI TRAILS

AT-A-GLANCE

Improvements in cross-country ski trail designs have resulted in better treads and longer seasons.

- **Planning:** Base your trail design on good information, including potential users, topography, and target user levels.

- **Layout and design:** Note striking features and drainage patterns and keep the route interesting.

- **Building trails:** Keep trails wide enough for grooming machinery.

Cross-country skiing, or ski touring, is a fun, inexpensive, and increasingly popular sport that provides great exercise (see figure 11.1). Many people consider cross-country skiing a life sport—an activity that is enjoyed for different reasons at different points throughout one's life. Private cross-country ski areas still attract a significant number of skiers seeking classical skiing in molded tracks and skate-skiing on firm smooth surfaces. Backcountry skiing, or skiing on ungroomed trails or in areas without trails, is popular with those looking for more strenuous activity in less populous environs. Opportunities for ski touring are widespread and exist in all degrees of difficulty, from a ski through the back yard to journeys into remote wildlands, and from family picnic outings at a local land trust property to multiday, cabin-to-cabin ski excursions.

As skiers have become more sophisticated through the years, trail maintainers have adapted to this trend by improving ski trails and tailoring them to specific types of skiing. In the past, adapting existing skidder trails, hiking trails, or roads into ski trails was the norm. Often these trails resulted in awkward

Fig. 11.1. A cross-country skier enjoying himself on a ski trail.

junctions, vast windblown openings, endless climbs, and near uncontrollable descents. Trails that are well designed for skiing are safe, enjoyable, and are more easily adapted for other sports, including snowshoeing, cross-country running, mountain biking, and hiking.

Ski touring trails need lots of snow or a smooth pre-snow surface. In most of the United States, the average snowfall has declined over the last twenty-five years. Winters are generally warmer, and most locations expect later snows, significant thaws, and earlier springs. The ski trail community has tried to mitigate this weather trend by preparing trails to higher standards. Trail surfaces have become much smoother and often incorporate extensive drainage plans. These built surfaces allow skiing with minimal snow and have proven relatively maintenance-free. The snow usually retains less water and dries faster, maintaining a higher quality surface for a longer time. These high-quality trails have become very popular destinations, sometimes because of a lack of reasonable snow elsewhere, but more often because the combination of dependable snow and fun terrain holds the interest of skiers.

New cross-country trails are being built in all snow-prone regions. Land trusts, schools, municipal and state parks departments, as well as clubs, ski teams, companies, and individuals are responding to requests for accessible and dependable outdoor winter recreation. From families looking to get out for healthy weekend activities to individuals who replace their daily run or walk with skiing, new users have created a pervasive trend in raising ski trail standards. Good ski trails are no longer only available at ski resorts; demand for skiing is bringing trails into local communities.

The AMC maintains backcountry ski touring trails in New Hampshire's White Mountains and has constructed ski trails in Maine. It also helps maintain other trails in New Hampshire, Massachusetts, and New Jersey, supporting ski touring as part of a spectrum of outdoor experiences.

PLANNING AND DESIGN

Development of a cross-country ski trail system begins with a determination of need, the expected users' experience level, and the expected number of users. A critical assessment of the topography and the users' expectations are essential. Review chapters 1 and 4 of this book for an overview of the applicable elements of hiking trail design.

Maintaining organizations should decide if they want to cater to one type of ski touring experience and level of expertise or all types and levels. The

11

Ski Trails

Whether molded by machinery or set by skiers, tracks (smooth parallel groves) are a precious commodity on ski trails, especially on un-groomed trails with little or no grade. Tracks help keep skis straight, and they offer a firm stable surface so skiers can propel themselves forward easily. Tracks are fragile. Snowmobiles, dogs, sleds, snowshoes, hikers, or discourteous skiers can easily destroy them. After a new snow, tracks that are "skied in" or mechanically set will need an hour for the snow crystals to freeze together before they can provide any firmness or durability. If you are not on skis, stay off the tracks!

Well-groomed ski tracks.

topography plays a significant role and will affect this decision. For instance, rough or extremely steep terrain will probably eliminate the possibility of novice trails, while flat terrain may not attract more-experienced backcountry skiers.

Determination of a standard degree-of-difficulty rating for your trails can be somewhat subjective, since it takes into account many varied factors, such as gradient, trail alignment, width, curve radius, and even the visual density of the trailside; use of the suggested standards will help keep you on track. Ideally, a ski touring trail system should contain approximately 50 percent novice-use trails, 30 percent intermediate-level trails, and 20 percent for expert-level skiers. Trail location, terrain, and land management goals often affect these percentages.

Assess the other ski touring opportunities in the region to see if there is a niche to fill, and investigate the potential of connecting with existing trails to provide a larger network. Also take the time to evaluate other recreational activities and land-management practices in the area. Watch for those that might pose conflicts, and minimize problems through trail layout and design. For example, snowmobiles and cross-country skiing are sometimes incompatible activities; you may want to keep them separate for reasons of aesthetics or safety. Check to be sure that timber management in the area does not pose problems for winter trail use.

Assess the opportunities for expansion early, and consider possibilities for future changes in operations. Planning and construction should allow for the possibility of operational changes and trail expansion. For instance, if you are planning on grooming in the future, design your trail system to allow grooming in loops and ideally, without traveling over any trail section more than once.

TRAIL LAYOUT

The best time to lay out any trail is in the late fall or winter, when leaves are off the trees and visibility is good. Before venturing out, consult topographic maps and aerial photos to get a feel for the land and location of predetermined control points. Remember the general trail layout considerations outlined in chapters 1 and 4 and the factors specific to ski touring described here.

Often it is good to review the trail layout on skis or snowshoes in the winter; this is an effective way to test a proposed line. Your route is often clearly marked by your tracks, and any brightly colored flagging tape stands out well against snow. This is a great opportunity to check approaches to scenic features and assure they are suitable when covered with snow. Winter layout also allows you to assess how existing drainage affects the snow quality and will help you identify problem areas for the construction or maintenance plans.

It often works best to lay in a curvilinear line or a route that drifts slightly across the terrain and limits long sight lines. Trails that use the existing terrain usually rest lightly on the land and save construction and maintenance expenses. Gentle curves add a sense of visual allure without breaking the flow or the rhythm of skiing. Always look to interrupt monotony; prolonged uniformity brings boredom. Mix forest and fields, light and dark areas, flats and rolling hills. Break up long climbs and descents with small flats to allow skiers to rest tired muscles or check their speed. Avoid abrupt changes in direction. Lay in lines that gently turn to avoid obstacles. Avoid overly sinuous trails that break rhythm, as well as long, flat, straight sections. Allow yourself to rethink and tweak your lines; often small changes that smooth turns and avoid difficult ground make huge differences in the construction phase. Walk or ski the route, uphill and downhill, in both directions to assess its suitability. Keep thinking of adding fun, a few challenges, and anything that is pretty to the route.

The best formats for ski touring trail layouts incorporate loops—single loops, stacked loops, or interconnected and compound loops (see figure 11.2). These configurations allow skiers to travel over several trail sections, cover variable distances, and return in the end to the same starting point. A series of loops with various levels of difficulty will serve a wide range of abilities.

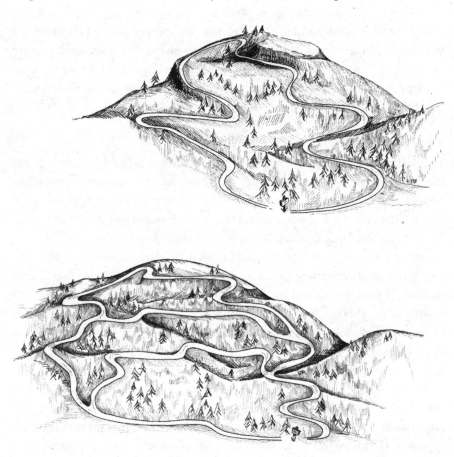

Fig. 11.2. Single loop (top) and stacked loop (bottom).

Consider a one-way traffic policy on steep trails, places where collisions are likely, or heavily used loops. One-way traffic reduces congestion and provides a greater sense of solitude for the skier.

Point-to-point trails take the skier to a place such as an outlook and must be backtracked to the starting point. Though this configuration is common for climbing mountain summits, it is less common or welcome for ski trails. Point-to-point trails are well accepted when connecting two ski trail systems or connecting a series of remote cabins. Sometimes terrain or landowner limitations prevent development of loop trails; if this is the case, use a point-to-point trail.

SPECIFIC LAYOUT CONSIDERATIONS

Ski touring trails need lots of snow or at least a smooth ground surface; the latter allows skiing on minimal snow. Most newly constructed ski trails use much higher standards than trails built even as little as ten years ago. Newer trails often have extensive drainage plans that include features such as ditches, culverts, grade dips, and broad water bars so snow can recover quickly from thaws or rain events. Siting trails on well-drained ground both saves construction efforts and maintains quality snow for longer periods.

Trails built on smooth and flat surfaces require the least amount of snowfall to open. Undulating terrain provides a more varied and interesting ski touring experience. Often old horse logging roads or naturally occurring benches make a smooth basis for a trail. Avoid very rough terrain that will demand lots of snow cover or significant work to smooth out. Build a terrace or bench on sidehill traverses to provide a flat stable ski surface. Grooming is often difficult, if not impossible, on unterraced sidehills. Avoid steep sidehills in the initial layout, as they are difficult and time-consuming to build, and they often create visual impacts inconsistent with the aesthetic sensibilities of most trail users. Terracing steep slopes usually demands significant downslope retaining walls and huge, often ugly, back slopes.

Slope aspect, or the direction a hillside faces, and type of vegetation are important factors in siting ski trails. South- and west-facing slopes usually receive the most sun, which means the snow there melts and evaporates faster, resulting in poor long-term snow retention. Also, crusts form earlier there, and these trails may demand more snow maintenance to keep them safe and usable. Conifers that shade the trail often mitigate impacts from the sun, but dense softwood stands hold much of the fallen snow off the ground. When

11

Ski Trails

this hanging snow is exposed to the sun or warm temperatures, it melts and drops as water onto the trail, creating crusty or icy conditions. Favor the cooler north- and east-facing slopes and areas of denser vegetation in hardwood or mixed stands when siting your ski touring trails.

It's also important to know where not to build ski touring trails. Avoid areas of known avalanche danger; hazardous crossings of lakes, ponds, and streams; and busy road crossings. Steer clear of or minimize conflicts with other winter recreation, such as snowmobiles, by separating them and providing adequate visual and sound buffers. It's also a good idea to site trails as far from roads as possible, as the traffic can be distracting and noisy. Avoid crossing bogs, ponds, and lakes; they are often windblown, icy, and can be dangerous when the ice is thin or wet. Also, boggy or wet areas often freeze late, if they freeze at all. If water crossings are unavoidable, provide alternative routes. Remember, one section of impassable trail can make the whole trail unusable.

CONSTRUCTION

Many of the techniques and tools used in hiking trail construction can apply to ski touring trails, but there are some specialized trail standards and construction techniques specifically for cross-country ski trails. Newer trail construction often requires heavy equipment, such as excavators, to establish the tread. These machines—even small, relatively inexpensive ones—can pull stumps, move rocks, flatten uneven ground, and complete a large amount of work very quickly. Choose your machine based on the trail width, parent material, and finish character of the trail. However, machine choice is often determined by availability. Mini excavators can usually be leased locally, but there is also the possibility that equipment time can be donated. Perhaps a volunteer who owns a backhoe will be willing to help. Some excavation companies or municipal road departments may also donate machine time to municipal parks or nonprofit trail groups. Many professional trail construction companies have specialized equipment and knowledge that can save many hours and leave behind a very attractive trail system.

Trail Width

Cross-country ski trails can be just about any width the planner desires, but designers usually balance the aesthetic nature of trails with skiers' needs. Commercial ski areas build trails wide enough to accommodate customers that skate, while some backcountry enthusiasts are let down if they don't brush snow off branches with their shoulders as they crank tight telemark turns. International guidelines for racecourses suggest widths of just under 20 feet. Many trails are wisely built wide enough to accommodate snow grooming equipment. Generally, plan to size groomed trails at least 2 feet wider than your grooming implements. Careful checks of machinery specifications and attachments for any grooming equipment is essential in the early stages of trail planning and certainly prior to any trail layout and design. Lately, trail designers have considered unpredictable snowfalls and in response have expanded openings in the tree canopy to allow snow to reach the ground. (Almost all trail maintainers establish trailside openings that receive and store snow for times when snow to cover bare or icy spots is scarce.)

The width of ski touring trails is also dependent upon difficulty level, type and volume of use, slope gradient, and trail layout. Easier trails often have a minimum tread width of 10 to 12 feet. Trails designated "more difficult" can range from 8 to 10 feet wide, while "most difficult" trails can be as low as 5 to 6 feet. Because skiers will have to snowplow while going down steep grades or herringbone while climbing them, the trail will have to be wide enough to accommodate these techniques. Curves are also wider to allow for turning and snowplowing. Generally, you will want to increase the trail width 25 percent for two-way traffic and add an additional 25 percent for grades over 10 percent or if you expect skiers to travel faster than 15 miles per hour.

Height

Remove branches to a height of 10 to 12 feet above the expected level of snow cover (see figure 11.3). Prune conifer limbs 14 to 16 feet above the average snow level, as they tend to hold snow and droop under the weight. Hemlock stands often keep snow from reaching the ground, and it is best to prune these to 16 to 18 feet.

Trail Tread

As noted earlier, the smoother the treadway, the sooner the trail can be used and the longer the skiing season will last. On the trail surface, maintain the natural sod or establish a vegetative covering. This plays a critical role in reducing erosion and catching and retaining the snow cover, especially on slopes. Remove rocks, logs, and other debris from the trail surface. Cut woody vegetation on the treadway flush with the ground. Avoid sandy soils on steep slopes since they are more susceptible to erosion and tend not to hold snow.

Ski touring trails are often built to permit other recreational activities during the snow-free seasons. These trails are built on stable, well-drained soils, and they are generally smooth and slightly crowned to allow surface drainage.

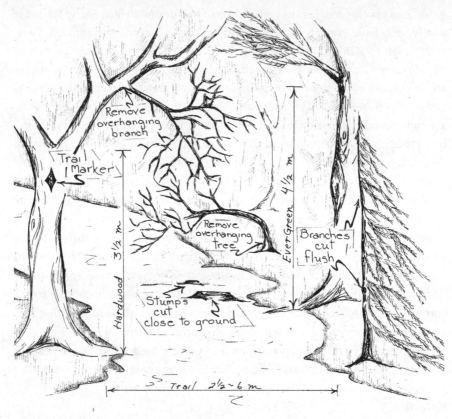

Fig. 11.3. Brush a ski trail right of way as shown.

Drainage devices such as ditches, culverts, water bars, and grade dips are all employed, and the trail surface is sometimes capped with a layer of wood chips, shredded bark, or gravel. Because machinery is often used to create these trails, the initial costs are relatively high, but a very durable, stable, and low-maintenance tread is the result. Skiing can start with very little snow cover, and in the summer, walkers, joggers, mountain bikers, and horseback riders can enjoy it.

During construction, seed or mulch to stabilize the soil where sidehill cuts occur or on steeper gradients where the tread construction has disturbed the native ground cover. At a minimum, place brush, logs, dirt, or wood chips in depressions and around high roots or rocks to provide fill on which snow will collect. Generally, wood chip and turf surfaces allow skiers to slide more safely across bare spots. Be sure that no obstacle protrudes more than 4 inches above ground level. On steep sidehill traverses, cut the sidehill to create a terrace that will hold snow and provide a level tread. The placement of logs, rocks, and

Fig. 11.4. Use log corduroy, conifer boughs, or hay in marshy areas.

brush on the downhill side of a sloped traverse can sometimes do the same job by collecting and holding snow to create a terrace.

Log corduroy, hay, or conifer boughs (see figure 11.4) can be used as a temporary solution to traverse short wet or boggy areas, but ditching and filling are more effective. Most wet areas will continue to melt snow or develop ice until more permanent solutions are employed. Adding fill on top of a geotextile fabric helps disperse loads and keeps fill from eroding. Open ditches that cross trails often require a small bridge, but culverts can also resolve this problem. However, culverts can result in large washouts if installed improperly or not maintained regularly, and they do occasionally freeze and clog. Be certain the culvert size is appropriate to the width of the treadway and the volume of water or snowmelt expected; it doesn't hurt to choose a larger diameter for good measure. Smooth-bore plastic culverts are more resistant to clogging than corrugated metal and are light enough to drag across a rough corridor when transporting them to the site.

Gradient

Variety and challenge should be objectives for any ski trail; avoid long flats and intersperse long climbing grades with level sections or short downhills. A good mix of terrain should include approximately one-third flat rolling ground, one-third uphill, and one-third downhill.

Sustained grades (about 200 feet) of 8 percent or less are recommended for novice trails, but maximum grades of 10 percent are acceptable for short distances (100 feet). Intermediate trails should have extended grades (about 300

| Grade | | Maximum Length in |
In percentages	In degrees	Feet to Reach 20 mph
10	6	250-300
12	7	100-125
15	9	80
20	12	60
25	14	40
30	17	30

feet) held at no more than 10 percent, and keep maximum grades of 20 percent to 300 feet or less. Expert trails can and should have long, challenging grades but, generally, grades greater than 15 percent get to be a slog after about 400 feet. A 40 percent grade is the maximum slope for even expert skiers. Short sections of higher-than-average grade are acceptable at all levels of difficulty.

Remember, steeper grades require a wider trail. The added width allows skiers to snowplow, sidestep, or herringbone. On curves, widening alone is not always sufficient. Provide appropriate run-outs on curves with slopes by clearing the outside of the curve from the top and continue along the width well past the curve exit. Also, the turning radius of curves should match the slope and the skiers' speed.

The table above shows the approximate distances a skier will travel in attaining speed on slopes of varying degrees of steepness. These estimates are useful for gauging suitable grades in combination with length of run-out, angles of turns, and trail widths.

Length

The length of your trails will depend on the type of skiers using them, but it is also helpful to look at statistics. Skiers usually travel at between 2 to 8 miles per hour, with most averaging a little over 3 miles per hour. The majority of trails range in length from 4 to 8 miles, and skiers usually plan outings of 2 to 4 hours. An integrated system of novice, intermediate, and expert trails provide opportunities for excursions of varied lengths and can accommodate the afternoon, evening, and full-day skier. Generally, novice trails are 3 to 5 miles long, and even less when geared toward young children or new skiers. Intermediate trails, usually 5 to 8 miles long, incorporate a combination of easier and more difficult terrain. Expert trails can be longer, but carefully consider the terrain; a trail that climbs for 6 miles may take longer to ski than rolling trail of equal mileage. Remember that long descents, especially after long climbs, often lead to very cold skiers.

STREAM CROSSINGS AND BRIDGES

While there may be sufficient snow to cover a ski trail, stream crossings, even small ones, may not freeze or may reopen during a thaw and prevent skiing. Natural stream crossings are cheaper and sometimes easier to maintain if the bank has a suitable slope. Choose natural crossings only if the stream is slow moving and not very deep; water needs to freeze early in the winter and remain frozen for the crossing to be useful. Trail maintainers have responded to several years of warm winter temperatures and low snow cover by constructing bridges, where in the past they have relied on ice and snow depth for the crossings. Generally, if the trail is dependent on a stream crossing, it is safest to bridge the stream since this can lengthen the ski season.

The same basic construction principles apply to ski trail bridges as they do to footbridges with several major differences: the width, the approach configuration, and grades onto and off of the bridges. Ski touring bridges should be built at least 8 feet wide, but up to 12 feet wide, if possible, to hold snow and compensate for crowning (see figure 11.5). If you plan to machine groom the trail, make the bridge at least as wide as the widest grooming implement and, preferably, as wide as the trail tread.

Align the ski trail to cross a bridge in a straight line. Avoid building a bridge as part of a curve in the trail. If the trail must curve to cross the stream, plan the trail so the turn is completed before the bridge crossing. Consider the expected speed of the skier when planning a bridge. It is best to have skiers cross a bridge in full control even if it means altering a trail design to slow their approach to the bridge.

Ideally, bridge approach grades should remain even with or be slightly above the trail grade, between 0 and 5 percent. If needed, raise the trail with a ramp or fill in a low spot with rocks and dirt. Skiers must not be able to catch ski tips under the exposed edge of a bridge deck. Placing a plank over the end of the stringers keeps this from occurring, and this method will also cover the end grain of log stringers, helping to keep precious snow from slipping between the stringers and decking.

Bridge projects can get very complex, especially if they involve long or multiple spans, very steep or unstable banks, and the need to support heavy grooming and trail building equipment. Consider seeking advice from a trail professional or civil engineer if you need to build more than a simple short-span bridge.

Fig. 11.5. Ski touring bridge.

Since ski bridges are covered with snow, decking can also be made from rougher materials, such as small-diameter logs, split logs, or rough-cut planking. If needed, place snow fence, hay, or conifer boughs to fill in large spaces between pieces of decking. Decking laid perpendicular to the direction of skier travel allows skis to slide over the board spaces if snow cover is minimal. Parallel stringers without decking can be used, but the stringers should fit tightly together or the gaps filled with sticks nailed into place.

If you must install railings, do so only on one side of bridges and make them at least 42 inches high. Allow for snow depth when determining the railing height, and do not leave railing ends protruding, especially if you expect skiers to cross at fast speeds. If the approach to a bridge involves significant speed, avoid railings unless the bridge is very high.

Shovel and pack snow onto the deck after the first snowfall to develop and maintain a better base. Since bridge snow tends to develop a distinct crown as the winter progresses, it may be necessary knock this crown down and spread it across the bridge. If the crown snow is thin, you may need to shovel more snow onto the bridge. Some maintainers leave a snow shovel hanging on the bridge or on a nearby tree for this work.

TRAIL SIGNS AND MARKING

Post trail difficulty rating signs and information about distances, current conditions, trail closures, and wax suggestions at the trailheads (see figure 11.6). Providing a large map of the entire area is always helpful. Also post a difficulty rating at each trail junction. If the trail system has a large number of intersections, the addition of intersection numbers or letters that correlate with a map is very helpful.

Four-inch, plastic, cerulean blue diamonds are the standard markers for most ski trails (see figure 11.7). Plastic diamond markers are available in a variety of colors if you wish to distinguish multiple trails. The standard difficulty rating markers used by most ski touring organizations are often printed on heavy plastic. A red exclamation point on a yellow plastic triangle is used to mark the beginning of a steep descent or a sharp corner. All plastic signs and

Fig. 11.6. Ski trail signs.

Fig. 11.7. Use 4-inch, plastic cerulean blue diamonds on ski trails.

markers can be purchased through the Cross Country Ski Areas Association (CCSAA), 259 Bolton Road, Winchester, NH 03470 (phone: 877-779-2754; fax 603-239-6387; www.xcski.org).

Place signs and markers approximately 5 feet above the highest level of snow cover. When attaching them to trees, use self-drilling torx head screws, but leave the heads sticking out about an inch to allow for tree growth. If you do not, the tree will grow over the screw, causing the sign or marker to pucker, rip, and eventually fall off. The torx head allows maintainers to apply enough torque to back the screw out even if the tree grows well into the exposed inch. Ski trail markings can also be painted if you are uncomfortable with buying and importing bits of plastic into natural environments. Areas that are treeless or that experience extremely deep snow conditions are marked using poles set in the snow or ground.

CHAPTER 12
KIOSKS & USER EDUCATION

AT-A-GLANCE

Before hikers begin their trip they should receive information about the trail, as well as safety tips and conservation messages.

- **Kiosks:** Convey information via a kiosk. Choose a design based on expected traffic, the feel of the trail, and user needs.

- **Construction:** Build the bulk of your kiosk off the trail site. Remember that construction can be time-consuming and expensive.

- **Information to include:** Post maps, a description of the trail's unique features, and safety information.

Kiosks, or information boards, play an essential role in introducing the visitor to a trail site. Signs, maps, Leave No Trace information, and other information are valuable to both the inexperienced and experienced outdoor traveler. Warning visitors of safety concerns and encouraging responsible use of the outdoors helps to set the stage for future generations utilizing our public lands. These are important messages to send to all visitors. While there are many different designs for kiosks, they all serve a similar purpose: to pass along information to the users of the trails.

In recent years there has been a notable shift in visitor use as day hiking has increased while backpacking has steadily declined. With a growing population taking interest in outdoor activities and recreational areas becoming more accessible, the potential for a less-experienced outdoor user group is relatively high. As a result, land managers and trail maintainers need to address this shift by reaching out to all experience levels. Well-designed information kiosks that address all visitors are a critical factor in the continued enjoyment of outdoor recreation areas.

KIOSK DESIGNS

Kiosks can range from a simple, single panel containing a limited selection of information about the area, to three or more panels with detailed information.

Fig. 12.1. Three-sided kiosk.

Fig. 12.2. Single-paneled kiosk.

They can be constructed in a linear fashion or angled in to surround the user. The size of the kiosk is determined by the type of use in that area, the number of visitors using that area, and the amount of information to be expressed to the user.

Many kiosks, like those used in the White Mountain National Forest in New Hampshire are three-sided with a roof to protect the panels (see figure 12.1). These are located at prominent trailheads throughout the forest that receive the greatest amount of use. At less-visited trailheads in the White Mountains, you will find single-paneled kiosks that relay key points (see figure 12.2).

Like a trail, the design of the kiosk must match the location, the needs of the user groups, and the feel of the trail. Kiosks should contribute to the user's experience, not detract from it. In remote areas, a rustic and simple design with basic information is most appropriate; however a residential park or highly populated and easily accessible area might call for a larger kiosk to reach a broader audience. Another style of kiosk, utilizing custom design work, uses the profile of a mountain range; you can see this, for example, on the Falling Waters/Old Bridle Path trailhead (see figure 12.3).

Selecting materials for the construction of the kiosk is as important as its design. Using materials that fit the landscape and meet the expectations of the user groups are essential to a successful kiosk design. Using full-round logs or hand-hewn lumber can provide a natural feel in remote locations. Materials such as milled lumber, metal, or cement are appropriate in a town park or

Fig. 12.3. A kiosk with the profile of a mountain range.

road-accessible area. Many kiosks have hinged panes of Plexiglas with a lock to easily and regularly rotate informational materials.

Also consider theft and vandalism when designing your kiosk. Selecting materials that are durable and anchoring the kiosk firmly in the ground can help prevent damage to the kiosk. Vandal-proof bolts and screws are also available, as discussed in the trail sign section in Chapter 10 and can help protect the structure and information panels.

CONSTRUCTION AND INSTALLATION

First, select your location. Kiosks can contain information that land managers and trail maintainers would like the user population to know. Local history, safety information, and maps are common topics included in kiosks. In most cases, addressing the user group as they begin their trip on the trail is best. Placing kiosks at the trailhead, parking areas, or campgrounds can draw users to the kiosk. Once you have selected a general location, consider the specific placement of the kiosk. Because many people will walk right up to the panels of the kiosk, the ground around the kiosk will be trampled significantly. Consider placing gravel or bark chips around the kiosk to protect the area.

Create detailed plans for the construction of the kiosk. An illustrated plan will help you determine material choices, style, and colors that will work best for its location. In many cases you will need comprehensive procedures and drawings to present to land managers for approval before construction begins.

Construction can be time-consuming and expensive. Working from your plans, pre-construct as much of the kiosk as possible before transporting the structure to the site. Fix the kinks while you have access to tools and equipment. With this step completed, installation can be done with a group piecing together the final product.

USER EDUCATION

Before you finalize the size and style of your kiosk, you must consider the information that will be placed on this structure. Since the trailhead is the introduction to a trail and you will not be there to greet them personally, you will want to carefully consider the information to be posted. At the trailhead, you can introduce visitors to the unique aspects of this location, quickly convey safety information, and focus on the importance of stewardship (see figure 12.4). If the kiosk is crowded with too much information the visitor will lose attention and will not get your message.

Fig. 12.4. A kiosk with regulations and information about safety and stewardship.

Concise and interesting signs attract the attention of trail users. If the signs are long, drawn out affairs with several "don't" messages, trail users will quickly move on without getting the whole message. Incorporating artwork, maps or photos can be very effective at keeping kiosks interesting.

When planning your kiosk, think about what important message you want to convey before they leave for their hike or outing. Resource conservation or stewardship? Dangers? A description of how the area is special is often important to point out. The real challenge is to keep the information interesting, simple, and relevant. Due to the limitless possibilities for informational kiosks, here are the basics to include:

- A map or layout of the land, including trail descriptions if appropriate.
- A quick description of the unique features of this site. Drawings or illustrations of plants or wildlife in the area can spark interest, or perhaps an important historical link is worth highlighting.
- Safety Information. It is impossible to insure the safety of each visitor, but they can be warned about the known dangers. This may include information about avalanche safety, stream crossings in high water, quickly changing weather, potable water, wildlife, poisonous plants, or poisonous snakes. The information can be clearly posted with suggestions for safe travel.

- Highlight Hike Safe principles, which encourage users to take responsibility for their trip.
- Stewardship Information: Cooperation in caring for the resource and how the visitor can get involved.
- Carry In/Carry Out message and the Leave No Trace principles all focus on taking steps to minimize human impacts on a resource.
- Contact information for your organization and land manager.

Once complete, the kiosk and its information can help in the outreach and education of countless users. However, the information that is placed on your kiosk must be regularly reviewed and updated, if necessary. Outdated information can lead to confusion, frustration, or even unsafe conditions.

When time and consideration is taken during the planning and installation of the kiosk, it can serve as a quality source of information and education for all visitors for many years to come.

GLOSSARY

adze To cut or shape wood with hard blows of a tool, like an ax.

backfill Mineral soil used to support a drainage structure. Backfill is used behind (downtrail) a rock or log water bar, or to reinforce a drainage dip.

basic maintenance (annual maintenance) Involves four tasks, listed in order of priority: cleaning drainage, clearing blowdowns, brushing, and blazing or marking. All should be done annually or more often if needed.

bevel An angle less then 90 degrees. In trail work it pertains to the angle of a tool's blade.

bog bridge A low, wood bridge used to help hikers cross muddy or wet sections of trail. Bog bridges are made of two base logs and one to three stringers.

bucking saw A crosscut saw used for applications other than felling. It is wider, stiffer, and heavier. It also has a straight back, unlike the concave back of the felling crosscut saw.

buffer zone The land area on each side of the trail treadway. Buffer zones shield the hiker from activities such as housing development, mining, or logging that are detrimental to the hiking experience.

check dams Step-like structures perpendicular to the trail that aid in soil retention. They can be made of either rock or wood.

check stairs These are used in areas where either livestock live, or the terrain is not steep enough to warrant rock stairs. They consist of a frame of either rock or wood, which is then filled with rock of graduating sizes, down to the stepping surface of gravel or mineral soil. They retain existing soil and prevent further erosion on a slope, while creating flat platforms that are pleasing to both hikers and pack stock. Also referred to as crib stairs or terrace stairs.

circle of danger The area surrounding a worker that is unsafe due to tool use. The inner (or primary) circle of danger is the area the tool can reach while the worker is using it. The outer circle of danger is the area the tool could reach if the worker lost control or let go of the tool.

crib stairs See *check stairs.*

cribbing A method of constructing a vertical support column for a bridge or pier that is typically made from short logs placed in an overlapping, log-cabin manner.

definers Used to channel or focus foot traffic onto a hardened or harder tread, thus protecting soils that may be wet, thin, or supporting fragile plant life. Scree and rock steps are examples of definers.

drainage Devices or structures, such as water bars, drainage dips, and ditches, that remove water from the trail tread or prevent water from entering the tread and thus limit or eliminate the effects of erosion.

duffing The process of scraping off leaf litter, pine needles, roots, bark, and the dark, organic, decomposed layer of soil below. It is the first stage in tread construction.

easement Grants a nonowner the right to use a specific portion of land for a specific purpose. Easements may be limited to a specific period of time or may be granted in perpetuity; or, the termination of the easement may be predicated upon the occurrence of a specific event. An easement agreement survives transfer of land ownership and is generally binding upon future owners until it expires on its own terms.

erosion control Includes work or devices designed to control surface erosion (drainages, hardeners, definers, and stabilizers).

felling saw A crosscut saw used for felling trees. A felling crosscut saw is narrower, and more flexible than a bucking crosscut saw, and has a slightly concave back. The increased flexibility and lightness make it easier to wield during the felling process.

grade A measurement of the rate of rise of a trail, road, or slope. Expressed as a percentage. A trail that rises 9 vertical feet in 100 horizontal feet has a 9 percent grade. Grade is different from angle; angle is measured with a straight vertical as 90 degrees and straight horizontal as 0 degrees. A grade of 100 percent would have an angle of 45 degrees.

gravel An assortment of small stones, often between ¼ inch and 1 inch.

hardeners Objects used to eliminate the impact of foot travel through wet areas. Hardeners include bog bridges, step stones, and turnpiking (constructing a raised tread).

hew see *adze.*

lease The grant of an interest in land upon payment of a determined fee. The fee does not have to be monetary, but some consideration must be given for the right to use the land or the lease will not be legally binding.

license In trail work, allows the licensed party to enter the land of the licensor without being deemed a trespasser.

mineral soil Found below the organic horizon, mineral soil is comprised of clays, silts, sands, and other inorganic materials. Mineral soils generally provide a stable and durable treadway when properly drained.

oral agreement Generally, a contract involving the sale of real estate is not binding unless it is in writing. Therefore an oral agreement that actually transfers ownership of land is not legally binding. Although some types of agreements for the use of land need not be written, an oral agreement will always be difficult to enforce because the parties may disagree over the original terms of their contract. An oral agreement is therefore inappropriate for use in a trail project except during the preliminary planning stages.

outflow The off-treadway ditch portion of a drainage structure, intended to remove all water from the trail.

ownership-in-fee (also known as fee purchase or fee simple) A complete transfer of land ownership from one landowner to another party, usually by purchase.

pin rock A medium-sized rock, usually 150–250 pounds, whose mass is used to anchor a log step or water bar.

pinned stairs Steps, of wood or rock, or an entire wood ladder secured to a slab rock surface with rebar.

protective zone See *buffer zone*.

rock treadway Used to harden the tread using well-placed flat rocks as the travel surface, much like a back-yard patio. Also called rock patio.

rubble Small- to medium-sized rocks scattered around the trail to prevent hiker traffic, particularly in alpine zones.

rubble wall A simplified version of a retaining wall, consisting of rocks that are not neatly placed together and used to help retain a slope or prevent hiker travel.

rungs A rod, bar, or piece of wood that forms the step in a ladder and is attached to the two side rails.

scree Material used to define a trail and/or channel hiker traffic. Made of medium to large rocks (but also fallen trees or large limbs), scree is set along rock staircases to stabilize soils and direct hiker traffic onto the staircase. Scree is also built into walls in alpine areas to define the treadway and keep hikers off fragile vegetation.

sidehill trail A sidehill trail, often literally cut out of the side of a hill, gains elevation by moving up a slope, gradually following the contour. To avoid a gully or ravine, a sidehill trail will turn in the opposite direction by using a switchback. Sidehill trails are well suited for accessible trails, trails used by pack animals, or other applications where a trail's grade must be limited.

stabilizers Used to hold soil in place and prevent erosion from water, feet, gravity, or other forces. Stabilizers include rock steps (used to stabilize steep gullied or eroding slopes) and cribbing (used to anchor soil above or below a trail on a slope).

step stones Large stones carefully placed in the tread to allow hikers to step from one to another in order to cross a small stream or long muddy section of trail.

stringers A horizontal structure in a bridge or wood turnpike that runs parallel to the trail and gives support to the bridge or turnpike.

switchback Used to gain elevation on sidehill trails. The switchback is a sharp turn in the opposite direction.

terminuses The trailhead or start of the trail (usually at roadside) and the destination (a mountain summit, waterfall, mill site, or similar feature).

trail *Webster's New World Dictionary* defines a trail as "a blazed or trodden path through a wild region," but it's more than that; a good trail also protects the region it passes through from damage.

trailhead The beginning of a trail.

trail corridor Includes the treadway, right of way, buffer zones, and all the lands that make up the environment of the trail as experienced by the hiker. The Forest Service has called it the "zone of travel influence."

trail right of way The area around the treadway that is cleared for the passage of the hiker. It is usually four to six feet wide, depending on vegetation density. If a trail has other uses besides hiking, such as cross-country skiing or mountain biking, the right of way will likely be wider. The term "right of way" also refers to legal right of passage, as would be the case with a protected trail on private land.

treadway The surface on which the hiker makes direct contact with the ground. It is the location for virtually all improvements intended to conserve soil resources.

turnpike A box made of log stringers or rocks and filled with smaller rocks and mineral soil. It is used to both harden and elevate the trail in a muddy or wet section.

visioning The first phase in the trail project planning process, which involves conceptualizing the trail project.

APPENDIX A

Suppliers of Tools, Equipment, and Materials for Trail Work

This list is not complete; the companies listed are some of the ones that AMC purchases tools and other supplies from most frequently. Many of the more common tools can be purchased from hardware stores, home supply centers, or other specialty stores closer to you. Most of these companies are wholesalers and/or manufacturers and may sell direct, but only in bulk. These brands can be found or ordered at many hardware stores, or you can call the company for the name of a local dealer.

American Coding & Marking Ink Co. 1220 North Ave., Plainfield, NJ 07062-1725; 800-913-9837 (toll free), 908-756-0570 (fax); www.americancoding.com. ACMI manufactures a brushable ink that we have found to be excellent for blazes.

Ben Meadows Company P.O. Box 5277, Janesville, WI 53547-5277; 800-241-6401 (orders and tech support), 800-628-2068 (fax); www.benmeaddows.com. Ben Meadows, like Forestry Suppliers, sells many of the tools and supplies a trail worker might need.

E.T. Techtonics P.O. Box 40060, Philadelphia, PA 19106; 215-592-620 (phone and fax); info@ettechtonics.com (email); www.ettechtonics.com. Supplier of engineered fiberglass bridges and building systems.

Forestry Suppliers, Inc. 205 West Rankin St., P.O. Box 8397, Jackson, MS 39284-8397; 800-647-5368 (orders), 800-543-4203 (fax); www.forestry-suppliers.com. Forestry Suppliers, like Ben Meadows, sells many of the tools and supplies a trail worker might need. For a catalog, call 800-360-7788.

Griphoist Division of Tractel, Inc. P.O. Box 188, Canton, MA 02021; 781-401-3288, 781-828-3642 (fax); griphoist.usa@tractel.com (email); www.tractel.com. AMC uses the griphoist most often with rock work, but recognizes it as an extremely durable and useful tool all around.

Labonville, Inc. 504 Main St., Gorham, NH 03581; 800-764-9969 (toll free), 603-752-7621 (fax); lab@labonville.com (email); www.labonville.com. Labonville is an honest-to-goodness North Woods logging supply company, with a long history of selling top-quality safety gear and clothing for the logger, as well as a full line of work and outdoor clothing, boots, tools, and other gear.

Leetonia Tool Co. 142 Main St., Leetonia, OH 44431; 330-427-6944, 330-427-6128 (fax); www.letoniatool.com. Leetonia makes many "high-grade construction, hardware, and marine tools." For the trail worker, Leetonia makes pick mattocks, picks, cutter mattocks, rock bars (which they call wedge point or pinch point crow bars), tampers, and other specialty tools. Their tools are very rugged and will hold up to many years of hard use.

O.P. Link Handle Company 403 S. Main St., Salem, IN 47167-1323; 800-992-9171 or 812-883-2981, 812-883-1672 (fax). Wooden tool handle manufacturer.

Trail Services P.O. Box 8057, Bangor, ME 04402; 207-947-2723, 207-945-6050 (fax); www.trailservices.com. Trail Services provides any trail tool, griphoists, rock drills, hand tools, light-weight generators, stone tools, and lots of good technical info in the yearly catalogs.

Trow and Holden Inc. 45 South Main St., Barre, VT 05641; 802-476-7221, 802-476-7825 (fax); info@trowandholden.com (email); www.trowandholden.com. Trow and Holden has been manufacturing stone cutting tools for 110 years. It produces stone cutting, carving, and shaping hand and mechanized tools and equipment.

Snow & Nealley Co. 609 Wilson St., Brewer, ME 04412; 800-933-6642 (toll free), 207-941-0857 (fax); www.snowandnealley.com. Snow & Nealley makes what we believe to be the best single-bit ax on the market today. In fact, new trails department employees are issued new Snow & Nealley 3½-pound axes as part of their orientation. S&N also makes draw shaves, bark spuds, broad axes, mauls, cant dogs and hooks, timber tongs, pulp hooks, and pickeroons. Their tools are American made and carry a lifetime warranty.

Voss Signs LLC P.O. Box 553, Manlius, NY 13104-0553; 800-473-0698 (toll free), 315-682-7335 (fax); sales@VossSigns.com (email); www.vosssigns.com. Voss manufactures stock and custom aluminum and plastic signs and markers for forests, parks, wildlife preserves, private property, and other applications. They specialize in custom signs and have complete typesetting and art facilities.

APPENDIX B

Recommended Reading

Birchard, William, Jr., and Robert D. Proudman. *Appalachian Trail Design, Construction, and Maintenance*, 2d ed. (Harpers Ferry, WV: Appalachian Trail Conservancy, 2000). 237 pp. Available at 304-535-6331 or http://www.atctrailstore.org

Birkby, Robert C. *Lightly on the Land: The Student Conservation Association Trail-Building and Maintenance Manual*. (Seattle, WA: The Mountaineers, 2005). 344 pp. Available at 800-553-4453.

Doucette, Joseph E., and Kenneth D. Kimball. "Passive Trail Management in Northeastern Alpine Zones: A Case Study." In: More, T. A., et al., eds. *Proceedings of the 1990 Northeastern Recreation Research Symposium*, Saratoga Springs, NY, Feb. 25–28, 1990. U.S. Forest Service, General Tech. Report NE-145:195–201.

Griswold, Stephen. *Trail Handbook: Sequoia and Kings Canyon National Parks.* (Three Rivers, CA: U.S. Department of Interior, National Park Service, 1991). 86 pp. Available at 209-565-3795.

Hallman, Richard. "Handtools for Trailwork." Gen. Tech. Rep. 8823-2601-MTDC. (Missoula, MT: U.S. Department of Agriculture, Forest Service, Missoula Technology and Development Center, 2005). 54 pp. Available at http://www.fhwa.dot.gov/environment/fspubs/05232810/lc05232810.htm

Hesselbarth, Woody, and Brian Vachowski. "Trail Construction and Maintenance Notebook." Gen. Tech. Rep. 9623-2833-MTDC. (Missoula, MT: U.S. Department of Agriculture, Forest Service, Missoula Technology and Development Center, 1996). 139 pp.

Michael, David, and Brian Vachowski. "Saws That Sing: A Guide to Using Crosscut Saws." 0423 2822. (Missoula, MT: U.S. Department of Agriculture, Forest Service, Missoula Technology and Development Center, 2004). 64 pp. Available at http://www.fhwa.dot.gov/environment/fspubs/04232822/lc04232822.htm.

Miller, Warren. "Crosscut Saw Manual." Gen. Tech. Rep. 7771-2508-MTDC. (Missoula, MT: U.S. Department of Agriculture, Forest Service, Missoula Technology and Development Center, 1988). 28 pp. Available at 406-329-3900.

Mrkich, Dale and Oltman, Jerry. "Hand Drilling & Breaking Rock." 8423 2602. (Missoula, MT: U.S. Department of Agriculture, Forest Service, Missoula Technology and Development Center, 1984). Available at http://www.fhwa.dot.gov/environment/fspubs/84232602/lc84232602.htm.

Parker, Troy Scott. *Natural Surface Trails by Design: Physical and Human Design Essentials of Sustainable, Enjoyable Trails.* (Boulder, CO: Natureshape, 2004).

Steinholz, Robert T. and Vachowski, Brian. "Wetland Trail Design and Construction 2007 Edition." 0723 2804. (Missoula, MT: U.S. Department of Agriculture, Forest Service, Missoula Technology and Development Center, 2007). 90 pp. Available at http://www.fhwa.dot.gov/environment/rectrails/trailpub.htm.

Webber, Peter, ed. *Trail Solutions: IMBA's Guide to Building Sweet Singletrack.* (Boulder, CO: International Mountain Biking Association, 2004). 272 pp.

Webber, Peter, ed. *Managing Mountain Biking: IMBA's Guide to Providing Great Riding.* (Boulder, CO: International Mountain Biking Association, 2007). 256 pp.

Weisgerber, Bernie and Brian Vachowski. "An Ax to Grind: A Practical Ax Manual." 9923 2823P. (Missoula, MT: U.S. Department of Agriculture, Forest Service, Missoula Technology and Development Center, 1999). Available at http://www.fhwa.dot.gov/environment/fspubs/99232823/lc99232823.htm.

Internet Links and Resources

www.americantrails.org: American Trails. Provides information on all types of trails, trainings, resources, library, calendar of events, online bookstore.

www.fhwa.dot.gov/environment/fspubs/index.htm: Forest Service Publications.

www.railstotrails.org/whatwedo/trailbuilding/index.html: Rails to Trails Conservancy. Information on trail project planning, funding, etc.

www.trailbuilders.org: The Professional Trailbuilders Association. A source for information on professional trailbuilders and contractors, resource links, equipment information, project solutions, employment opportunities, training.

INDEX

AMC
VOLUNTEER
VACATIONS

GET OUT, GET DIRTY, GIVE BACK!

Join an AMC Volunteer Vacation and help maintain and repair trails in spectacular locations throughout the Northeast. You'll meet new people, discover new places, and feel good knowing you're giving back to the landscape you love.

- One- to Three-week Vacation Crews in the White Mountains, the Berkshires, Baxter State Park, and Acadia National Park

- Crews just for Teens or Adults

- Weekend Vacation Crews at the Maine Woods, Cardigan Lodge, and the Delaware Water Gap

- Day Work Parties throughout the Northeast

- No experience necessary— we'll train you!